Secondary Traumatic Stress and the Child Welfare Professional

Also Available from Oxford University Press

Child and Family Practice: A Relational Perspective
Shelley Cohen Konrad

Social Work Practice with Families, 2E
Mary Van Hook

Social Service Workplace Bullying
Kathryn Brohl

Civic Youth Work
Ross Velure Roholt, R. W. Hildreth, and Michael Baizerman

Navigating Human Service Organizations, 3E
Rich Furman and Margaret Gibelman

Evidence-Based Practices for Social Workers
Thomas O'Hare

Getting Your MSW: How to Survive and Thrive in a Social Work Program, 2E
Karen M. Sowers and Bruce A. Thyer

Advocacy Practice for Social Justice, 2E
Richard Hoefer

The Recovery Philosophy and Direct Social Work Practice
Joseph Walsh

Clinical Assessment for Social Workers: Qualitative and Quantitative Methods, 3E
Catheleen Jordan and Cynthia Franklin

The Costs of Courage: Combat Stress, Warriors, and Family Survival
Josephine G. Pryce, David H. Pryce, and Kimberly K. Shackelford

Social Work with HIV and AIDS
Diana Rowan

Secondary Traumatic Stress and the Child Welfare Professional

Josephine G. Pryce

Kimberly K. Shackelford

David H. Pryce

OXFORD
UNIVERSITY PRESS

Oxford University Press is a department of the University of Oxford. It furthers the University's objective of excellence in research, scholarship, and education by publishing worldwide. Oxford is a registered trade mark of Oxford University Press in the UK and certain other countries.

Published in the United States of America by Oxford University Press 198 Madison Avenue, New York, NY 10016, United States of America.

© Oxford University Press 2016

Library of Congress Cataloging-in-Publication Data

Pryce, Josephine G.
  Secondary traumatic stress and the child welfare professional / Josephine G. Pryce, Kimberly K. Shackelford, David H. Pryce.
    p. cm.
  Includes bibliographical references and index.
  ISBN-13: 978-0-190615-91-8
  ISBN-10: 0-925065-90-0
  1. Secondary traumatic stress. 2. Child welfare workers—Job stress.
  I. Shackelford, Kimberly K. II. Pryce, David H. III. Title.
  RC552.P67P75   2007
  362.7—dc22

                                                         2006100860

                    ISBN 978-0-190615-91-8

To the countless child welfare workers who over the years have given of their hearts, souls, and lives for the protection and well-being of our most vulnerable; to the families and children who suffer; to the children whose suffering ended in death at the hands of those they looked to for protection and love; and to BreAnna

Those who work with the suffering suffer themselves because of the work.

C. R. Figley, *Treating Compassion Fatigue*

It is an ethical imperative. We have an obligation to our clients—as well as to our-selves, our colleagues, and our loved ones—not to be damaged by the work we do.

Saakvitne and Pearlman, *Transforming the Pain*

Contents

Tables

About the Authors

Josephine G. Pryce, MSW, Ph.D., is associate professor at the School of Social Work at the University of Alabama. Jo earned her BSW and MSW from Our Lady of the Lake University, and her doctorate in social welfare from the University of California, Berkeley. She teaches a variety of courses in social work practice, research, and traumatic stress. Jo is the recipient of several awards for teaching excellence. The focus of her scholarship and writing is military families, veterans, lesbians and gay men, and secondary traumatic stress and self-care for helping professionals.

Kimberly K. Shackelford, MSW, Ph.D., is associate professor of social work at the University of Mississippi. She was previously the director of training for the Mississippi Department of Human Services–Division of Family and Children's Services and before that was a front-line child protection social worker and child protection supervisor. She continues to work with the Mississippi child welfare agency staff and other community service agencies for the continued improvement of services delivered to the children and families of Mississippi.

David H. Pryce, MA, MSSW, is a retired army colonel and a twice-wounded veteran of the Vietnam War. He received his MA from the University of Nebraska, and his MSSW from the University of Texas, Arlington. He is a social worker, author, and trainer specializing in secondary traumatic stress in the helping professions. He also serves as a secretarial appointee to the Department of Veterans Affairs National Advisory Committee on the Readjustment of Veterans.

Preface

Dear BreAnna,

    I just wanted to let your know that I've had you on my mind. The call came in last night. You were en route to the hospital—maybe you would live. The phone kept ringing. Every thirty minutes or so the updates came—abdominal bruises—fractured wrist—cracked ribs—punctured lung—no brain activity. . . . Maybe you will live. . . . I waited and prayed . . . why I'm not sure. If you lived, what would you be—and the other choice was dying—but why? We started our investigation; three counties worked together and three counties waited. Everyone wished we had a prior report. Anything to work with, anything but this.

    I interviewed a child that morning and had a meeting at noon. The rest of the day we shared news about you. During some quiet moments, when defenses were down, the question came—What did you go through? What went through your mind? You are two. Nowhere to go or to even know that you should go. Too little to reach a doorknob—too tiny to run. A picture of your eyes comes to mind. Terror. And I wonder. . . . Did you call for your mama. Last year someone turned your name in at Christmas. You were an angel on our Christmas tree. Someone drew your name and gave you a good Christmas. Just a little while ago.

    Today a man inflicted more injuries on your little body in a few moments than most bodies experience in an entire lifetime. I am sorry BreAnna. I wish we had known about you. Then two calls came in close together. Three p.m.—a man killed himself—he was going to be arrested for felonious child abuse as soon as they found him. Three forty-five p.m.—the last information about you. You died a few minutes ago. No charges. No court. No trial. No hope. Three counties of social workers stop. Newspapers and television question the workers—"What is it like to work a case like this?" For today, they get no response.

    The struggle begins to fight the questions, but the questions creep into our minds. What does it feel like to be beaten to death, BreAnna? Did you hold your tiny arms up for help? Did you try to get away? Did you cry? Several people ask what a two-year-old toddler could do to make a man so mad. The answer—nothing. She could do nothing.

    Five o'clock came and we went home, knowing more about life than we wished we had to . . . and my daughter asks, "What's wrong, Mom?" with eyes alive and bright and fearless. . . . I tell her, "Nothing." My husband asks about my day. "Interviewed a child this morning, had a meeting at twelve, phone calls and paperwork all day." Oh, and a child died today.

    You were an angel on the Christmas tree last year. Goodbye BreAnna. I am sorry this happened to you.

    The story of BreAnna was written by Lori Woodruff, LMSW, who served the Mississippi Department of Human Services for many years as a front-line social worker, supervisor, regional director, and training director for the state. The BreAnna story was used by Lori Woodruff and Kim Shackelford in training sessions with Mississippi Department of Human Services child welfare workers. The story evokes emotional responses similar to what child welfare workers in the field experience after working with abused and neglected children. This story was used during the initial training of child protection workers in Mississippi to demonstrate the emotions that workers would experience with some of their child protection cases. After reading the story, the new child protection workers were encouraged to talk about their emotions, and they were then taught the possible effects of working with traumatized clients and the symptoms of secondary traumatic stress. The story has been used for years. Lori Woodruff and Kim Shackelford are sisters, but it was only after Lori was asked if the story could be used in this book that she shared the truth behind the story. She asked Kim if she had ever told her about the writing of the letter, and for the first time, almost twenty years after the death of BreAnna, Lori shared the following:

> I did go home after BreAnna died that day. I was the supervisor for three counties. We were all numb at work and couldn't talk about it. The man who murdered BreAnna had killed himself and we were supposed to move on and act like nothing had happened. I couldn't go to sleep that night, and when I did, I had a nightmare of two horses fighting to their death and there was nothing I could do to stop them. The gore and the blood and the death woke me and I was shaking and crying. I knew I had to get control of myself, and I got out of bed and wrote a letter to BreAnna. Writing, to me, was always a way to express thoughts that couldn't be said out loud. I wrote it and remember being exhausted and thinking, "There, it is done." I laid the letter on the kitchen counter, planning to take it to work with me, and went back to bed. My husband got up before me and found the letter. He said, "When you write stuff like that, don't leave it lying around." I knew he couldn't deal with and did not want to hear about what I deal with everyday, but I remember that it also made me feel so very alone. I remember thinking, "How am I supposed to help my workers, when I don't know how to deal with it myself." One of the most agonizing things about this event was the community members calling to make themselves feel better. The callers needed someone to talk to because they had heard BreAnna cry or had suspicions about the abuser and they were trying to find someone who would understand or relieve them of the guilt they were feeling. The workers and I talked about this and discussed how we wanted to scream at them that if they had done what they should have, BreAnna would be alive. Of course, being the empathetic social workers that we were, we listened and also felt their agony. I still get choked up and tearful when I read the story of BreAnna.

It took Lori almost twenty years to discuss the trauma she went through on that day. Many workers have never discussed the cases that brought the most trauma into their lives and do not realize that the reactions they have are symptoms of secondary traumatic stress. This book is the result of years of research and study regarding the prevalence of secondary traumatic stress among child welfare workers. It is our hope that it will help the countless child welfare workers affected by secondary traumatic stress to work through what has happened and is happening to them. We also hope that it will give others the information they need to recognize the symptoms as they occur.

Advice to the Reader

This book contains both qualitative and quantitative information. The information is sometimes graphic and painful. The content may evoke difficult memories in the reader. We suggest that staying cognitive while reading this text will make the content more understandable and usable. Please take this into account and plan your reading accordingly. When possible, it may be beneficial to discuss the content in groups. While much of the content is centered on traumatic situations and the negative results of working with trauma victims, we also discuss successful outcomes for children and families and rewards of working in the field of child welfare.

Acknowledgments

WE WOULD LIKE TO EXPRESS OUR THANKS TO THE CHILD WELFARE WORK-ers, supervisors, and administrators who made our research on secondary traumatic stress and child welfare possible and who shared their stories and experiences with us. We also want to thank them for the work that they do everyday to protect children and preserve families.

Numerous people have generously supported this project. We want to thank our social work librarian at the University of Alabama, Lynn Tobola, for her professionalism and commitment to this project. Professor Cindy Roff, former dean of the School of Social Work, University of Alabama, supported the project with resources and encouragement. We also want to thank Professor James Leeper for his assistance with data analysis and his critical review of Appendix A, and Teresa Golson, University of Alabama, for graphic art support.

Lori Woodruff, University of Southern Mississippi School of Social Work, and Crystal Collins-Camargo, University of Kentucky College of Social Work, have shared their ideas and provided much-needed feedback. Dr. Kristina Jaskyte, University of Georgia School of Social Work, assisted with the data management. The late Judy Birmingham, former director of the Child Welfare Center, University of Texas at Arlington School of Social Work, recognized the importance of this project from the beginning and supported its development. Hugh McKay, Fort Worth Vet Center, contributed to the development of the initial training in 1995. We also thank the Frank and Simon family and Julia Hartman for their support, as well as our helpmates Angie Mills, Regina Wilson, and Jessie Jones.

Several students have worked on this project since its inception. We wish to express our appreciation to Grandville Andrews, Angela Curl, Tamika McDowell, and Fang "Sandy" Lin for their invaluable assistance.

We thank our family and friends who listened, supported, and encouraged our endeavor. We especially want to thank Kim's children, Amanda, David, and Ben, for their patience as their mother's time was absorbed by this project.

We also want to thank David Follmer and Sonia Fulop of Lyceum Books, Inc., for their support and guidance.

Introduction

Would you have become a child protective services worker if you knew that in three months you could not do paper work properly, in six months you would not know when a child was abused and neglected, in nine months you would not be able to trust anyone, and in a year you would be in need of tranquilizers and looking for a new job that might not even be in social work?

S. D. Lee, "Staying Alive in Child Protective Services"

THIS BOOK ENDEAVOR BEGAN TEN YEARS AGO WHEN A SOCIAL WORK EDU-cator in one state and a child welfare director of training in another, unaware at the time of each other's existence, recognized that both child welfare social work masters students in a part-time program and child welfare professionals working in the field were experiencing problems associated with their work. While an abundance of literature suggested that burnout is a problem for the child welfare professional, it seemed to both of these independent observers that the problem might be more than burnout, or perhaps something entirely different. Burnout is most often associated with high stress coupled with heavy demands and low personal and professional reward in the workplace. These are conditions inherent in child welfare work. Burnout is a phenomenon that occurs gradually. It takes time to burn out, and some of the students and child welfare workers with whom the authors were working were relatively new to the field of child protection. However, they still seemed to be experiencing problems associated with the work. When Charles Figley's *Compassion Fatigue* (1995), which addressed secondary traumatic stress (STS), was published, the question was raised whether or not these child welfare students and workers were experiencing STS.

Figley identified factors that make helping professionals vulnerable to STS. The factors are highly characteristic of child welfare professionals and include empathic engagement with clients, having experienced personal trauma in childhood or as an adult, having a past traumatic experience that is affecting the present due to one's exposure to another person's trauma, and working with traumatized children. Child welfare work requires regular use of empathic engagement to help clients share with the worker what their traumatic experience has been. We know from experience and research that many students become interested in child welfare because of their own personal histories of trauma. Most, if not all, of the children with whom workers are involved have had traumatic experiences, and some may well be horrific. We hypothesized that unresolved trauma experienced by the worker might be drawn to the surface and could possibly affect the worker in a variety of ways. It seemed logical that STS might be what the child protection workers and the MSW students were experiencing, rather than burnout.

With the possibility that STS was affecting this group of part-time child welfare social work students, an intervention was arranged by the professor and a readjustment counselor from the Fort Worth Vet Center in Texas. The professor and counselor made a joint presentation on posttraumatic stress in general and STS in particular. They discussed how trauma affects people as well as individual coping strategies and the use of social support to work through STS. As part of the presentation, students were asked to share anonymously any traumatic experiences they had experienced either in childhood or as an adult that were somehow related to their work by describing the experience on a five-by-seven note card. The students revealed an abundance of trauma responses consistent with STS. After gaining knowledge about how the trauma of child welfare work was affecting them, the students asked the professor to develop a workshop that could be shared with child welfare staff throughout the state.

THE STS AND CHILD WELFARE WORKSHOP

A committee was expeditiously formed and was charged with developing the STS and Child Welfare Workshop. Child welfare workers and supervisors, educators with expertise in trauma and stress, a vet center readjustment counselor, and a technical writer/trainer with considerable knowledge of traumatic stress developed a six-hour psychoeducational workshop on compassion fatigue. The workshop had several goals. The first was to increase participant knowledge of traumatic stress and its impact on child welfare professionals, with the objectives of addressing the differences between burnout and STS and identifying how people respond to trauma and ways to categorize the responses. The last objective was to identify typical patterns of attitudes and behaviors of child welfare professionals and traumatized clients and how attitudes and behaviors affect the relationship.

The workshop also focused on individual coping skills that can be learned and used by child welfare professionals to reduce the impact of STS. The objectives included identifying personal factors influencing readiness to effectively manage STS, professional factors influencing readiness to manage STS, and the need to balance personal life, professional life, and agency demands. The final three objectives addressed how quality supervision mitigates the negative effects of STS, how to identify signs of a failing system of self-care, and how to identify both positive and negative coping behaviors that contribute to successful and unsuccessful management of STS.

The last goal of the workshop was to increase knowledge of the role of social support in reducing the effects of STS on child welfare professionals. This goal was supported by four objectives. The first objective was to gain an understanding of the difference between the social support of colleagues and that of families. The next objective was to increase understanding as to how multiple interpersonal interactions among members of an individual's support system and the affected person might reduce a stressed person's discomfort. The last two objectives were to increase understanding of the structure and use of both personal and professional social support systems and understanding of the behavioral roles of support seekers and support providers.

The workshop was highly interactive and incorporated several practical exercises. The centerpiece exercise began by randomly assigning roles of supervisor, caseworker, and fellow caseworker to participants working in small groups. The participants were then presented with scenarios describing either the death of a child, the removal of children from a home, or the sexual assault of a child. The participants then worked through the exercises by responding to questions that linked the education they received in the workshop to the scenario events. One group worked through the requirement from the caseworker's perspective. The other two groups worked through the same scenario from the perspective of supervisor or fellow caseworker. The last activity was to share what had been learned in the group exercise with the other workshop participants.

The workshop has been presented to hundreds of child welfare workers in several states and has consistently received positive participant evaluations since its inception almost ten years ago. At the beginning of the workshop, participants were asked to complete the Compassion Fatigue Self-Test (Figley, 1995). Data from five states have been collected and are an integral part of this text. As we presented the material, gathered data, and interacted with several hundred child welfare workers, we hypothesized that STS is a phenomenon affecting child welfare professionals and possibly contributing to the current worker retention crisis.

ONE AUTHOR'S EXPERIENCE AS A CHILD WELFARE PROFESSIONAL

Three years prior to meeting the other two authors of this book, Kim Shackelford was employed as a child welfare supervisor. She was supervising nine workers in two counties. At the time, she had seven years' experience with the public child welfare agency, five of which were as a direct-line worker in child protection and foster care. She had worked with hundreds of abused and neglected children. Before becoming supervisor, Shackelford had been the advanced social worker responsible for the more difficult and horrific sexual abuse cases within a twenty-county area.

While she was a supervisor, two cases occurred at the same time in which she was unable to keep the children involved from being sexually abused again, even after they became involved with the child welfare system. The first involved a five-year-old boy who, despite the recommendation of the child welfare worker, was allowed unsupervised visitation in the paternal grandparent's home by a judge's order. The outcome was that the child was sexually abused again by his father. Only then did the visits stop. The other situation involved a five-year-old girl whose stepfather involved her in child pornography. Because the stepfather was highly educated and of a higher socioeconomic class, the judge could not believe the child was telling the truth. The child continued to have unsupervised visits with her mother and stepfather and continued to be sexually abused.

These two incidences together were stressful to Shackelford. She became angry and irritable. She had nightmares about children being harmed. Intrusive thoughts and rumination were continuous. There was no time when she did not think about how to protect the little girl from further harm. She was constantly trying to figure out ways to prove the abuse was happening and to get the decision-making powers to listen and act to protect the child. Shackelford tells about being in church and looking around the congregation and being angry at everyone there for being naive and stupid about how bad the world really was. This was not Shackelford's normal worldview prior to this point in her life and is not now. She knew at that point that something was wrong. She doubted her effectiveness as a child welfare professional. She had lost perspective and felt like she could no longer be useful in protecting children. Even though she had planned to make child welfare a lifelong career, she turned in her resignation notice.

The resignation was met with anger and resentment from coworkers. The social workers she supervised told her that they felt betrayed and hopeless and that they could not believe she was giving up. Her peers, other supervisors and administrators, were disappointed in her. Her supervisor and others told her that she was "just burnt out" and could not "cut it" anymore. Shackelford reports thinking that she did not feel burned out, but maybe everyone was right and she really could not cut it anymore. She remembers: "I knew something was wrong. I didn't think I was burned out. I was changed somehow, different. . . . I just didn't have a name for what was wrong." She went to work in another setting for two years. It took that long for her to return to a worldview that people are mostly good and that the world is full of people who want to protect children from harm. She was then offered a job in the training unit of the public child welfare agency. She had been working for the public child welfare agency for over a year (the second time around) when she met Jo and Dave Pryce.

Kim Shackelford attended an STS presentation given by the Pryces at a Mississippi and Alabama social work educators conference. The presentation helped her to understand what had happened to her while working with the particularly difficult child sexual abuse cases in which all her efforts to protect the children were to no avail. Shackelford remembers blinking back tears and trying very hard to control herself as a lump began forming in her throat; her heart began racing, and her stomach started twisting. As she listened to the presentation on secondary traumatic stress and its symptoms, she realized that she had not burned out and that there was a name for what had happened to her. She also realized that no one with whom she previously worked understood STS. The realization was exciting and a relief at the same time. She recalls being overwhelmed with gratitude and, for the first time, understanding of what had happened to her as she approached Dave and Jo Pryce to thank them for their work and their presentation. Shackelford knew that this information was needed by all child welfare workers. She quickly arranged for the training for all child welfare workers in her state.

ABOUT THIS BOOK

Meeting for the first time at the conference, the three of us recognized that we shared common concerns for child welfare practitioners and their well-being. We have made numerous presentations regarding STS. Each time the result is that several child welfare workers thank us for helping them understand what happened or is happening to them. Many are in tears as they share their experiences, but all are excited regarding their new knowledge and understanding.

This book represents what we have learned from many workers, supervisors, and administrators. It focuses solely on child welfare professionals and how the data we have collected demonstrate how they are affected by STS. The book also discusses coping strategies and how to use social support to mitigate the effects of STS. We explain how to recognize when self-care strategies are failing and what to do when this occurs. The book also discusses supervision and what supervisors can do to help workers who are experiencing STS. We discuss how organizational culture affects the working environment and how the organizational acceptance of STS as a normal reaction to child protection work can help workers deal with the effects of STS. We examine what works and does not work in child welfare administration with regard to workers and supervisors and the mitigation of the effects of STS. We explain why STS is an occupational hazard in child welfare work and how it may result in an occupational stress injury. We try to help child welfare professionals stay in child welfare and find meaning in their work as they give up innocence for wisdom. Finally, we address implications for social work education with regard to STS and child welfare.

The epilogue summarizes the content and suggests areas for future research on STS and child welfare. While this book focuses on child welfare workers, its content may be relevant to other helping professionals who work predominately with vulnerable and traumatized populations. The authors recognize the outstanding work of the many scientists, scholars, and educators who have contributed to the field of traumatology. Their work has allowed us to deepen our understanding of how traumatic stress affects child welfare practitioners and what can be done about it.

1

Traumatic Stress in Child Welfare

TRAUMATIC STRESS AND CHILD WELFARE ARE LIKELY PAIRED TERMS, AND IT would seem obvious that the relationship between the two would have been explored since the beginning of professional involvement with abused and neglected children. The literature, however, is not replete with studies of traumatic stress and child welfare. On the contrary, the discussion and study of problems associated with social workers being affected by indirect trauma is relatively new (Bride, 2004; Figley, 1995; Pearlman & Saakvitne, 1995). In a review of the literature, Bride found only fifteen published studies of empirical research on secondary traumatic stress and vicarious traumatization in psychosocial service providers.

We have been immersed in the study of child welfare and traumatic stress and therefore tend to bring these topics into professional discussions involving many of the problems associated with the child welfare system, especially discussions about worker retention and turnover. Our pleas for others to pay attention to this phenomenon are often dismissed by those we are trying to convince. Our passion for helping child protection workers deal with the traumatic stress of the work has not always been understood by other professionals. Many times the lack of understanding or dismissal comes from child welfare administrators and social work educators. This is puzzling, as it would seem that if understanding the effects of traumatic stress improved the retention of workers in the field and strengthened the services to children and families, then knowledge in this area would be sought. We have found the study of trauma to be riddled with fits and starts and lack of acknowledgment in more than one professional field. This may seem like a strange place to start a book about traumatic stress and child welfare, but bear with us, and the following discussion and history will have relevance for what will follow in the rest of this chapter. Through the examination of the history of the study of trauma, we have found possible answers as to why the effects of traumatic stress have not been acknowledged in the field of child welfare.

SILENCING THE STUDY OF TRAUMA

Herman (1992) claimed that because of the inherent nature of studying trauma, which requires the student to face unspeakable events, over the past century there have been periods of attention to the problem and periods in which "lines of inquiry have been taken up and abruptly abandoned, only to be rediscovered

much later" (p. 7). Herman described a typical traumatic event as having a perpetrator and a victim and possibly a bystander. She exposed the bystander's dilemma
in that victims plead for help and ask something of the bystander, whereas perpe-
trators only demand silence from the bystander: "If [the perpetrator] cannot silence
her absolutely, he tries to make sure no one listens. To this end, he marshals an im-
pressive array of arguments, from the most blatant denial to the most sophisticated
and elegant rationalization. After every atrocity one can expect to hear the same predictable apologies: it never happened; the victim lies; the victim exaggerates; the
victim brought it upon herself; and in any case it is time to forget the past and move
on" (Herman, 1992, p. 8). Herman compared the attempt to silence the victim to
the suppression of the study of trauma. The literature on the study of psychological
trauma reveals a constant debate regarding the realness of the effects of trauma and
the veracity and level of suffering of trauma victims. She also claimed that the political climate has not always been supportive of trauma studies. "Repression, dissociation, and denial are phenomena of social as well as individual consciousness"
(Herman, 1992, p. 9). Like the bystander, even though out of curiosity we might
want to glance at a victim of trauma, as a society, many of us do not want to face all
that the trauma entails.

Herman referred to the public's reception of Freud's discovery of childhood sexual abuse in his female patients as an example of the attempts of professionals and
society to suppress the study of trauma by finding fault with victims and those who
study their plight.

> Freud's investigations led the furthest of all into the unrecognized reality of women's
> lives. His discovery of childhood sexual exploitation at the roots of hysteria crossed the
> outer limits of social credibility and brought him to a position of total ostracism
> within his profession. The publication of *The Aetiology of Hysteria,* which he had ex-
> pected to bring him glory, was met with a stony and universal silence among his elders
> and peers. As he wrote Fliess shortly afterward, "I am as isolated as you could wish me
> to be: the word has been given out to abandon me, and a void is forming around me."
> (Herman, 1992, p. 18)

McFarlane and Van der Kolk (1996) echoed Herman's thoughts by emphasiz-
ing the lack of attention given to trauma by medical school departments of psychiatry. Despite the fact that almost three million children in the United States were
abused and/or neglected in 1992, and it had been shown that a substantial number
of these children would develop trauma-related psychiatric disorders, by 1996,
there was only one published controlled psychopharmacological study of the treatment of posttraumatic stress disorder (PTSD) in children in existence. Compared to
the thirteen studies of this type regarding children with obsessive-compulsive disorder and thirty-six studies of this type regarding children with attention-deficit/
hyperactivity disorder (ADHD), McFarlane and Van der Kolk found the world to be
lacking in studies regarding psychopharmacological treatment of PTSD in children.
The researchers also noted that no past trauma history was discussed in the ADHD
studies even though girls with attention-deficit/hyperactivity disorder have been

shown to have a strong possibility of sexual abuse in their past (McFarlane & Van der Kolk, 1996).

When discussing the effects of trauma on the individual, Van der Kolk, Weisaeth, and Van der Hart (1996) exposed the historical questioning of patient malingering, moral weakness of the individual, or the inability of the person to take charge and responsibility for his or her own life. Herman (1992) professed that "It is not only the patients but also the investigators of post-traumatic conditions whose credibility is repeatedly challenged" (p. 9). She discussed the professional isolation that occurs for persons who research trauma "beyond the bounds of conventional belief" as being susceptible to becoming "suspect among their colleagues" (Herman, 1992, p. 9).

Just as Freud and his colleagues were silenced at the end of the nineteenth century, women were continuously kept from talking about their traumas. Throughout the twentieth century until the 1990s, women were not to speak of rape, domestic violence, childhood sexual abuse, or any exploitation, and to do so would be met with ridicule, humiliation, disbelief, and resulting feelings of shame and guilt (Herman, 1992). Until the 1970s and the women's liberation movement, women's trauma and resulting traumatic disorders were not recognized. As Van der Kolk, Weisaeth, and Van der Hart (1996) noted, "Between 1895 and 1974, the study of trauma centered almost exclusively on its effects on white males" (p. 61).

A BRIEF HISTORY OF TRAUMATOLOGY

The study of psychological origins of traumatic stress has included two paths that joined in 1980 when posttraumatic stress disorder was first included in the American Psychiatric Association's third edition of the *Diagnostic Statistical Manual* (Figley, 1995; Herman, 1992; Van der Kolk, Weisaeth, & Van der Hart, 1996). One path began with the study of hysteria and the other began with the study of the traumatic neurosis of war (Herman, 1992). The study of hysteria began in the late 1800s but was ignored throughout the twentieth century until the 1970s, when it reappeared in a line of inquiry regarding trauma in the lives of women and children (Herman, 1992). A divergent path from each line of research was the study of civilian trauma and natural disasters (Van der Kolk, 1984; Van der Kolk et al., 1996). These types of studies started later than the two initial streams of research but fed into the information used to determine the elements of posttraumatic stress disorder (Van der Kolk et al., 1996).

The field of traumatology has its roots in war and combat stress. Weisaeth (2002) refers to World War I as a "watershed" of knowledge regarding shell shock or combat trauma (p. 443). Unfortunately, once a war is over, interest in soldiers quickly evaporates, and caregivers in the next armed conflict have to learn all over again. Even with the significant knowledge gained during World War I about shell shock, soldiers were abandoned in hospitals following World War I. In 1935, Brigadier General Smedley Butler, United States Marine Corps, who twice received the Congressional Medal of Honor, toured the nation's hospitals for World War I veterans. He wrote:

On a tour of this country, in the midst of which I am at the time of this writing, I have visited 18 government hospitals for veterans. In them are a total of about 50,000 destroyed men—men who were the pick of the nation 18 years ago. The very able chief surgeon at the government hospital in Milwaukee, where there are 3,800 of the living dead, told me that mortality among veterans is three times as great as among those who stayed home.

Boys with a *normal viewpoint* were taken out of the fields and offices and factories and classrooms and put into the ranks. There they were remolded; they were made over; they were made to "about face"; to regard murder as the order of the day. They were put shoulder to shoulder and, through mass psychology, they were entirely changed. We used them for a couple of years and trained them to think nothing at all about killing or being killed.

Then, suddenly, we discharged them and told them to make another "about face"! This time they had to do their own readjusting, sans mass psychology, sans officers' aid and advice, sans nation-wide propaganda. We didn't need them anymore. So we scattered them about without any "three-minute" or "Liberty Loan" speeches or parades.

Many, too many, of these fine young boys are eventually destroyed, mentally, because they could not make that final "about face" alone. (Butler, 1935, pp. 33–34; italics added)

Following World War I, interest in combat stress lagged. During World War II the lessons from World War I had to be relearned, yet the same faulty practices for treatment of combat stress were employed. Between World War II and the Korean War, the long-term effects of combat-related trauma proved to be significant. A study by the U.S. Department of Veterans Affairs (1994) found that 22,273 veterans spent 2,005,404 days in the hospital for mental illness with an average stay of 90 days. Two longitudinal studies (Archibald, Long, Miller, & Tuddenham, 1962; Archibald & Tuddenham, 1965) demonstrated that fifteen and twenty years following World War II what was then called combat fatigue syndrome was chronic. The veterans had symptoms of what we now know as posttraumatic stress disorder.

It was largely the Vietnam War that brought about the beginnings of a deeper understanding of what trauma is and what it does to human beings. Veterans returning from Vietnam did not find a welcoming atmosphere or assistance from the Veterans Administration health-care system. Some veterans responded by gathering in rap groups in major cities and beginning the process of talking about what they were experiencing as they tried to readjust (Scott, 1993). At the veterans' invitation, psychologists, psychiatrists, and social workers joined the groups. Collectively, the groups began to understand that the veterans, especially those who had experienced heavy combat, demonstrated similar reactions to their combat experience. The cluster of reactions was also similar to what had been observed in the longitudinal studies of World War II veterans.

Mental health professionals and other clinicians who treated patients for non-combat-related trauma, such as burn victims or victims of sexual assault, took the cluster of reactions to the American Psychiatric Association. War neurosis was replaced in the third revision of the *Diagnostic and Statistical Manual of Mental*

Disorders with the diagnostic label posttraumatic stress disorder (American Psychiatric Association, 1980; Scott, 1993). Since 1980, many advances in the treatment of traumatic stress, regardless of the cause, have occurred. This progress in mental health knowledge and practice is one of the positive legacies of the Vietnam War and its veterans (Pryce & Pryce, 2000). As a result of the work that followed, the Veterans Administration established storefront community-based centers to provide readjustment counseling for Vietnam veterans. These vet centers have proved to be a most effective model for enabling the readjustment of combat veterans (Pryce & Pryce, 2000).

Advances in the treatment of trauma resulted in increasing numbers of clinicians working with trauma clients and researchers conducting studies that validated the theory underlying PTSD. In 1991, Donovan transformed the term "traumatic stress" into "traumatology," effectively making it the term used for the field of study. Donovan defined the term as the study of trauma and its social and psychobiological effects. The field includes study of predictive and preventive factors, and interventions that evolve from research (p. 434). The field of traumatology has grown quickly and has produced a variety of constructs related to trauma as well as journals and traumatic stress organizations (Morrissette, 2004). It remains a young field with the potential for continued growth, and the interventions that come about continue to contribute to trauma healing.

THE EMERGENCE OF COMPASSION FATIGUE AND SECONDARY TRAUMATIC STRESS

In 1995, Figley raised the question of what happens to the clinician who treats traumatized clients. He wrote: "Perhaps even more important, the burnout and countertransference literature suggests that therapists are vulnerable to experiencing stress as a result of their jobs, yet few studies can identify the active ingredients that are most connected to this job/profession-related stress. It appears that secondary traumatic stress—or, as we prefer, compassion fatigue—is the syndrome that puts most therapists at risk" (p. xiv).

In previous writing, Figley (1989) voiced concern that colleagues were leaving the field because of the pain of working with traumatized people. He theorized that just as a traumatized person can traumatize others in his or her family by sharing traumatic experience, it is equally possible for the traumatized client to traumatize the clinician working with him or her. As Figley (1995) pointed out, the focus of the traumatology field and work has been on the clients, not on those who care for them. It was time to examine secondary traumatic stress and learn if and how clinicians become traumatized by their clients.

Figley (1995) defined STS as "the natural consequent behaviors and emotions resulting from knowing about a traumatizing event experienced by a significant other" (p. 7). He argued that STS is equivalent to PTSD with the exception of the etiology; STS comes from the relationship between a traumatized person and a caregiver, either family or professional. The cluster of reactions to being a witness to a traumatized person is the same as those of PTSD. The traumatized person shares information of an abnormal experience that is severely distressing, and subsequently the listener may reexperience the episode through recollection, dreams, intrusive thoughts, and reminders of the event. Avoidance and emotional numbness may also be reactions. The consequence is avoidance of thoughts and feelings or situations that serve as reminders of the trauma, psychogenic amnesia, withdrawal from others, a loss of interests, feeling flat, and in some cases a loss of a sense of future. The person may also experience persistent arousal, trouble sleeping or staying asleep, outbursts of anger, difficulty concentrating, hypervigilance for the traumatized person, exaggerated startle response, and physical reactions to reminders of the trauma.

STS is not to be confused with either countertransference or burnout. STS is a much broader concept than countertransference. Countertransference occurs in the context of a clinical therapeutic relationship between a professional and a client. Countertransference concerns any response, personal feelings, and memories a clinician has relating to a client and may be conscious or unconscious (Friedman, 2001; Pearlman & Saakvitne, 1995). Countertransference is likely to occur when there are likenesses between the client's experiences and the therapist's experiences that are sufficiently strong to elicit feelings, memories, and physiological reactions in the therapist (Friedman, 2001). As Figley (1995) pointed out, STS may include countertransference, but it is the product of caring between two people, one of whom has been traumatized, and the other who is listening to her or him talk about the trauma. It can occur within a professional or a nonprofessional relationship. Although it often happens to workers who have a personal history of trauma, it is also possible for the witness not to have had traumatic experiences and yet, through empathic engagement, become traumatized by the experience of the client. It is possible to experience STS with several clients who have been traumatized, particularly if they are children or vulnerable in some other way.

BURNOUT

Burnout is a different phenomenon from STS. Burnout is anchored in the organizational culture and work environment and is associated with low personal reward and high work-related demand in an unsupportive environment (Freudenberger, 1974; Harrison, 1983; Maslach, 1982; Maslach & Jackson, 1981). Burnout is strongly associated with human service agencies (Bhana & Haffejee, 1996; Daley, 1979; Drake & Yadama, 1996; Felton, 1998; Harrison, 1980; Himle, Jayaratne, & Thyness, 1991; Jayaratne & Chess, 1984; Myung-Yong & Harrison, 1998; Poulin & Walter, 1993; Shinn, Rosario, Morch, & Chestnut, 1984; Soderfeldt, Soderfeldt, & Warg, 1995; Treadwell, Saxton, & Mulholland, 1995). It takes time to be affected by burnout, in some cases years. Burnout does not occur in the first weeks or months on the job. In contrast, STS can occur with the first traumatized client the clinician works with in the first weeks or months of work. Another difference that Figley pointed out is that a practitioner can recover more quickly from STS than from burnout.

It may be necessary to leave the work environment in order to recover from burnout. Burnout comes from the organizational culture, and that culture may be an artifact of the nature of the work. It may not be possible to change the work environment or the factors that are contributing to burnout. If workers have little or no ability to affect or change burnout factors that affect their work, then what they can change is where they work and with whom they work. Being affected by one's work is not the same thing as being unfit to do the work. Many competent and qualified workers leave child welfare for less stressful and more supportive work environments.

TRAUMATOLOGY AND CHILD WELFARE PROFESSIONALS

When Figley (1995) addressed the concept of STS, he argued that four factors make for vulnerability to compassion fatigue: empathy, personal trauma history, unresolved trauma, and children's trauma. One professional area where these factors are often found is child welfare. This raised for us the question of whether or not child welfare professionals are being affected by STS and mistaking it for burnout.

Retention is a major problem in child welfare (Bernotavicz, 1997; Ellett & Leighninger, 1998; General Accounting Office, 2003; Rycraft, 1994). Workers often leave within months of finishing training. This loss contributes to unstable relationships between clients and the agency and is also an economic loss, given what it costs to train workers. If child welfare workers are leaving because of STS, we believe it may be possible to find ways to support them so they can learn to master the work and simultaneously cope effectively (Pryce & Pryce, 2000).

APPLYING TRAUMA THEORY TO CHILD WELFARE WORK

It is difficult for anyone but child welfare professionals to understand the work they do. The public in general certainly doesn't understand. All too often the only media attention child welfare receives is negative, often involving a child's death. The successes are seldom known or interesting enough to be considered newsworthy by the press. Child welfare workers often work with the darkest side of humanity; people do evil things to children and adolescents. The communities in which they work and the homes they visit are often among the poorest. Unemployment is high and drugs abound. They work in social conditions that are plagued by epidemics such as the use of methamphetamine. The abuse and neglect of children and adolescents is horrific and runs the gamut of sexual, physical, emotional, and psychological contexts.

The organizations in which child welfare workers work, filling out endless forms and writing case notes, are not necessarily the most supportive, nor are state officials, who can conjure up some of the strangest policies in pursuit of organizational effectiveness or lawsuit avoidance. Policy, often defined by lawyers or administrators who do not know or understand the work, can change daily and often does. There are never enough resources or foster homes in which to safely place a child.

Workers are constantly aware that the assessments they do will affect the well-being and safety of children.

Fear is a factor in child protection work, and it may spring from either indirect or direct sources. One worker told us about a judge to whom a case was presented. The judge wanted to return an adolescent girl to the home where, the girl's older sisters had shared with the worker, their father's sexual abuse of them began at the client's age. The judge stated that the child had not been abused and ordered her return to a known abuser. The worker feared greatly for the child. There is always the threat of danger. Danger may come from a wayward bullet in a run-down neighborhood or a client who is determined to "get" you. Another worker told us about an adolescent client who, in a psychotic state, took a butcher knife and chased the worker back to her car.

Trauma abounds in this work, yet little attention has been given to child welfare professionals and how their use of empathy and relationship may contribute to their own traumatic stress. In 2001, there were 37,777 child protective service workers involved with 1,460,239 children whose caregivers were being investigated for abuse and neglect (U.S. Department of Health and Human Services, 2004). These data underestimate the number of child protective service workers in the United States because six states did not provide data. The figure also does not include other types of child welfare workers such as foster care workers.

In applying trauma theory to child welfare work, it is important to explain how we use Figley's term "secondary traumatic stress" and McCann and Pearlman's term "vicarious traumatization." McCann and Pearlman (1990) describe how vicarious traumatization is a process that alters the inner life of the clinician and ultimately his or her personal and interpersonal behavior. We think the process of vicarious traumatization can lead to STS symptoms and ultimately to STS disorder. Our hypothesis is that child welfare professionals using empathic engagement and relationships with clients, who are most often children and adolescents, experience vicarious traumatization that results in the development of STS. Child welfare is a predominately female profession, and we hypothesize that many of these women have experienced childhood trauma, which may increase their vulnerability to STS. Without intervention and over time, childhood trauma can become STS disorder. This is both a process and an outcome and is best understood through McCann and Pearlman's use of constructivist self-development theory.

CONSTRUCTIVIST SELF-DEVELOPMENT THEORY

Constructivist self-development theory asserts, among other things, that each individual has fundamental psychological needs: safety, dependency/trust, power, esteem, intimacy, independence, and a frame of reference through which life is experienced and interpreted (McCann & Pearlman, 1990, p. 137). From the time a child is born to the present moment of his or her life, these cognitive schemata are in a constant state of development and change based upon the individual's life experiences.

For example, a baby who is cared for and fed, gets his or her diapers changed in a timely manner, and is held and consoled when he or she cries develops knowledge and experiences of safety, trust, intimacy, and being able to make things happen. With time, cognitive schemata continue to grow and change based upon new life experiences. As time passes and growth continues, the child proceeds to adulthood with a set of cognitive schemata based upon his or her life experiences. If the child is cared for, then his or her development is likely to be positive, and his or her frame of reference or worldview is likely to be positive. For the most part, when negative things happen they can be interpreted and integrated into the psychological frame of reference in a meaningful way.

Another example: you are driving along and someone in another car hits you. You are shaken up, but it is not a bad accident and everyone is okay, and there has been minimal damage to the vehicles. When you get back into your car to drive home, your sense of safety and trust in other drivers are shaken. The experience of being hit has altered your cognitive schemata. The next time you get into your car to go somewhere, you may feel a bit of anxiety, question your safety, and be somewhat hypervigilant regarding other drivers. As you continue to drive without another accident happening, your experience will transform the experience of being in an accident into a broader psychological frame of reference.

Cognitive schemata represent our belief system, the assumptions we make about the world and what we expect will happen. It is through these schemata that life experiences are filtered and interpretation and meanings of experiences are developed. These schemata are also influenced by experiences across the life span and the environment in which social interactions take place. McCann and Pearlman (1990) also find other aspects of self to be influential to cognitive schemata. Ego resources influence social interactions and include aspects of self such as intelligence, reflection, initiation, insight, and self-awareness that shape the interpretation and meaning of experience, which in turn contributes to shaping psychological needs. Self-capacities regulate self-esteem and also influence the interpretation and meaning of events. They include the ability to tolerate strong effect, to be comfortable when alone, to be able to calm down when needed, and to regulate negative thoughts and feelings toward oneself. It is also important to understand cognitive schemata from the perspective of development (McCann & Pearlman, 1990). Cognitive schemata develop across the life span and develop in a social environment. At any point in time in an individual's development, traumatic events can disrupt the developing schemata, challenging beliefs, assumptions, and expectations about life and other people.

Depending upon factors that influence self-development, the continuum of cognitive schemata is such that they may constitute a highly positive worldview or an extremely negative worldview. Cognitive schemata that constitute the individual's worldview are highly individualized. It is important to understand that traumatic experiences or stress will be uniquely experienced by the individual and not necessarily shared by others having the same or a similar experience.

When traumatic experiences occur, cognitive schemata are altered, and the effects may be permanent (McCann & Pearlman, 1990). Like the soldiers General Butler wrote about, the child welfare professional experiences changes from a normal viewpoint to an altered viewpoint or worldview. Child welfare professionals repeatedly see and listen to children's and adolescents' accounts of their traumatic experiences. They record these accounts with precision and detail. They recall these accounts with supervisors and other administrators. They also guide the child or adolescent through a system of other professionals in which their experiences are repeated over and again. McCann and Pearlman (1990) argue that clinicians may internalize the memories of their clients, which may alter their own memory systems (p. 142). It is just as likely that child welfare professionals experience alterations in their memory systems, and they may start to see the world through their clients' frame of reference rather than their own. Without an opportunity to share what they are experiencing, these professionals may use avoidance, numbing, and distancing to cope with their distress, which may affect their work with their clients and their relationships with colleagues and significant others.

As McCann and Pearlman (1990) argue, the more connected the client's trauma experience is to the worker's life experiences, particularly if the worker has a childhood trauma history, the more entrenched the memory may become to the child welfare professional. Pearlman and Saakvitne (1995) further hypothesize that working with traumatized clients can "disrupt an individual sense of meaning, identity, connection to others and their worldview to include affect tolerance, psychological needs, beliefs about self and others, interpersonal relationships, as well as sensory memory" (p. 151). The client's trauma becomes the child welfare professional's trauma; he or she is literally infected. Furthermore, the larger child welfare system can become infected as each person involved with the case becomes familiar with the client's traumatic experience.

The application of trauma theory to child welfare professionals is timely. Consistent, ongoing personnel turnover has created a national crisis in the field of child welfare (General Accounting Office, 2003). Drake and Yadama's 1996 study found a turnover of 46 to 90 percent among child welfare workers. This compromises the profession and children's and families' continuity of care. It may also lead to negative outcomes for families who must deal with several workers rather than being able to build an effective relationship with one worker. If child welfare professionals are experiencing STS, there are interventions that can be put into place to help these professionals cope and therefore avoid negative changes in their cognitive schemata and frames of reference. It may be possible to learn to manage the outcomes hypothesized by Pearlman and Saakvitne (1995). It is possible to intervene in the organizational culture and make changes that would create a supportive environment and build cohesion among colleagues.

EMPIRICAL EVIDENCE OF STS AMONG HELPING PROFESSIONALS

There is a growing abundance of literature regarding compassion fatigue among a wide range of helping professionals. Empirical studies of compassion fatigue or vicarious traumatization, still an emerging field, are few but growing. Bride (2004) found fifteen independent studies of the impact of trauma work on professionals providing psychosocial services to clients. The following represents a summary of that review.

In the studies reviewed, the greater the exposure to trauma, the stronger the trauma symptoms. In five studies no strong support for changes in cognitive schemata was found. There were mixed results regarding general psychological distress, which appeared most strongly in sexual assault trauma counselors and child protective service workers. One study of community-based case managers who met the criteria for PTSD due to secondary exposure to trauma showed that some managers experienced greater psychological distress than others. Five of seven studies found no relation between secondary trauma and age. Among sexual assault counselors, a younger age was related to a greater number of secondary trauma symptoms. Gender was not a factor except in two studies. One study found female trauma therapists had greater STS than male trauma therapists. Another found differences between male and female child protective service workers' symptoms of psychological distress.

Bride found a few studies that examined academic and professional roles. A study comparing psychologists and social workers found social workers had higher levels of STS, which were unrelated to the level of their educational degree. A study of child welfare workers found no relationship between education level, discipline, and STS. Another study found no relationship between STS in community mental health caseworkers and discipline or appointment level. Although the sample was small, one study did find increased stress disorder among administrators working at the Oklahoma City bombing scene.

A study comparing length of professional experience and psychological distress or STS found mixed results. Six studies found no relationship between the variables. Two studies found an inverse relationship between length of experience and trauma reactions. In contrast, three studies found that length of experience working with traumatized clients increased trauma symptoms. Five of the studies reviewed found that trauma symptoms in clinicians were associated with clients with an experience of sexual trauma. At the same time, two other studies found there was no relationship between these two variables. Only two of the fifteen studies examined childhood trauma in relation to trauma work, and these did not find an increase in trauma symptoms among clinicians. Having a personal trauma history was found to be associated with an increase in trauma symptoms in four studies but was not found in two other studies. Social support was found in one study to be associated with fewer trauma symptoms, and another study found that the use of negative coping strategies correlated with increased trauma symptoms.

The studies are too few and varied in methodology and comparison of variables to draw any substantive conclusions. The wide variety of professional backgrounds may also influence the mixed results, as do the variety of measures used. As Bride noted, more empirical research is needed in this field, and longitudinal research is needed to better understand the phenomenon. Only two of the studies reviewed addressed child welfare professionals.

CHILD PROTECTIVE SERVICES: THE IMPACT ON PROFESSIONALS

A small body of literature addresses how child welfare professionals are affected by the work they do. Lee (1979) wrote:

> Child protective service in a public welfare agency is a difficult and thankless task for the social worker and supervisor. The brutality of child abuse and futility of child neglect is readily apparent to most observers, but what effect this has on the CPS worker and supervisor is not so easily seen by the untrained eye. What happens to the CPS worker in a matter of months may happen to other workers over a period of years. . . .
>
> From champion and protector of children's rights to tranquilized victim, the CPS worker's ability to make sound decisions dies under the cancer-like frustrations of ever-increasing caseloads (the better you do, the more difficult cases you get), insensitive administration (you're doing a good job, but document it with these forms so we can justify keeping your position), the demands of clients (you promised me that I could have my child back), and failing physical and mental health. (pp. 195–196)

Lee could have written this today, and it would still be relevant. Although he fully understood the problem from having been a worker and supervisor, he did not have the theories we have today about what happens to professionals who work with traumatized clients. Another point Lee made that is relevant today is that social workers are by their education trained to help others. There is little in social work education that addresses the impact trauma work can have on the social worker and ways to cope.

Morrison (1990) raised issues about the emotional effects of child protection work on workers, especially with the emergence of child sexual abuse as a major social problem. One of the issues is the survival message of "don't feel, be strong, and don't admit mistakes" (Morrison, 1990, p. 255). In other words, if you have the "right stuff," the work won't affect you. Another issue is that the majority of child welfare workers are female, but administrators are predominately male. Child welfare management is modeled after business. A consequence can be "an under-valuing of the validity of feelings, or worse, a belief that feelings demonstrate incompetence or weakness" (Morrison, 1990, p. 256). The lack of qualified, trained supervisors is another problem for child welfare workers, who have nowhere to turn to address the emotional feelings the work brings up for them.

Morrison (1990) urged child welfare professionals to move this problem out of the closet. Morrison used an adaptation of Summit's (1983) model of family dynamics in families in which sexual abuse is taking place to understand how the unsupportive organization may victimize workers. Morrison compared the victimized child welfare worker to the sexually abused child in Summit's model. His model provides an understanding as to why disclosure may take years. Summit argued that abused children adapt to the pressure of secrecy and being helpless in a world of adults in which they should be protected. The child assumes responsibility for the abuse and tries to be a "better child" in a hopeless situation. When the child does disclose the abuse, the family dynamics may subvert his or her telling about the whole experience, leading to questions about the truth of the child's allegations. It may give credence to the perpetrator's argument that the child is not telling the truth and cannot be believed. The consequence is that the child experiences another trauma when his or her disclosure is rejected. The child is abandoned by the family, who should be protecting him or her from harm, and then abandoned by professionals who are also supposed to protect and not cause further harm.

Summit (1983) wrote that the child sexual abuse accommodation syndrome has five stages: secrecy, helplessness, entrapment and accommodation, delayed unconvincing disclosure, and retraction. He argued that applying this model makes it easier to understand the dynamics that surround the child and to be an advocate for the child.

Morrison (1990) applied the model to the child welfare workers in an organization under stress. Child welfare practitioners work in dangerous conditions where families abuse children, and it is their job to protect them. It is questionable if administrators and supervisors acknowledge and respond to their distress when workers return to the office, especially with difficult cases. Morrison quoted Summit but changed references from children and parents to staff, agencies, and colleagues: "Acceptance and validation are crucial to the psychological survival of the victim. A worker emotionally abused by clients and rejected by colleagues or agency is psychologically orphaned. Agencies must anticipate the self-camouflaging and self-stigmatizing behavior of workers, and not see this as a reason to disbelieve them" (p. 262).

Morrison then drew analogies between the family dynamics of the abused child and the organizational dynamics of the agency and the worker. She argued that secrecy, helplessness, entrapment and accommodation, delayed or unconvincing disclosure, and retraction constitute the dynamic components that promote unhealthy compliance.

Practitioners do not talk about the emotional stress of the work, and many do not have an understanding of traumatic stress and what it does and how it changes their psychological frame of reference or worldview. Often administrators do not acknowledge or address the stress and do not admit that the work requires workers to observe evil, danger, and trauma on a daily basis, and that these things affect workers. Secrecy is reinforced with trite statements such as "You'll get over it," or "If you can't take the heat, get out of the kitchen."

When practitioners know they are adversely affected by the work and feel helpless, they keep it to themselves, knowing that no one in authority wants to hear about their feelings. It is believed that a mature professional adult isn't supposed to feel helpless. Organizational culture asserts that professional objectivity should keep the practitioner in a cognitive mode and not be emotional about cases. Agencies expect the practitioner to protect him- or herself and not bring additional problems to the organization because he or she isn't capable of adjusting to the stress of the work.

The belief that "If I were competent I wouldn't feel this way" reflects self-camouflaging in the practitioner as he or she assumes responsibility for painful responses to the work that are perfectly normal and consistent with being a mentally healthy person. Morrison (1990) argued that this is being "trapped in a value distortion" (p. 263). This produces internal conflict that goes unresolved; the practitioner believes that feeling abused must be his or her fault, not the agency's. The practitioner's suppression of distress is caused by overwhelming numbers of cases and the sadness and horror of child abuse. The agency's failure to acknowledge this distress may cause anger and self-destruction as the practitioner engages in unhealthy compliance. But it is a false front, like that assumed by the sexually abused child, and masks what is actually happening.

Disclosure may never come, and the practitioner may decide to find work elsewhere, or it may come as an eruption of pent-up distress. It may show up in negative interactions between colleagues or adverse responses to being questioned about a case. It may show up as the practitioner becomes withdrawn and socially isolated. It may reveal itself in angry outbursts in staff meetings. The distress that has finally surfaced may be invalidated by others through suggestions that the person is not a good fit for the agency because he or she can't handle the work. In contrast, practitioners may try to mask their feelings and manage their distress by doing more and more and doing it well. This may lead administrators and supervisors to think that the practitioner is fine.

Finally, there is the stage of retraction, which is when the practitioner dismisses the distress as not due to the work but caused by some other matter. Administrators and supervisors may not pursue the matter or may make it clear that expressing distress is not acceptable or professional in this particular agency. The problem is that dismissing it doesn't mean it is gone. The child who retracts will continue to be abused. The practitioner who retracts will continue to feel distressed. For both, the problem continues.

Supervisors and administrators are in a good position to keep practitioners from minimizing their distress and to help them cope. Child welfare professionals who underestimate their own psychological distress can be supported by supervisors and administrators who understand that the stress of this work creates an occupational hazard for workers (Pryce & Pryce, 2000). This can be done by increasing knowledge through professional development education about vicarious traumatization and STS, improving management and supervision skills, and providing a supportive organizational culture. But it must be from the top down and directed toward removing the taboos regarding the impact of the work (Morrison, 1990, p. 265).

EMPIRICAL EVIDENCE OF STS IN CHILD WELFARE WORK

A few empirical studies have been done regarding child welfare and traumatic stress. Meyers (1996) studied 205 child protective services workers in a southern state. The study assessed the severity of STS symptoms and factors associated with

STS symptomology by using Derogatis Brief Systems Distress Scale. Meyers (1996) hypothesized that severe symptoms of STS were related to length and intensity of children's traumatic stress and the worker's gender, personal trauma history, and family-of-origin interaction patterns. Meyers found that the longer the person had been a child welfare worker, the greater the number of symptoms. Workers with a year of experience had greater anxiety symptoms than did workers with less than one year. The intensity of symptoms of STS was found to be associated with working forty or more hours per week. Women reported more reexperiencing of traumatic events, avoidance, numbing, and persistent arousal than did men. They also reported more physical and medical problems than did men. When family of origin was examined, the result indicated that individuals from enmeshed families have more symptoms of STS, and those from disengaged families experience more symptoms of poor mental health. Meyers also found more severity of symptoms among individuals with a personal trauma history than among workers who did not have one.

Gold (1998) used participatory research to enable child welfare workers and supervisors to talk about how their work affects them. Thirty female workers and ten female supervisors were placed in focus groups and asked about the positive and negative aspects of the work. They were also asked how the work affected their physical and mental health and how they coped and took care of their health. One positive aspect of the work was that they found it exciting, challenging, and rewarding, especially when clients grow and change. The women felt proud to be in child welfare. There were several negative aspects of the work: impossible expectations, heavy caseloads, the feeling that child welfare is a dumping ground for cases other professionals don't want, the lack of time management and unpredictability of the work, court decisions that interfere with the work, insufficient resources, unsupportive or negatively critical supervisors, lack of agency recognition and/or praise, role strain, role ambiguity, and role conflict.

In addition to these factors, the focus group participants identified how gender affected the work. Physical danger was always a risk factor, and many women expressed concerns about being attacked or hurt. Sexism was a factor in that males move quickly into administration and females are left to do the grinding work. Sexism also applies not only to taking care of the work but also to taking care of homes and families. Many men have wives to do the home and family part. The discussion addressed traumatic stress. Although the women did not use the term "traumatic stress," they did describe it in another way: "It's seeing people's pain and being part of their pain" (Gold, 1998, p. 708). Another woman said, "It's being day-to-day, hour-to-hour, minute-to-minute, face-to-face with human suffering. It doesn't matter what the case number is, these are human beings, and there is so much suffering in this job" (Gold, 1998, p. 708). Another phrased it this way: "We are sponges for pain. We just soak it up" (Gold, 1998, p. 709).

Most of the study participants reported that their physical health had suffered. Many reported having chronic illnesses that were hard to cure and feelings of chronic exhaustion. One individual shared that she rarely feels well. Although they did not call it numbing or dissociation, some of the women felt alienation from their bodies. The child welfare professionals also reported compromised mental health. They identified mood swings, anger, depression, fearfulness, anxiety, paranoia, low self-esteem, and self-doubt, and a few experienced nightmares. Many reported that their worldview had changed. As one woman put it, "I don't see the world with any normalcy any more. I only see it through the eyes of child abuse" (Gold, 1998, p. 712). Several reported feeling jaded, cynical, and mistrusting of other people and that they had become overprotective of their children.

What Gold found were symptoms of STS in forty child welfare workers, although they were not yet labeled STS. Gold reported that the women used both emotion-focused and problem-focused coping strategies. Several used cognitive reframing. Most indicated that having a personal life and leisure was important. Sex was found to be a good stress reliever. They also found humor and social support in the work-place essential to managing the work. Women spoke of being surrounded by pain and human suffering. Feeling alienated from their own bodies could be dissociation or numbing. In particular, the women reported changes in their worldview.

Horwitz (1998) examined social worker trauma and how to build resilience in child welfare workers. He then applied his findings to a case study. He argued that the social worker is affected by trauma when the social worker experiences events with which he or she cannot readily cope. The events usually involve danger. The events may affect clients and have an indirect impact on the social worker, or they may directly affect the social worker. Direct trauma arises in four ways (Horwitz, 1998). Social workers experience assaults and vandalism, verbal abuse, threats of assault, and public scorn from a lack of understanding of what child welfare work is about. Some workers also report experiencing direct trauma that can come from organizational demands.

In contrast with direct trauma, indirect trauma occurs when the client's traumatic experience affects the child welfare worker. The worker is exposed to the impact trauma has on the child and the way the child shares what has happened to him or her (Horwitz, 1998). Horwitz referred to it as the emotional contagion that occurs when the worker experiences sadness and anger with the client over what has happened. He also argued that there are three things that influence how workers are affected: children's deaths, the belief (which may be unrealistic) that the worker might have been able to prevent what happened, and the degree to which the worker identifies with the victim and his or her family. Another factor posited to influence indirect trauma is personal vulnerability such as past experiences, coping style, or current life situation and trauma history. Horwitz argued that the way in which the worker chooses to cope and integrate the experience will most likely influence future functioning. Active supervision can help the worker throughout the experience. Creating a safe work environment for the worker following traumatic events, directly or indirectly experienced, is essential (Horwitz, 1998). Once the worker feels safe, it is possible to examine and express his or her feelings about what has happened. He argued that support from supervisors, colleagues, family, and friends is necessary for the worker.

Another factor that facilitates integration of the impact of the trauma is crisis debriefing for all involved. Horwitz used a model for building resilience in children and applied it to child welfare workers; the model has four elements. The first is risk reduction, followed by reducing and avoiding negative chain reactions. The third is protecting and building self-esteem in the worker. The last is maintaining openness to life opportunities.

Horwitz then used a case example of a child welfare worker who goes through an indirect trauma involving a child who is severely harmed. The worker has managed the work well up until this event and has successfully balanced her work and her private life. Following the event she begins to question herself and wonders if she could have prevented the event. She knew the child well, which makes his being harmed particularly painful. She also wonders if she will be blamed as the situation is investigated. The worker is supported throughout the investigation by her supervisor and colleagues. As days pass, she begins to process her feelings and wonders if she should leave the work. As the child recovers and the investigation indicates that there was no way the worker could have prevented the child's injury, the worker is in a better position to move on knowing she is respected and supported at work.

Horwitz argued that creating a safe working environment, protecting and building self-esteem regarding worker competency by respecting the worker, avoiding a negative chain of events that leads to the worker being blamed, and helping the worker stay open to future possibilities and opportunities will help build resilience in child welfare workers. In many ways Horwitz was addressing protection of the worker's worldview and psychological frame of reference. This is also a way of helping the worker maintain balance in his or her worldview. If the organizational culture is one of safety and support, then the work environment will facilitate worker resilience in the face of direct or indirect trauma.

Dane (2000) examined the ways in which STS affects child welfare workers. Focus groups were used to gather data on workers' reactions. Two three-and-a-half-hour focus groups were conducted with ten child welfare workers. All ten workers experienced sadness regarding the work. All the workers entered the work right after college and were enthusiastic about working in the agency. Two workers talked about the painfulness of removing a child from his or her home and how they were haunted by having done so. They all noted that they had experienced changes in behavior in an effort to cope. The coping strategies included detachment, staying busy, accepting limitations, and setting limits. All the focus group participants agreed that the death of a child is most stressful, especially if the media blames the worker. They also said they experienced symptoms of STS: inability to concentrate, irritability, increased startle response, feelings of vulnerability, anxiety, sleeplessness, and intrusive images of the trauma.

Seven workers reported that there are successes that make the work worthwhile. Building relationships and trust was the most important aspect of success, and all took pleasure in the work when clients changed in positive ways. All the focus group participants agreed that the agency, daily working conditions, and the community were significant sources of stress.

Dane also asked about the impact of spiritual and religious beliefs. Spirituality was important and reinforced the workers' ability to find meaning in the work. Many workers reported relying on God to help them maintain their beliefs when work is particularly horrific, and many maintain a prayer life that buffers the work. At the same time, some workers wondered why God allows the pain and suffering of children who are so vulnerable.

The results of the focus groups were then used to develop a two-day workshop attended by eighteen workers. The workshop utilized small group discussion, experiential learning, art, relaxation techniques, and working on restoring the workers' worldviews (Dane, 2000, p. 33). One day was dedicated to self-care interventions for STS. Workers responded positively to the workshop and made recommendations for the workshops to be followed up six months later. They also thought it would be good to have small monthly groups for discussion of trauma issues. Another recommendation was for a spiritual consultant to be made available to workers when children die. A final suggestion was to have a group to provide support when workers experience soul sadness. Dane recommended the integration of knowledge of STS into social work education and that a university-agency partnership be formed to infuse knowledge of STS and needed interventions into child welfare work. The two-day workshop increased workers' knowledge of trauma, facilitated finding ways to cope with the trauma of the work, and emphasized the importance of supporting each other.

The Children's Aid Society of Toronto in partnership with the University of Toronto conducted a study of the stressors in child welfare (Howe & McDonald, 2001). One hundred seventy-five survey respondents and twenty interviewed participants provided information about levels of posttraumatic stress, depression, and general stress in child welfare work. The findings indicated that workers are subjected to a great amount of direct and indirect trauma. Half of the respondents had been verbally attacked, and many had experienced physical assault. One-fourth of the workers had children die, and a few had adults in their caseloads die. More than 80 percent of respondents had experienced work-related trauma, and 70 percent reported having emotional distress following their experiences.

Data collected in the study corroborated workers' experiences of trauma and distress. More than two-thirds of respondents scored well above the cutoff score (26) for posttraumatic stress disorder on the Impact of Events Scale (IES). Individuals with higher support scores had lower depression scores. High levels of support did not correlate with traumatic stress on the IES. Howe and McDonald (2001) questioned how staff members' posttraumatic stress affected their decision making and the conclusions they drew about clients and families. They also considered how it might affect the agency as a whole, especially supervision and policy development. They concluded that this needs further examination.

Howe and McDonald also addressed the use of the peer support team (PST). This is a fourteen-person team of child welfare staff trained in critical incident stress debriefing for traumatic events in child welfare. The PST responded to 189 traumatic stress events in the agency. Participation is voluntary, services are provided in a timely manner, and it is encouraged, user friendly, and separate from internal and external review, thereby allowing child welfare staff to feel free to discuss their experiences and feelings. These program characteristics build worker trust in the PST program.

This study is consistent with others identifying direct and indirect stress as factors in child welfare work. Interestingly, increased social support was not correlated with decreased posttraumatic stress symptoms. Further research is needed to understand how social support relates to traumatic stress. Evaluation of the peer support teams will also demonstrate if they are effective in reducing traumatic stress in child welfare.

Regehr, Chau, Leslie, and Howe (2002) examined the impact of inquiries into the deaths of children in care on child welfare workers and the organization. The study had two components. The first was a survey assessing stress and trauma following a child's death and all the attending procedures. The second part was an interview of individuals who had experienced a formal review following a child's death and individuals who had been involved in a coroner's inquest. Twenty workers were interviewed regarding their experience; ten had direct experience with a coroner's inquest and ten had indirect experience. Semi-structured interviews of one to three hours long were conducted with each individual. Questions involved experience with death inquiries, the impact of these events, the review of these events, and organizational and personal support. The quantitative study demonstrated that workers find the death of a child to be the most painful experience in child welfare. Workers rank this experience above physical assault and threats. A child's death, according to workers, produces depression, problems sleeping, nightmares, and preoccupation with the event. Workers also report that removing a child from a home, especially if they have a relationship with the family, is almost as stressful as a child's death.

The authors of this study found that children's deaths produced symptoms of traumatic stress in the worker and those involved in the inquest, and that traumatic stress permeated the organization. One of the intense effects of traumatic stress on the worker is the recollections, reexperiencing, and reminders of the death that come from being asked repeatedly about the child's death. The constant questions and testimony that must be provided affect self-esteem and make the worker wonder if it is worth doing this work. Workers report feelings of isolation and the withdrawal of support from others. The traumatic stress is ongoing, and even when it is over, workers are left doubting themselves. In addition to the trauma the workers experience, the authors found that the distress spread to anyone remotely related to the events, even the clerical staff who transcribed the death reports. The intrusion of the press and public was also felt by workers and the organization. The media coverage is usually negative, and often unfair judgments are made by the press and the community.

This study also observed positive outcomes. The authors reported that cohesion among direct staff, supervisors, and management followed the experience of a death. The agency provided the organization with an employment assistance program and a peer support team to serve as a support system during critical events. Another positive aspect workers identified was internal efforts, through self-examination, to improve child welfare practices. Workers also indicated that there were some negative experiences such as a change in the way services were delivered. Following the inquests there seemed to be more emphasis on policy and procedures than on bringing about changes within families.

The study by Regehr, Chau, Leslie, and Howe demonstrated how both direct and indirect traumatic stress affect child welfare workers as well as the agency as a whole when a child dies. First, the worker is traumatized by the child's death. Second, the worker must reexperience the child's death repeatedly as he or she explains how the death happened. Other agency members must listen to the details of the child's death, and they have the potential to be affected by STS. Finally, by responding empathically to the worker who experienced the child's death, fellow workers may also be affected. When a child dies, direct and indirect traumatic stress have the potential to permeate throughout the agency.

Bride (in press) studied the prevalence of secondary traumatic stress among 600 masters-level social workers randomly selected from 2,886 licensed social workers. With a response rate of 47 percent ($n = 282$), Bride found that 70.2 percent had experienced at least one symptom of secondary traumatic stress during the week preceding the survey. The symptoms included intrusion, avoidance, and arousal. The most frequently reported symptoms were intrusive thoughts, avoidance of reminders of clients, and numbing responses. Bride found that 55 percent met the diagnostic criteria for at least one of the core symptom clusters. Bride also discovered that 15.2 percent of the respondents reported secondary traumatic stress symptoms that meet the diagnostic criteria in the fourth edition of the American Psychiatric Association's *Diagnostic and Statistical Manual of Mental Health Disorders* for posttraumatic stress disorder.

Bride, Jones, and MacMaster (in press) measured the prevalence of secondary traumatic stress in child protective service workers in a southern state through the use of the Secondary Traumatic Stress Scale (Bride, Robinson, Yegidis, & Figley, 2004). This study received 187 completed surveys—which was a 56 percent response rate. The study did not delineate the type of degree held by respondents, but 87.2 percent had a bachelor's degree and 11.7 percent had a master's degree. The study showed 92 percent of the respondents experienced at least one symptom of secondary traumatic stress occasionally in the week preceding the survey. During the same time frame, 59 percent of the participants reported one or more symptoms occurring often, and 34 percent of the respondents met the core criteria for posttraumatic stress disorder.

In the final study, childhood abuse history and STS among child welfare workers were examined (Nelson-Gardell & Harris, 2003). This study included 166 child welfare workers and conference participants who attended an innovative workshop on STS. At the beginning of the workshop for child welfare workers, participants were asked to complete the Compassion Fatigue Self-Test (Figley, 1995), a knowledge survey, and a demographic survey. At the close of the workshop, participants were asked to complete a knowledge survey, an analog application of STS knowledge, and a workshop satisfaction evaluation. Six weeks later, participants who agreed to participate in this part of the study were asked to complete the Childhood Trauma Questionnaire, or CTQ (Bernstein & Fink, 1998). This instrument measures emotional, physical, and sexual abuse, and emotional and physical neglect. The second group contributing to the data collection attended an STS workshop given at a professional conference. At the beginning of the workshop, the same instruments provided to the first group were administered to attendees. The two groups were compared in terms of age, education, gender, years of experience, CTQ scales, burnout, and STS; the first group was slightly younger; this was the only difference between the two groups. The data were combined for the following analysis.

In a stepwise regression analysis, it was found that a worker's risk of STS increased when the worker had a personal history of childhood trauma, especially child abuse and neglect (Nelson-Gardell & Harris, 2003). The findings also demonstrated that a combination of more than one type of abuse or neglect increased risk for STS and that emotional abuse or neglect produced the greatest risk for STS among workers. It was also found that younger workers had a higher risk for STS than did older workers when trauma history was controlled for. As Nelson-Gardell and Harris (2003) concluded, "The good people trying to make a difference in the lives of vulnerable children are sustaining blows to their long-term emotional and physical well being" (p. 23). The authors recommended that child welfare educators incorporate information about the use of empathy in relationships with traumatized clients in their classes as well as inform students about personal risk factors related to STS. They also recommended that child welfare administrators and supervisors be prepared to educate workers about STS, develop support groups, and ensure that insurance plans have mental health coverage.

CONCLUSION AND IMPLICATIONS FOR CHILD WELFARE

Even though traumatic stress and child welfare seem to be likely paired terms, traumatic stress has not received the much-needed attention of child welfare administrators, trainers, supervisors, child protection workers, and social work educators, just as the results of trauma have been dismissed throughout history, and only when victims of trauma were given a voice that could not be ignored was a diagnosis of posttraumatic stress given credence. It is our belief that the trauma experienced by child protective service workers has been dismissed. It must be seen as real and in need of attention. Society has a history of blaming the victim, and we have blamed the child protection social worker by sending the message that if you can't cut it, then you can leave—it is not the agency's responsibility to help. The message that has been sent to child protection workers when symptoms of distress occur makes it clear that it is the worker, not the work, that is the problem. Child protection workers have told us that they suffer in silence—just as many victims of trauma have been silenced throughout the years. If history repeats itself, it does not appear that acknowledgment and responsibility will be forthcoming from persons with the power and resources to offer services and help to child protection workers suffering from secondary traumatic stress without the workers' demand for acknowledgment. With knowledge and understanding of vicarious traumatization and secondary traumatic stress, child protection workers may be empowered and find their voice to bring attention to their needs. Without it, the child welfare system, families, and children will suffer.

Child welfare work has been associated with burnout in many articles and studies. Only recently has the effect of worker trauma begun to be recognized. We hypothesized that STS is being mistaken for burnout, and we began to determine if, in fact, that was the case. Many symptoms of STS identified by Figley (1995) came up frequently in conversations among child welfare workers concerning the impact of the work on them (Pryce, personal communication, spring 1996). It is also clear that workers can be affected by both primary and secondary traumatic stress due to the dangerous environment in which they work and clients who make threats and are physically aggressive. There appears to be evidence that a personal trauma history may greatly influence vulnerability to STS.

The good news is that STS is more treatable than burnout. Theoretically, educating workers about STS, differentiating it from burnout, teaching about coping, and using social support within the organization can protect the worker's worldview and psychological frame of reference. If child welfare workers who are leaving the field are affected by STS more so than by burnout, then the use of interventions might positively affect retention. The following chapters will share what we have learned in the past ten years about traumatic stress and child welfare workers.

2

Who Are Child Welfare Workers, and What Is the Cost of Losing Them?

Becky became a foster child at the age of fifteen. Her father had sexually, emotionally, and physically abused every older female child in the family. Becky had endured the physical and emotional abuse and knew it was her turn to be his sexual partner, so she ran away from home. Her father hunted for her with a shotgun, threatening to kill her and anyone who helped her. Her mother disowned her and her siblings would not speak to her, as she had brought shame to the family. Becky had previously been sexually abused by another family member when she was seven. Becky suffered terrible abuse at the hands of those persons who were supposed to love and care for her. However, as an adult, Becky tells anyone who will listen that the worst situation she ever dealt with in her life was when her social worker left her to take another job.

The problem in child welfare is that many foster children are suffering from grief and loss not only from being taken away from their parents but also from losing another important person in their lives—their child welfare worker. It is important to look at the rate of child welfare worker turnover to understand how many children and families this affects, and also to look at what effect the loss of a child welfare worker has on the child, the family, the social worker, the agency, and society. We cannot understand the high turnover rate without first looking at who becomes a child welfare worker and then examining why anyone would continue in the child welfare field. This chapter examines in detail turnover and retention and their effects.

WHO BECOMES A CHILD WELFARE WORKER?

Before we can examine the reasons child welfare workers leave, it is important to understand the reasons why anyone would enter this field of work. When a child welfare worker tells another person what he or she does for a living, the response is usually one of the following:

- ◆ "Are you one of those people who take people's kids away?" After this introduction, the term "baby snatcher" often comes up in the conversation.
- ◆ "I don't know how you can do that kind of work—isn't it depressing? Doesn't

seeing all that abuse bother you?" Many times it is a police officer, nurse, counselor, or other professional who works with persons in crisis who is asking this.

◆ "I am having a problem with my food stamps *or* TANF *or* child support. . . ." The person expresses a total lack of knowledge regarding the professional child welfare worker.

◆ "I want to ask you about some kids I know who are being abused or neglected." The person proceeds to tell the social worker about a terrible situation in which a child welfare worker somewhere did not do the right thing and the children involved are still in a dangerous situation. This usually leads to the child welfare worker being blamed for any mistakes made by the profession in general.

◆ "Are you going to try to tell me that I can't spank my kids?" The conversation moves toward the subject of the state trying to control how parents discipline their children and usually gravitates to how parents not whipping children has led to the downfall of society today. The person cites some religious beliefs or verses from the Bible to support his or her denigration of the entire child welfare system.

People have a hard time understanding the work of a child welfare worker. In many places the job description involves being on call twenty-four hours a day, seven days a week, and being responsive to family situations that involve physical abuse, sexual abuse, psychological maltreatment, ritualistic abuse, and neglect of children. The situations may involve infants left alone; starving and malnourished children; filthy, lice-ridden children; children without shelter; HIV-infected children or children with other sexually transmitted diseases; children who have been intentionally burned; shaken babies; children of all ages with bruises and broken bones; homeless children who are not being educated; children locked up in dark basements and closets; sexually abused children; exploited children used for prostitution or child pornography; and children who have been raped. The child welfare worker sees many children with tortured souls and empty eyes.

The parents of these children are often substance abusers or victims of domestic violence, or they themselves may have been victims of child abuse, sexual abuse, or neglect. They may be depressed, poor, hopeless, and helpless. The parents may be angry and violent. They may be rich and emotionally detached. A parent may be alienated and alone or the most popular person in an elite social club. Parents may be intelligent and educated or illiterate. The parent may be a pedophile. It is hard to grasp why someone would go into this type of work.

The caseloads are heavy, and the work is dangerous. Child welfare workers and their families and children are often threatened and at times actually are physically harmed. Children of child welfare workers are sometimes harassed at school. The amount and type of work put child welfare workers at risk for depression, anxiety disorders, and posttraumatic stress disorder resulting from either direct or indirect trauma. The stress can lead to health problems. Child welfare workers' families suffer as the job takes them away from their own families to take care of other children. Many child welfare workers are not compensated for overtime, and many agencies offer little opportunity for career advancement or raises for length of employment, education, or skill improvement. In some states the pay scale begins at $24,000. Nationally, the average pay is $35,000.

States vary in their education requirement for the child welfare worker position. Some states require a bachelor of social work or a master of social work while others allow workers to hold a related degree. The research on the topic of secondary traumatic stress at times delineates between persons with degrees in social work and degrees in other fields; some research refers to social workers, and other studies discuss child welfare workers. Our focus is on child welfare workers regardless of the worker's degree.

Research does not help us understand who would go into this type of work, as there have been few studies that ask that question. Hodge (2004) stated that "almost nothing is known about the national population of social workers" (p. 261). He reported that there is a lack of knowledge concerning the demographics of social workers. Gibelman and Schervish (1997) stated, "We still know very little about the larger population of social workers in the United States" (p. 15). The National Association of Social Workers (NASW) comprises about one-third of the social workers in the United States (Hodge, 2004). Eighty-five percent of the NASW membership have master's degrees in social work (Hodge, 2004). Bureau of Labor statistics reveal that about two-thirds of social workers have bachelor's degrees (Gibelman & Schervish, 1997). Many social workers working in the field of child protection are not members of NASW. These workers report not being able to afford the dues due to the low salaries so common to the field. Therefore, studies regarding demographics of NASW membership may not be useful in describing the child welfare worker population.

Hodge (2004) highlighted a few demographics concerning social workers in the United States. In comparing social workers to the general population, he found that social workers were less likely to be married and just as likely to have lived with two parents when they were sixteen years old, had fewer siblings, were more likely to have lived in the city at age sixteen, and were more likely to have moved from the city in which they lived at the age of sixteen. Hodge (2004) also found that social workers were "more likely to rate their lives as exciting, to live in racially mixed neighborhoods, to be stronger proponents of controversial speech, and to be perceived by interviewers as friendlier than the general public" (p. 1).

California-based researchers Nissly, Mor Barak, and Levin (2005) conducted studies on stress, social support, and workers' intentions to leave their jobs in child welfare. They collected demographic information on 418 public child welfare workers from a large urban agency. Twenty-seven percent of the workers were under the age of twenty-nine, 26.6 percent were thirty to thirty-three, 22.2 percent were forty to forty-nine, and 23.9 percent were over fifty. Collection of data regarding gender revealed 77.2 percent to be female. African American workers made up 18.9 percent and Asian American workers made up 8 percent, while 32.2 percent of workers were

Caucasian, and 35.8 percent of workers were Latino. As to workers' marital status, 41.6 percent were married, 39.4 percent were single, and 13.9 percent were divorced. Also, 49.3 percent of the workers had children. The researchers examined agency tenure and found that 26.1 percent had less than a year with the agency, 18.9 percent had one to three years, 16.7 percent had three to five years, and 38.2 percent had more than five years. Line workers represented 88.3 percent of the respondents, and 11.7 percent were supervisors. Education levels indicated that 34 percent had bachelor's degrees and 66 percent had graduate degrees.

Harrison (1995) studied factors related to intent to leave among 260 child welfare workers in Ohio and found some differing and some common demographics. Harrison achieved an 86.9 percent response rate ($N = 226$). The respondents were predominately female (83.2%), young adults (median twenty-eight years old, mode twenty-four years old), and Euro-American (70.8%); had no children (63.3%); and had never married (46.9%). Almost 24 percent of respondents were African American, and 38.1 percent of respondents were married. The median length of time in public child welfare was three years, and the mean was five years. However, the median length of time in the current job was one year and the mean was 1.8 years. Differences among workers may be related to the geographic area in which the workers lived, as racial and ethnic makeup varies.

Black, Jeffreys, and Hartley (1993) compared masters-level social workers ($n = 195$) and masters-level business students ($n = 151$) to examine the extent of psychosocial trauma in the early lives of these students. The types of childhood trauma examined were alcohol and drug abuse; physical, sexual, and emotional abuse; physical and mental illness; death and suicide of significant others; and separation or divorce of parents. Social work students were found to have experienced a frequency of trauma in their childhoods that was significantly greater than that of the business students. Demographics showed most of the MSW students were female and most of the business students were male.

Marsh (1988) similarly compared undergraduate social work students and business students and found business students to be "achievement oriented," while social work students were "other oriented." Marsh noted differences between social work students and business students regarding alcoholism and drug addiction of family members. Marsh found that 80 percent of the social work students had an alcoholic family member, but only 59 percent of the business students had an alcoholic family member. Family member addiction to a drug other than alcohol was reported twice as often by social work students as by business students.

Black, Jeffreys, and Hartley (1993) discussed studies by Lackie done in 1982 and 1983 that found two-thirds of a sample of social workers to be overly responsible and that they acted as mediators in their families. These social workers described themselves as "parentified children," those who assume a caretaking role in the family. Rompf and Royse (1994) also discussed Lackie's study and stated that Lackie found 61 percent of 1,577 social workers with master's degrees experienced stressful family situations during their childhood. Rompf and Royse pointed out that the Lackie study did not have a comparison group.

Rompf and Royse examined the influences of life events on social work students and non-social work students. Their findings suggested social work students were more likely to report problems such as alcoholism and emotional illness in their families of origin, and that the social work students attributed their life experiences to their career choice. There was statistically significant difference between social work students and non-social work students regarding parents' marital happiness, alcoholism and drug addiction within families, and occurrences of child abuse or neglect. Russell, Hill, Coyne, and Woody (1993) also found the MSW students came from families with alcohol or drug abuse more frequently than did other graduate students in the fields of guidance and counseling, business, and education. They also found that social work students were significantly more likely to have a family member who was a victim of a violent act and were more likely to have been sexually abused.

Rompf and Royse (1994) concluded that a hypothesis that early-life psychosocial trauma is associated with the selection of social work as a career is logical, but that there is an argument that social work students are able, through their education, to recognize the trauma and are more willing to disclose past trauma. They offered other possibilities regarding the choice of social work as a career. Being able to address social problems, be personally involved in creating a better world, have opportunities to be creative, and work independently were suggested as possible reasons to choose social work as a career.

Rompf and Royse discussed other studies that revealed that other helping professionals also have stressful life events or family dysfunction in their backgrounds. The researchers found that a study done by Frank and Paris (1987) revealed that "psychiatrists expressed more disappointment in their parents than did nonpsychiatrists" (p. 2). Rompf and Royse stated that Gockel (1966) explored why students choose social work as a career and decided the reason was that the social work students want to work with people.

These studies look at a few of the demographics and some of the reasons for choosing social work as a career, but no study was found that asked why a person would choose to go into child welfare work. We have asked several child welfare social workers and students this question. The consistent answer is that social workers and social work students want to make a difference in the lives of abused and neglected children. They understand child abuse and neglect. Perhaps this is due to a high incidence of trauma in the social workers' own lives, or perhaps it arises from their education. The social workers want to stop the abuse and neglect of children and give children a chance to reach their optimal level of development. This field is consistently described as the job in which a social worker can have a huge impact on the lives of children, and one in which the biggest difference can be made.

As professors of social work and past supervisors and trainers in public child welfare agencies, we have witnessed countless new child welfare workers enter the profession with hope, enormous amounts of energy, high levels of ability, and on fire to eradicate child abuse and neglect, at least for the children they will encounter. We have been told that the work they are about to do in child welfare is all they ever wanted to do and they can't wait to begin. They enter with so much excitement and vision for the families and children on their caseload, and they know that their work will make a difference in children's lives. What happens after these enthusiastic beginnings?

A LOSS OF INNOCENCE?

We have seen some child welfare workers lose their zeal within weeks of beginning employment. Some may take longer, but few are able to withstand the problems that plague the child welfare system and the families involved in it. We have watched people who began as child welfare workers with sparkle and light in their eyes begin to resemble the haunted, dim-eyed children with whom they work. Most of the workers who leave report not being able to make a difference, and the ones who stay somehow continue to believe they are making a difference. We need to know what personality characteristics and organizational characteristics enable them to stay. They all have stories about children they could not save from abuse and neglect, and some have stories of children who died from abuse or neglect. They all have suffering children in their minds and memories. It is clear that they all care deeply about children and families.

We have worked very closely with these workers and have wished many times that there was a way to shield the twenty-two-year-old newly graduated social worker from the evil and suffering he or she is about to encounter upon entering the world of child welfare. A new child welfare worker sees more evil and suffering within the first few months of work than anyone should ever have to see in a lifetime. Samantrai (1992) reported that child welfare workers are excited about their work for about six to nine months, but by the time they have been on the job for one year, the new workers report disillusionment. "Loss of innocence" is the term Samantrai heard used by child welfare workers to describe this apparently altered worldview.

THE BIGGEST COST OF LOSING CHILD WELFARE WORKERS: THE COST TO CHILDREN AND FAMILIES

The biggest cost of child welfare worker turnover is the emotional cost to the children and families. It is impossible to assign a dollar amount to this cost. When a child enters foster care, his or her entire world has been shattered. The child's family has been torn apart, and the feelings of shame, guilt, loss, confusion, and anger are strong. The neglect and/or abuse the child has suffered may disable the child's ability to trust in others.

The child welfare worker's first task is to develop a relationship with the child and family members. This relationship is at the core of the social work process. Without the helping and working relationship, nothing will happen, and any work will be an effort in futility. Rubenstein and Bloch (1982) noted that "motivation," "movement," and "emotion" all stem from the same Latin root, *movere*. Without emotion, there is no motivation for the client to change and therefore no movement in a positive direction. Building relationships is a dynamic process that must involve emotion and connection. Establishing emotional connectivity and sensitivity to the client's problems is the only way to make a difference in the lives of children and families. Rubenstein and Bloch stated that building a relationship is like building a supportive, reliable bridge that requires compassionate connectiveness between one person and another. They wrote: "When I know that you feel with me, that you care about me, that you understand what my reasons and reactions are, then I am more likely to care about you, to want your approval, to listen to you, to take your hopes and encouragement into myself and to open my mind to your suggestions or opinions" (Rubenstein & Bloch, 1982, p. 9).

Levine and Sallee (1999) stated that there is a need in child welfare for a "warm and supportive relationship between the child and social worker in which the child feels respected, accepted, and understood" (p. 167). Building this type of relationship takes time, skill, and the ability to give of oneself. The child or family member must relinquish strong defense mechanisms in order to try to trust the social worker. When the client begins to believe that the social worker understands what the situation is actually doing to the client and what the client feels and wants, and when the client believes the social worker cares, then the movement toward resolution of the problems begins.

The social worker must be trustworthy in order for a relationship to be established. This requires the social worker to be honest, genuine, available, and helpful; have the client's best interest at heart; and follow through on promises. If the client believes that the relationship is strong and worthy of trust, it is reasonable for the client to believe that the relationship will last as long as needed. Damage to the client's ability to trust occurs when this process has been initiated but is abruptly terminated. How can we measure the cost of losing a social worker when the loss results in the devastation of a child who has trusted someone for the first time in his or her life? How much is lost when a parent is working toward gaining custody of his or her child but the person who instilled hope that things could be different for the client's family leaves? What is the price tag attached to the lost possibility of a child living with his or her own family and not being abused?

It is important to note that not all social workers are able to establish this type of relationship with their clients. It is very possible that heavy caseloads, limited time, lack of skill or desire, and the effects of secondary traumatic stress or burnout prevent workers from being able to establish a good working relationship with children or parents in their client caseload. The devastation that is felt when a client is transferred to a new worker's care does not occur when the first worker never establishes a strong relationship with the client, but the reasons for the limited ability to establish the relationship required to effect change are part of the problems found in the child welfare system, and this creates a frustrating amalgamation of issues.

The child welfare agency's ability to retain workers is directly attached to the immeasurable cost to society when a child's safety, permanency, and well-being are at risk. When the Child and Family Services State Reviews were established, the

Children's Bureau put in place a mechanism for assessment of state child welfare systems in the areas of safety, permanency, and well-being of children and families (Courtney, Needell, & Wulczyn, 2004). The Children's Bureau reviewed states to determine their compliance with outcome-based standards in child welfare and found that no state was in full compliance with federal standards (Pear, 2004). All state child welfare agencies were failing to keep children safe, give foster children permanent homes, and meet children's needs.

ATTACHMENT IN FOSTER CARE ISSUES

Crosson-Tower (2004) listed several problems that occur when a child's attachment to someone is disrupted, including loss of empathy, loss of affection, cruelty, self-destructiveness, destructiveness, and anger. A recipe for creating a dysfunctional adult with similar problems is to take an abused or neglected child with no ability to trust away from family, siblings, and familiar places; forbid the child from having contact with extended family members; make the child change schools frequently; and bounce the child from foster home to foster home in a child welfare system in which the social workers change frequently. Every attachment possible for a child is broken. What is the cost to the person whose fate after a series of broken attachments is to become a mean, uncaring, untrusting, unaffectionate person? What is the cost to society when this person is housed in prison, a mental health treatment center, a homeless shelter, or a substance abuse treatment center after his or her predictable anger has resulted in crime and harm to others?

The Northwest Foster Care Alumni Study (Pecora, Kessler, O'Brien, Downs, English, White, et al., 2005) examined outcomes for foster care alumni (persons placed in family foster care as children). Case records were reviewed for 659 alumni, and 479 alumni were interviewed. These individuals were in care between 1988 and 1998 and were between the ages of twenty and thirty-three years old at the time of the study. The study revealed 54.4 percent had clinical levels of at least one mental health problem and 19.9 percent had three or more mental health problems within the previous twelve months. "Posttraumatic stress disorder (PTSD) rates for alumni were up to twice as high as for U.S. war veterans" (Pecora et al., 2005, p. 1). Within the previous twelve months, 25.2 percent of the alumni had experienced PTSD.

Fromm (2001) estimated the economic costs associated with child abuse and neglect. She reported that three million children are reported to be abused and neglected each year in the United States, and that three children die each day from abuse and neglect in this country. The direct costs to the nation of this abuse and neglect are $6,205,395,000 for hospitalization, $2,987,957,400 for chronic health problems, $425,110,400 for mental health care, $14.4 billion for child welfare costs, $24,709,800 for law enforcement costs, and $341,174,702 for costs associated with the judicial system (Fromm, 2001). This is a total of over $24 billion in direct costs, and Fromm estimates another $94 billion in indirect costs. The indirect costs include special education, mental health and health care, juvenile delinquency, lost productivity to society (which was estimated at $656 million but is sometimes claimed to be as high as $1.3 billion), and adult criminality (Fromm, 2001).

Research has shown that abused and neglected children placed in foster care who do not receive needed help burden society later in many ways. Kools (1997) stated that failure to attend to the needs of adolescent foster children in a "humanistic and individualized manner" may lead to "mental illness, criminality, and inability to function productively and independently in society" (p. 268). According to Kools, the lives of these foster children are ones of dependence and dysfunction. The 1999–2000 Committee on Early Childhood, Adoption, and Dependent Care reported abused and neglected children are at great risk for not forming healthy attachments to anyone. This committee noted that children with attachment disorders often grow up to "vent their rage and pain on society" (Miller, Gorski, Borchers, Jenista, Johnson, Kaufman, et al., 2000, p. 1145). The researchers involved in this committee's work also stated that "having at least one adult who is devoted to and loves a child unconditionally, who is prepared to accept and value that child for a long time, is the key to helping a child overcome the stress and trauma of abuse and neglect" (Miller et al., 2000, p. 1152).

Foster care can be a secure, safe place in which healing can begin, and a social worker can be the person who ignites a child's trust. Sometimes the social worker is the child's only link to family. The social worker is the person who knows what happened and where the child is from—historically and geographically. More often than not, the social worker is the only adult in the foster child's life who is devoted and supportive and who accepts and values the child.

Crosson-Tower (2004) stated that child protection is a field fraught with difficulty. She claimed that the child welfare worker must advocate for the client in the system, and this requirement, added to the daily caseload, is overwhelming. High turnover rates and staffing shortages leave the remaining workers with not enough time to make home visits, and these factors limit the frequency of visits with children (General Accounting Office, 2003). Crosson-Tower (2004) called for professionals to recognize the need for consistency in the lives of troubled children. One way to start giving consistency to children's lives is to tackle the issues that lead to social workers leaving the child welfare agency.

OTHER COSTS OF LOSING CHILD WELFARE WORKERS

The biggest cost of losing child welfare workers is the immeasurable damage that occurs when children's needs are not met, but these costs do not get legislators' or administrators' attention as much as line-item dollar amounts in agency budgets. The turnover of child welfare workers has been estimated to be between 30 and 40 percent annually nationwide (General Accounting Office, 2003). The American Public Human Services Association (APHSA) report from the Child Welfare Workforce Survey (2005) revealed that child protective service worker turnover averaged 19.9 percent in 2000 and grew to 22.1 percent in 2004. The upper range of child protective service worker turnover grew to 67 percent percent in 2004 from 38 percent in 2000 (APHSA, 2005). The amount of this turnover that could have been prevented was 60 percent for child protective service workers and 69 percent for in-home protective workers. APHSA defines preventable turnover as a staff person leaving the child welfare agency for reasons other than retirement, death, marriage/parenting, returning to school, moving due to a spouse's job, or interagency transfers. It is important to note that only 24 percent of the forty-two states completing the survey actually completed the section regarding preventable turnover in the state agency. This may account for the discrepancy in estimations between the General Accounting Office (GAO) report and the APHSA report.

Not only are social workers leaving their agencies for preventable reasons but the positions are remaining vacant and no one is there to work with the children and families in the vacant caseload. The APHSA report showed vacancies are staying open longer compared to the results of the 2000 report. The average amount of time a position in child protection remained vacant was ten weeks and foster care and adoption positions stayed vacant for thirteen weeks (APHSA, 2005). On the average, a child will not have a worker for thirteen weeks if his or her worker leaves the agency. So not only is the child adjusting to the loss of his or her social worker, but there is no one there to take the social worker's place and see that the child's needs are met. The average tenure of child welfare workers is less than two years (General Accounting Office, 2003); social workers are not staying long enough to develop relationships with the children and families or to achieve the skill level needed to do the job well.

What this means for local agencies and foster children is that between one out of five and two out of three social workers leave a caseload every year. The APHSA (2005) report showed average caseloads of child protective service workers to be twenty-four children (upper range of one hundred children), forty-two children (upper range eighty children) for in-home protective service workers, twenty-three children (upper range eighty children) for foster care and adoption workers, and twenty-seven children (upper range eighty children) for multiple-program workers. The lowest number of children that could be affected is twenty-three children per year for every five social workers, assuming one worker leaves. This could be as many as one hundred children for every five workers, and in the worst scenario, two hundred children will lose their social workers every year for every three social workers hired by an agency, assuming two of these workers leave. These children will be without a social worker for an average of thirteen weeks.

Out of the twenty-six states reporting in the APHSA survey, the average number of full-time equivalent (FTE) positions for child protective service workers in a state was 787. The FTE position average for in-home protective service workers was 353, for foster care and adoption workers it was 225, and for multiple-program workers it was 421. If one in five foster care workers leave the child welfare agency, an average of forty-five social workers will leave an average of at least 1,035 foster children and up to 3,600 foster children in each state, depending on the size of the caseload of the exiting social worker. A minimum of 51,750 foster care children in the United States are affected. The figure could be 180,000 foster children. The Adoption and Foster Care Analysis Reporting System report showed 532,000 children in foster care on September 30, 2002. Thirty-four percent of the children in foster care could be without a social worker at any point in time with the current turnover rates. The figure is worse if the larger number of child protective service workers is used as the base figure. It is safe to say that hundreds of thousands of children are affected by child welfare worker turnover each year.

The APHSA (2005) report compared the vacancy rates of child protection positions with those of state and local government positions on the basis of the Bureau of Labor Statistics' November 2004 report and showed that the vacancy rate for all state and local government positions was 1.5 percent, while the vacancy rate for child protection social positions was 8.5 percent. Comparisons of the same data revealed the turnover rate for state and local government workers to be 9.6 percent, but the child protection social worker turnover rate was 22.1 percent.

ECONOMIC COSTS OF TRAINING NEW CHILD WELFARE WORKERS

The APHSA (2005) report used a figure at 70 percent of the worker's annual salary for cost of turnover but also reported that some estimates use 200 percent of the worker's annual salary for an estimate of the cost of turnover to the agency. The average salary of child protection social workers noted by the report was $35,553. Every social worker who leaves the agency costs the agency a minimum of $24,888.

The cost of initially training a new child welfare worker is a portion of the cost of worker turnover. The cost of initial training can be figured by calculating the child welfare worker's weekly salary plus benefits for time spent in training, per diem for food and lodging during training, mileage to the training site, materials such as training manuals, and trainer salaries. A conservative estimate is $1,300 to $1,500 per trainee per week, plus an estimated $1,000 in salary per week for each trainer involved in the training. This figure does not include the use of a training room and the associated costs for providing a training facility, trainer equipment, and offices and expenses. If there are four weeks of initial training, each new social worker costs at least $5,200 in individual expenses.

Graef and Hill (2000) used more than actual training costs to determine the cost of child protective services staff turnover. The researchers studied one Midwestern state to determine the actual cost to a child welfare agency that accrued over one year and could be attributed to staff turnover. The factors included administrative costs of separation functions and replacement functions as well as training. For the agency that was studied, the per-vacancy average cost of child protection services worker turnover was conservatively estimated to be $10,000 (in 1995). In times of fiscal restraint, it is vital that agencies have a plan to decrease worker turnover. Graef and Hill (2000) also stated:

> Even moderate levels of staff turnover can create crisis conditions in any type of work organization if there is a shortage of trained replacements readily available to assume the workload. In the child protection field, the exit of an experienced investigator or

case manager can have an overwhelming effect on the workload of the remaining staff in the work unit. The challenge of providing even basic coverage for the vacated caseload, much less a level of continuity in service to those families, is a daunting task. . . . The continuous cycle of turnover in many CPS work units means that operating understaffed has become the norm, rather than the exception. (p. 518)

CHILD WELFARE WORKER TURNOVER: WHY DO THEY LEAVE?

A review of the literature regarding issues related to child welfare worker turnover revealed a mix of factors associated with either organizational structure or the nature of the work. The 2005 APHSA report from the 2004 Child Welfare Workforce Survey found heavy workloads, heavy caseloads, after-hours work, amount and type of paperwork, insufficient resources, lack of career advancement or promotional opportunities, and low salaries to be organizational structure factors that contributed to child welfare worker turnover. Some of the same issues—heavy workloads, heavy caseloads, amount of paperwork, and low salaries—were also found to contribute to worker turnover in the Child Welfare League of America study (2001).

Russel (1987) also discussed heavy caseloads, after-hours work/on-call duty, lack of career advancement or promotional opportunities, and low salaries as reasons for leaving employment as a child welfare worker. Russel identified inadequate training as an additional factor in the decision to leave the work. Jayaratne and Chess (1984) revealed that the best predictor of job satisfaction in child welfare was promotional opportunity. Samantrai (1992) stated that the inflexibility of the job was a factor that led to child welfare worker turnover. Dickinson and Perry (2002) and Smith (2004) reported that the environmental factor of the availability of other jobs was a factor in whether or not a child welfare worker remained employed by the public child welfare agency. Fryer, Miyoshi, and Thomas (1989) found that both workers who stayed and workers who left were disgruntled, and both groups felt burdened by heavy caseloads. However, they found a statistically significant difference between the groups in that the group of workers who left the agency "had been more inclined to express that they did not plan long-term service to the child protection field than workers who remained" (Fryer et al., 1998, p. 347).

Harrison (1995) surveyed child welfare workers from a public agency in Ohio, and out of the 266 respondents, 47.4 percent said that they thought about leaving often or very often, 58 percent had applied for another job, and 55.3 percent said they would attempt to find a new job within the next year. Harrison found a strong correlation between intent to leave and fifteen composite variables. In order of strongest correlation ($p < .01$), the variables were commitment to the organization, psychological rewards, commitment to child welfare, job frustration, interest in the job, financial rewards, administrative support, supervision, job clarification, perceived efficacy, job utility, paperwork, concern for safety, monitoring, and independence. Harrison used multiple regression analysis to find that nine predictor variables explained 50 percent of the total variance. Harrison reported that commitment to the organization was the most important predictor. Other predictor variables for less intent to leave were a stronger commitment to one's career, more years in public child welfare, more adequate training, a high degree of psychological rewards, more vertical (administrative) support, not having had a student field placement/internship in child welfare, and having a current assignment in protective services other than those in foster care and adoption. Case workers were also less likely to leave if they did not have children of their own between the ages of thirteen and eighteen.

The other factors in the literature regarding child welfare worker turnover are associated with the nature of the work, rather than organizational issues. Stress is named as a factor by Dickinson and Perry (2002) and Russel (1987). Dickinson and Perry also found that burnout was a factor in worker turnover and that emotional exhaustion was the main factor associated with workers leaving the child welfare agency. The Maslach Burnout Inventory was used in this study to measure emotional exhaustion, depersonalization of self, and lack of personal accomplishment. The only statistically significant factor was emotional exhaustion. This was consistent with the study done by Drake and Yadama (1996) in which emotional exhaustion was found to be associated with child welfare workers leaving their jobs. Anderson (2000) found 62 percent of the 151 front-line child protection workers in her study scored in the high range of emotional exhaustion.

Low job satisfaction was found to be a factor in child welfare worker turnover (Dickinson & Perry, 2002). Beaver (1999) found client violence toward the social worker to be significantly correlated with job dissatisfaction and professional burnout. Beaver stated that social workers who were younger and had a bachelors-level education were more likely to be the target of client violence. Beaver (1999) also reported that "work related characteristics of less social work experience, governmental auspice, non-private settings, and tenure on current job were significantly related to incidence of client violence" (p. 153). All these factors describe many child welfare workers. Beaver (1999) found "levels of job satisfaction to be negatively and significantly related to intent to seek another social work position in the next year" (p. 153).

The above studies looked mostly at child welfare workers and some looked at social workers in general. Jayaratne and Chess (1984) compared the self-reports of child welfare workers, community mental health workers, and family service workers regarding job satisfaction, burnout, and attributes of jobs and organizational variables related to job stress. All respondents had masters-level social work degrees. All groups reported a high level of job satisfaction, but a large number of individuals reported that they would be likely to "make a genuine effort to find a new job with another employer in the next year" (Jayaratne & Chess, 1984, p. 449). That included 44.6 percent of the child welfare workers planning to leave, if possible. The child welfare workers had the highest percentage of workers intending to leave.

Jayaratne and Chess (1984) reported that "On three dimensions (role conflict, value conflict, and challenge), the child welfare workers reported an environment that was significantly worse than those reported by their colleagues in family services and community mental health" (p. 450). The researchers suggested child welfare workers often find themselves in dilemmas concerning what is in the best interest of the child and what the court is ordering and also that their role as a social worker often conflicts with their involvement in investigations that might be more typical of police work. Moral dilemmas occur when court orders force the removal of children from their own homes or the return of children to potentially dangerous homes, either of which may be against the recommendation of the worker, forcing the worker to take action that he or she believes is harmful to the child.

The researchers also claimed that the lack of challenge that child welfare workers see in their work surfaced due to their perception that they are not being allowed to grow psychologically and their perceived inability to have an impact on the environment. The researchers stated that this could be attributed to the restrictive nature and minimal choices of the child welfare agency environment. The research clearly showed child welfare workers to be under more stress than family service workers or community mental health workers, but there was no significant difference between the three groups regarding burnout.

These factors all relate to the nature of child welfare work. The job is stressful and emotionally exhausting. Two studies that attempted to measure burnout revealed that the really salient issue was emotional exhaustion. There has been no research regarding worker turnover and the existence of secondary traumatic stress. Both role conflict and values conflict occur in the child welfare field. The nature of the work is dangerous, and people who abuse their children can become violent or threatening toward the worker. This is especially true when the parents have a history of substance abuse or mental illness, a tendency to become violent, and irrational thought processes, or they feel threatened by the possibility of having a child removed from the family's care. In the qualitative portion of his study, Harrison (1995) stated that the workers who said that they liked the work with children and families still had a general mood of unhappiness. Harrison (1995) reported the work to be stressful and demanding and said one caseworker described this mood as a feeling that one is "responsible for everything, [with] control over nothing" (p. 119).

The most consistent finding in the literature is that the supervisor is an important factor in worker turnover. Lack of supportive supervision and supervisor problems appear in numerous studies regarding child welfare worker turnover (APHSA, 2005; Child Welfare League of America, 2001; Nissly, Mor Barak, & Levin, 2005; Reagh, 1994; Russel, 1987; Rycraft, 1994; Samantrai, 1992; Smith, 2004). The lack of supportive supervision is mentioned more than any other factor in worker turnover studies. This is a major factor affecting worker retention. It is also a vital factor in workers' abilities to deal with secondary traumatic stress. An upcoming chapter is devoted to child welfare supervision.

DISBELIEF AND DISMISSAL TRAUMA

We believe there is another type of trauma involved in the nature of the work in child welfare. In interviews about their work, child welfare workers often discussed role and value conflicts. They often told about not being believed by judges, police officers, attorneys, and other community professionals regarding the occurrence of abuse or the child's resulting trauma. Some of the abuse that is discovered by child protection workers is so atrocious, heinous, and horrific that it is almost beyond human comprehension. Persons who do not work in this field do not understand how torturous and terrible an adult can be to a child. Child welfare workers often reported times when they were not believed by another professional or a person in the community, and they stated that they understand that they are not believed because the abuse is beyond the person's ability to comprehend. Baranowsky (2002) calls this process the "silencing response."

This section represents what we have learned from workers, supervisors, and administrators in discussions about work during STS workshops, child welfare training, and other interactions. The times that the concept of dismissal and disbelief trauma comes up are too numerous to ignore. We hypothesize that this is a very real phenomenon but have not found empirical studies consistent with our observations. It is a phenomenon that demands research.

Social workers have told us stories about not only not being believed but being accused of manufacturing stories of abuse or abusing the child through their work. For example, when a social worker told a district attorney that a five-year-old had told her about being sexually abused by five different men, the attorney responded with, "What do you do, sit around and think this stuff up?" Another social worker who was on the witness stand after an emotional and stressful investigation of the sexual abuse of several children was accused of sexually abusing the children herself through the interview process. Countless times, child welfare workers have told us that they are laughed at and ridiculed for the stories they tell about children being abused. They are often told that the story can't be true or that they are embellishing the story.

Other professionals attack the credibility of the child welfare workers when they cannot fathom such acts, or when they want to disprove the allegations. Sometimes they do not believe the details of the abuse, and sometimes there is disbelief that the accused person actually committed the abuse. Sometimes the attack involves a lack of respect for the child welfare profession in general. For example, in a meeting with a new prosecuting attorney, an experienced child welfare worker asked the attorney what information he wanted from the agency regarding referred felony cases, and the attorney's response was, "Well, first I need to determine if there are any false allegations in any of these cases." It is very damaging to child welfare workers to have what they know to be true not be believed and to have their abilities, credibility, and reputation questioned. The situation worsens if a child is left in or returned to an abusive situation due to that disbelief.

We became aware of the injury this type of treatment causes in workers during interviews. If a child welfare worker is questioned about a time when he or she was not believed in spite of tremendous evidence, the worker will usually be quick to talk about the event. It does not seem that the worker has a difficult time remembering these incidents. Even though these situations may have occurred many years ago, the worker is usually able to retell the conversation in detail, and emotions come up during the process of telling what happened.

We have labeled this type of trauma "disbelief and dismissal trauma" for want of a better description. This occurs when the worker's knowledge, experience, and belief systems are violated. The worker may begin to doubt his or her own capabilities and adopt a protective stance in the face of disbelief. The child protection worker may talk about his or her anger toward another professional or refuse to work with that person. If there is a general lack of support for the work being done to protect children, the workers may feel like they have to fight people who should be on the workers' side in the war against child abuse. Examples of persons who are reported to have treated workers in demeaning ways are law enforcement officers, judges, prosecuting attorneys, court-appointed special advocates, guardians *ad litem*, counselors, physicians, and social workers in other human service agencies such as advocacy centers or trauma centers.

An unhealthy transformation may occur so that the worker can deal with disbelief, dismissal, and criticism from other professionals, community members, and sometimes friends and family members. Sometimes the worker quits trying and succumbs to performing less effective investigations, not wanting to know what is really happening because no one will believe it anyway. At times the worker's skills may be doubted just because he or she works for the public child welfare agency, and this can lead to the worker doubting his or her own abilities. The worker may readily accept others' opinions regarding a child's situation when the other person is less than qualified or just wrong. Continuous disbelief from persons in power or other professions can lead to the worker giving up the fight and moving into another line of work.

Disbelief and dismissal trauma for child welfare workers can be compared to the trauma experienced by sexual abuse victims when they are not believed (Morrison, 1990; Summit, 1983). Sexual abuse victims often state that the sexual abuse was bad, but the worst part of the situation was when their nonoffending parent or other nonoffending adults did not believe them (Morrison, 1990; Summit, 1983). Victims often report having a more difficult time dealing with their parent's or other adults' failure to believe them and protect them than with the abuse itself. It is the same for child protection workers. It is bad enough to hear a child tell about an adult doing terrible things to the child, but it is worse not to be believed by those who are supposed to be a part of the solution. It is worse still if, due to the disbelief he or she encounters, the worker is unable to protect the child and the abuse continues.

HOSTILE WORK ENVIRONMENT AND ADMINISTRATIVE BULLYING

Throughout our years of training child welfare workers and working for child welfare agencies, we have observed and been told by child welfare workers that a hostile work environment exists in some child welfare agencies. This particular type of stressor has been described by many as separate from the nature of the work, not exactly a factor of the organizational structure. This environment creates a climate in the agency that is uncomfortable for many and unbearable for some.

The hostile work environment often occurs due to the actions of upper-level administrators appointed to powerful positions and sometimes, but less often, the actions of middle managers. The individuals in authority who are creating the added workplace stress are often but not always from backgrounds other than child welfare. The behaviors described include unrealistic demands for work, demands for unnecessary work, micromanagement regarding issues about which the administrator has little knowledge, and micromanagement that fails to do the right thing for children and families. It may include orders to take action that is in conflict with the social work code of ethics; orders to take action that is not in the best interest of a child or could be harmful to a child; or interference in casework for political favors, personal reasons, or just to demonstrate authority. It may consist of refusals to ask for resources needed to do the job (i.e., more funding, more staff, resources for children and families), cutting of programs and services for no empirically based or financial reason; the addition of programs, services, and work with no added staff for political reasons; or the promotion of or participation in public demeaning of agency staff in general or the blaming of one person or unit when a child dies from abuse or neglect.

The last type of incident is especially damaging when the worker is not at fault, but "someone's head will roll for this" is the administrator's attitude. Sometimes the media names workers and supervisors concerning the death of a child. Child welfare workers have been suspended and fired for the deaths of children in their caseloads, and this has occurred even when policy and appropriate practice were followed. Often, workers state that the child's death could be traced back to lack of staff, lack of resources, and heavy workloads, but the administration would not admit this. Instead, administration found it more politically palatable to blame the worker and/or supervisor. Child welfare workers discuss the lack of support they receive from agency administrators and the perception that some agency administrators do not care or understand the work that they do. This is damaging to morale and the reputation of the child welfare agency in the community. When the nature of the work and organizational issues already lead to worker turnover, the addition of agency administrators who do not understand the work of child welfare professionals can lead to more workers leaving child welfare.

There is another type of administrative behavior that occurs in some child welfare settings that can do more damage than the type of administrative behavior described above. There are some administrators who can be described as bullies. Research regarding workplace bullying was found most often in studies done by researchers in Europe and Australia. Most of the research on bullying regarded corporations and the nursing field. No research has been found regarding bullying in the child welfare setting. Bullying has been defined by Einarsen (1999) as "the systematic persecution of a colleague, subordinate or superior, which, if continued, may cause severe social, psychological and psychosomatic problems for the victim" (p. 16).

Tehrani (2004) conducted a study of 165 caregiving professionals to establish the incidence of bullying in the workplace. She found that 67 had been bullied, and 113 had observed bullying taking place. The types of bullying that were most prevalent were unfair criticism, intimidation, unpleasant personal remarks, public humiliation, and malicious gossip.

Butler (2002) also discussed bullying in the workplace and described it as repeated behavior that is inappropriate for the workplace. This behavior may come from either a supervisor or a coworker and may take place in front of coworkers or clients; it can be distinguished from legitimate negative feedback on job performance.

Butler also described behaviors associated with bullying as aggressive eye contact, glaring, giving the silent treatment, intimidation, physical gestures such as finger pointing or slamming/throwing things; yelling; screaming; cursing; angry outbursts or temper tantrums; nasty, rude, or hostile behavior; accusations of wrongdoing; insulting or belittling; excessive or harsh criticism; breaches of confidentiality; unreasonable work demands; withholding of needed information; and taking credit for another's work. The target feels disempowered. Targets are often nice people who are not likely to confront the bully; vulnerable people; or the "best and brightest," who are perceived as a threat to the bully.

Bullying was one of the reasons given as to why a child welfare worker with fifteen years of experience and no desire to leave her public child welfare agency left with no notice of resignation. The worker was told by an administrator that she needed to find a job that was a better fit for her even though she had excellent performance evaluations and was consistently informed by her direct supervisor that she was doing a great job. She was not allowed to make decisions or to be part of the decision-making process regarding her work. She stated that upper management often created barriers that made it difficult for her to do her work, put little or no thought into their decisions, and created chaos in the unit that she supervised. Her supervisees were often given instructions by management without her knowledge or even her supervisor's knowledge. She described the environment as hostile and petty with no concern shown by upper management for agency employees. Training, professional development activities, community networking, and meetings were thought to be wasted time, and staff was accused of using this time to goof off. She described morale as low and good employees who were committed to child welfare leaving to avoid mistreatment by the administration. The administrator often yelled at and criticized staff members and would do so in front of colleagues while making unrealistic demands for unnecessary work. The administrator showed little knowledge of child welfare practice or policy and made no effort to learn. The worker stated that she knew she was not the only person being treated this way. She also reported physical illness attributed to the tremendous amount of stress at work caused by this administrator. Her experience and knowledge were not valued, and she received no respect, which was made worse by harsh criticism during everyday communication. She left the agency to take a job at two-thirds pay and with no retirement benefits.

Matthiesen and Einarsen (2004) studied the distress and symptoms of PTSD in victims of workplace bullying (a sample of mostly educated women working in a white-collar profession) and determined that there were indications "that psychiatric distress and post-traumatic stress disorder may be widespread among victims of bullying at work" (p. 348). In this study, it was found that 63 percent of the respondents had been exposed to bullying for a period of two years or more. The most frequent types of bullying in this study were "ostracism (social isolation), being devaluated, holding back information, calumniation, and frequent attacks or criticism against one's person" (Matthiesen & Einarsen, 2004, p. 340). Using the work of Lerner (1980), Matthiesen and Einarsen (2004) suggested that "our need to believe that we live in a world where people get what they deserve and deserve what they get, seems to be shattered by the experience of being bullied" (p. 349). They considered bullying at work to be a socially created cumulative trauma in which the victim often feels that there is no escape.

Our hypothesis is that child welfare workers commonly see and experience things that alter their belief in a just world. The nature of the work, the organizational structure of many child welfare agencies, attacks by other professionals and community members, and the presence of administrative bullies all play a part in the stress and trauma child welfare workers face everyday while trying to protect children. We have heard repeatedly that child welfare workers knew going in about the nature of the work and the heavy caseloads, but that their experiences of disbelief and dismissal trauma and the lack of support from administrators or administrative bullying made staying in the field difficult or in some instances unbearable. The child welfare workers who leave know that the children they leave behind will miss them, and that the departure of yet another worker from the child welfare field will cause more loss in children's lives.

CHILD WELFARE WORKER RETENTION: WHY DO THEY STAY?

Worker retention has been found to be a separate construct from worker turnover. Even though some issues coincide, factors associated with worker retention differ from those associated with worker turnover. Ellett (2001) asserted that it was more productive to determine why workers stay employed in public child welfare than to examine why they leave. It is also important to note that child welfare workers may be committed to the field of child welfare practice but not remain employed in the public child welfare agency. Landsman (2001) examined commitment of workers in public child welfare and learned that "Findings from this study support the primary notion that public child welfare employees may hold dual commitments to the organization and to the occupation. First, job satisfaction, commitment and intent to stay in the organization, and commitment and intent to stay in child welfare practice are each distinct constructs" (p. 405).

A review of the literature revealed that some of the factors associated with child welfare turnover are associated with child welfare worker retention. The 2005 APHSA study showed fair compensation benefits to be one of these reasons. A reasonable number of cases and manageable workloads were found to be retention factors (APHSA, 2005; Landsman, 2001; Samantrai, 1992). Promotional opportunities were also named as a factor that helped agencies retain child welfare workers (Dickinson & Perry, 2002; Landsman, 2001). Samantrai (1992) found that flexibility of job assignments would aid in keeping child welfare workers with the agency. Smith (2004) reported that an ability to maintain a life-work balance and a lack of availability of other jobs contributed to worker retention.

The most strikingly evident factor in several studies was good supervision (APHSA, 2005; Dickinson & Perry, 2002; Ellett, 2001; Landsman, 2001; Rycraft, 1994; Samantrai, 1992; Smith, 2004). Dependable management was also found to be a factor in employee retention in child welfare (APHSA, 2005; Ellett & Millar, 2001; Landsman, 2001).

Variables associated with child welfare worker retention can be divided between agency factors and personal characteristics of the worker. Agency factors that influence the agency's ability to retain workers in child welfare include learning and growth opportunities (APHSA, 2005; Dickinson & Perry, 2002; Reagh, 1994), peer support (Dickinson & Perry, 2002; Ellett & Millar, 2001; Reagh, 1994; Samantrai, 1992), recognition (Dickinson & Perry, 2002; Reagh, 1994), and the worker's authority to make decisions (Dickinson & Perry, 2002). Jones (2002) reported that Title IV-E trained workers had longer periods of tenure with the agency than did non-Title IV-E trained workers. These reasons seem to be more connected to organizational culture than to agency policy. Ellett and Millar (2001) found organizational culture positively linked to retention of child welfare workers. Mentoring; professional sharing and support among colleagues; administrative support; and agency vision, professionalism, and commitment were all positively related to employees' intent to stay.

Personal characteristics were shown in several studies to be related to employee retention in child welfare. Researchers linked worker self-efficacy to retention in several studies (APHSA, 2005; Dickinson & Perry, 2002; Drake & Yadama, 1996; Ellett, 2001). Studies have shown other personal characteristics such as human caring (APHSA, 2005), altruistic tendencies (Landsman, 2001; Reagh, 1994), personal identification with child welfare (Reagh, 1994), an ability to find meaning in the work (Reagh, 1994), and organizational commitment (Landsman, 2001) to be related to child welfare worker retention. Besides good supervision, Rycraft (1994) found that the intent to remain employed by the child welfare agency related to a "goodness of fit" with the agency; investment in the relationship with colleagues; investment in the agency, social work, and child welfare; and a personal mission that coincided with the work. The personal mission was described as a desire to be of service to others, with a focus on children and families. The commitment to protecting children and strengthening families was strong in the workers intending to stay. Rycraft stated that even the dedicated and committed child welfare workers sometimes questioned their sense of mission, but the ones who stayed showed the ability to accentuate the positive rather than the negative. Global satisfaction with the job was a reason for staying in the studies done by Dickinson and Perry (2002) and Landsman (2001).

The most powerful reasons for social workers to stay in the field, however, have to do with the children and the families whom they serve. The personal rewards are tremendous when individual lives are transformed due to the efforts of the child welfare worker. Dickinson and Perry (2002), Drake and Yadama (1996), and Reagh (1994) all cited a sense of personal accomplishment as a reason workers stay. One worker described the gratification she felt when a child she had rescued many years before won a beauty contest. The day of the rescue, the worker had been urinated and thrown up on and had had feces thrown at her. She and a coworker had been exposed to scabies and lice. She later ceremoniously burned the clothes she had worn that day in a cleansing ritual for herself and the children. Now, watching from the audience, the worker remembered the day she removed the little girl and her brothers from their home and she cried tears of joy as she reflected upon the girl's transformation from a neglected and sexually abused child to a confident and happy young lady with a loving family. For every negative outcome that a worker experiences, there is a positive outcome in which one child's life is saved, and that life is a reminder that the social worker can make a difference.

It is possible that the child welfare agency could have an effect on some of the personal characteristics associated with retention of workers. Agency supervisors and administrators who put into place policies, programs, and practices that increase worker self-efficacy, help the worker see personal accomplishments, bring out evidence that the worker is making a difference, and help the worker find meaning in the work by accentuating positives in everyday work may influence the personal characteristics associated with retention. Team-building activities may relate to organizational commitment, investment in the agency, and investment in relationships with colleagues. The personal characteristics that seem to be required in order for a worker to stay are human caring, altruistic character, a goodness of fit, and a personal commitment to protect children and strengthen families.

Most child welfare workers profess commitment to the prevention of childhood abuse and neglect and to service focused on helping vulnerable children and families. Child welfare workers may have this commitment due to past trauma in their own lives or from being educated about the need for work in this area and the opportunity to make a difference in the lives of children and families. Why do some stay, yet many leave the work that they were initially committed to doing? Some reasons for worker turnover involve agency structure, and some involve the nature of the work. Reasons why workers stay in child welfare may coincide with reasons for leaving related to agency structure (salary, workloads, caseloads, flexibility of job assignments, and life-work balance), but many of the reasons for staying are different from those for leaving. Some of the reasons for staying involve agency structure, but some also involve the worker's personal characteristics. Supervision is the factor that is found in most studies to affect worker turnover and worker retention. According to child welfare worker reports, disbelief and dismissal trauma and administrative bullying seem to play a part in worker turnover. These two phenomena demand further research. The need for child welfare agencies to put in place policies and practices to prevent worker turnover and to retain workers is evident in the cost to children, families, the worker, the agency, communities, and society when the turnover rates are as high as they currently are.

3

Educating Child Welfare Workers about Secondary Traumatic Stress

LEARNING TO COPE AND TO HAVE A STRONG SOCIAL SUPPORT SYSTEM IS crucial to managing the effects of the traumatic stress of child welfare work. What complicates coping and social support for child welfare workers is that there is a need to have a professional support system and, at the same time, a separate, but equally important, support system of family and friends. Legal issues and the need to maintain clients' confidentiality prevent child welfare workers from being able to discuss their work with friends and family. Telling family and friends that you had a hard day at work may be all that can be shared. The worker is not able to say, "I interviewed a five-year-old little girl today who had been sexually molested by five different men who were also having sex with the child's mom, but the mom was drunk and passed out, and then I listened to an eight-year-old boy tell me that his stepfather burns him with cigarettes, and then I was called by the hospital because the emergency room had just admitted a baby who had been shaken and had head injuries. The baby will probably die or be a vegetable because the mom lost her temper. That was how my day was—how was yours?"

A PSYCHOEDUCATIONAL MODEL FOR SECONDARY TRAUMATIC STRESS EDUCATION

Between 1997 and 2004, we conducted workshops with child welfare professionals in five states. Figley's Compassion Fatigue Self-Test was used, along with a demographic questionnaire, to collect information from participants regarding symptoms of secondary traumatic stress and burnout. The data analysis and findings can be found in Appendix A. The key findings were that child welfare professionals are affected by STS, and less so by burnout. Younger workers and workers with less experience in the field were more affected by STS. Individuals who had experienced childhood trauma had high STS scores. The 666 child welfare professionals we studied reported being affected by STS, and many had ten symptoms of secondary traumatic stress, as described by Figley. More than 50 percent of participants in all states reported feeling trapped and hopeless about their work with clients, being in danger while working with clients, avoiding thoughts and feelings about their clients, and having experienced trauma in their own lives as adults.

We used a psychoeducational model as the basis for developing our educational materials (Simon, 1997; Simon, McNeil, Franklin, & Cooperman, 1991). This approach incorporates emotional issues as part of the educational process. One of the first steps in coping is to develop knowledge and understanding of STS and how it is different from burnout. The second is to develop an understanding of how people normally respond to trauma and how it changes their worldview or psychological frame of reference. Third, a thorough understanding of the relationship between a worker and a traumatized client or clients must be achieved. Once this knowledge is acquired and participants have a conceptual framework for understanding how they may be traumatized by the work, then it is time to concentrate the educational process on coping and social support in both personal and professional arenas.

STAYING COGNITIVE DURING STS EDUCATION: THINKING ABOUT FEELING

One of the most important things we have learned about introducing the concept of STS to child welfare workers, supervisors, and administrators is that workshop participants need to stay at a cognitive level and not let their emotions and memories of past experiences overwhelm them. In every child welfare workshop we conducted there was an abundance of work-related traumatic experience among the participants. We learned early on that if participants allow emotions to overwhelm them, it then becomes difficult to stay focused on learning. This is particularly important if the worker or the organization has recently experienced a traumatic event.

For example, in one workshop, a foster care worker had recently been chased by a psychotic adolescent wielding a butcher knife. The participant began emotionally breaking down when her feelings were aroused by memories of that event during a practical exercise using a fictional case example. One of the presenters took her aside and helped her regain her composure. She decided that the trauma was too fresh in her mind and that she could not continue in the workshop that day.

The way in which we help participants stay at a cognitive level is to encourage them to think about feelings rather than allow themselves to focus on their emotions during the workshop. It is important for participants to stay cognitive and in a learning mode. Staying cognitive also helps to prevent the workshop from disintegrating into a gripe session. Visual reminders are posted in the classroom to help keep the participants thinking and learning.

GENDER ISSUES

We have also learned the importance of having two educators, preferably one male and one female, deliver the workshop. First, one of the educators may need to leave to assist someone who has become emotionally affected and in need of support. Second, if there are ongoing tensions in the workplace and participants are angry, two presenters can better diffuse the negativity that can detract from education. Third, because of the overwhelming number of women in the field, it helps the few males present to address any gender issues that may affect their traumatic stress experiences in child welfare. Evidence suggests that men and women react differently to traumatic stress (Meyers & Cornille, 2002; Peirce, Newton, Buckley, & Keane, 2002; Tolin & Foa, 2002). It is important that all reactions and individual differences be acknowledged and respected.

DIFFERENTIATING STS FROM BURNOUT

Many workers and supervisors intuitively understand that they are affected by their work, but most often they use the term "burnout" to describe what is actually STS. Developing a distinction between the words "trauma" and "burnout," and the experiences they represent, is one of the first participatory activities in the STS educational experience. STS workshop participants are asked to develop a list of descriptive words that they associate with trauma/traumatic stress—words that reflect their experiences with the work they do. Participants work in groups to generate lists of terms. Participants are presented with this statement: "When I hear the word 'trauma,' I automatically think _____." They are instructed to fill in the blank with as many terms as they think of. The lists in table 1 were developed in seven workshops recently attended by child welfare workers, supervisors, and administrators.

Table 1. Terms Generated by Workshop Participants to Describe Trauma/Traumatic Stress

Group 1	danger, blood, emergency, pain, injury, emotional upset, anger, betrayal, death, destruction, fear, anxiety, 911, traumatized, harm, hurt, helplessness, hopelessness, sudden, panic, chaos, reactive, uncertainty
Group 2	disaster, severe accident, turmoil, tear, emergency room, pain, victim, death, hurt, abuse, sick, rape, unhealthy, helpless, hopeless, isolated, blood, cuts
Group 3	physical injury, emotional upset, violence, crisis, death, helplessness, hopelessness, loss, pain, blood, burn, broken bones, bruises, emergency room, sickness
Group 4	life threatening, change, mass destruction, emergency room, fear, powerlessness, terror, paralysis, loss of control, shock, helplessness, hopelessness, low self-esteem, death, injury, accident, loss of family, loss, rape, abuse, violence
Group 5	emergency, disaster, harmful, serious injury, despair, grief, life altering, devastation, blood, graphic images, stress, violence, pain, major event, chaos, hopeless, helpless, victim, scarring emotions, loss of control, death, emergency room, super-intense, impact
Group 6	bad, pain, danger, frighten, shock, sudden, crisis, harm, stress, hurt, anger, scared, anxious, helplessness, hopelessness, blood, cut, depression, emergency room
Group 7	pain, injury, suffering, fear, disruption, loss, stress, death, disability, loss of control, assault, anxiety, helpless, hopeless

Once this list has been discussed, the participants are then asked to list terms they associate with the word "burnout." The participants are instructed to complete the statement "A burned-out colleague is _____." The lists are shown in table 2.

Table 2. Terms Generated by Workshop Participants to Describe Burnout

Group 1	tired, underpaid, angry, frustrated, abused, immobile, unwilling, unfocused, unappreciated, ineffective, invisible, absent, physical, overwhelmed
Group 2	irritable, tired, don't care, messy desk, irrational, angry, late, apathetic, tardy, resistant, frustrated, uninvolved, unmotivated
Group 3	lethargic, passive-aggressive, apathetic, overwhelmed, dangerous, dumped on, stressed, not appreciated, low evaluation, angry, irritable, sarcastic, cusses, hopeless, not productive, frustrated, postal, depressed, withdrawal, absent, insecure, paranoid
Group 4	tired, irritable, frustrated, pregnant, stressed, don't perform, passive-aggressive, procrastinate, uncaring, absent, hostile, uncooperative, impatient, insubordinate
Group 5	depressed, stressed, blaming, job paralysis, no control, no way out, overwhelmed, dreading to work, rigid, combative, ready to quit, no empathy, no creativity, absent, tired, snappy, can't make a decision
Group 6	tired, detached, ineffective, emotionally blunt, overwhelmed, noncompassionate, angry, unproductive, don't care, procrastination, hopeless, resentful, agitated, absent, mentally stressed, unfulfilled, irritable, frustrated, postal, nervous, blaming, confrontational
Group 7	tired, hopeless, unmotivated, uncooperative, late, passive-aggressive, nonchalant, irritable, bipolar, apathetic, immobile, rationalize behavior, defensive, insensitive, negative, nonproductive, absent, isolated, paralyzed, self-destructive, postal, witch, cancer sore, self-medicating

When the participants compare the two sets of terms, there are a few similarities, but there are many more differences between the lists. For example, "death," "pain," "injury," and "emergency room" don't appear on the list of terms related to burnout, nor do "blood," "burns," "broken bones," and "bruises." Traumatic stress is a different phenomenon from burnout, and as we found in our study, STS is more pervasive than burnout. The sources of the phenomena are different. Traumatic stress comes from the helper's relationship with a traumatized client or clients. Burnout occurs in organizations typified by high demands and low personal rewards. Workshop participants will say that they knew something was wrong and they didn't think they were burned out, but they didn't have a term for what they were experiencing. The bad news is that there is not much that can be done about burnout other than changing the organizational culture or changing where one works. In contrast, there are effective interventions for STS, and that is the good news.

HOW HUMAN BEINGS RESPOND TO TRAUMA

The next issue addressed is how people respond to trauma. Continuing to work in their groups, participants were asked to identify the ways people respond to trauma on an emotional, cognitive (intrusive and perceptual), physiological, behavioral (acting), and interpersonal (interacting) level. The groups' responses (shown in table 3) are consistent with what theory predicts and research demonstrates (Figley, 1995; Morrissette, 2004) and what is found in the diagnostic criteria for 309.81 Post-traumatic Stress Disorder.

Table 3. Terms Generated by Workshop Participants to Describe Responses to Trauma

Emotional	Feeling stressed, anxious, overwhelmed, fearful, fatigued, guilt, numb, tearful, depressed, angry, sad, enraged, a loss of control, worried, shameful, lonely, shocked, frustrated, edgy, guilt, helpless, hopeless
Intrusive Cognitions	Having thoughts of the event when you are trying to not think about it, dreams, nightmares, flashbacks, ruminations
Perceptual Cognitions	Experiencing an altered outlook, memory loss, a decreased interest in favorite activities, dissociation, a loss of innocence, detachment, impaired cognition (inability to think straight), paranoia, a decline in intellectual functioning, poor concentration, thoughts of harming others, a lack of focus, an altered worldview, jaded thoughts
Physiological	Developing clinical depression, ulcers, headaches, migraines, immune system malfunctions, hypertension, hypotension, anxiety disorders, irritable bowel syndrome, crying spells for unknown reasons, memory loss, fatigue, chronic fatigue syndrome, sweating, hyperarousal, substance abuse problems and addictions, overeating, illnesses, sweaty palms, panic attacks, trembling, gastrointestinal problems, chest pain, adrenaline rushes, sleep disruptions, changes in appetite, an increased startle response
Behavioral	Being tearful, overreactive, numb, forgetful, sleepy, unable to concentrate, nervous, an excessive substance user, socially withdrawn from others, oversensitive, blameful, easily irritated, paranoid, less spiritual, detached, aggressive, impatient, nervous, overprotective of children, hateful, inappropriate with laughter, untrusting, hurtful to self or others, negative, a thrill seeker, unsympathetic, judgmental
Interpersonal	Experiencing codependency, isolation from others, loss of trust, withdrawal, loss of interest in sex, loss of intimacy, withdrawal of support for others, blaming others, family problems, problems with coworkers, problems with children, damaged relationships, divorce, inappropriate relationships, loss of friends

Child welfare workers, supervisors, and administrators are fairly consistent in their thoughts about emotional reactions to trauma. Many report numbing and distancing in order to be able to intervene in a traumatic situation. They also share that it is sometimes difficult to get in touch with their feelings because so much of the work is painful. They agree that this makes maintaining interpersonal relationships a challenge. Participants in the STS workshops clearly want to leave the work at the workplace when they go home, but the nature of trauma makes that difficult. They indicate that it is difficult to stop thinking and worrying about the children and families with whom they work at the end of the day. It is not uncommon for these professionals to experience intrusive thoughts or to ruminate about a difficult case, especially if they have become hypervigilant about a client or more than one client. Several workers reported that they had been at the movies on the weekend and suddenly became anxious about a client or case, rendering them unable to concentrate on the movie. Others reported being in church and finding themselves thinking about a child or a family. These professionals experience a fair amount of work-related intrusion into their personal time that often prevents them from staying present for family, friends, or themselves.

Child welfare workers are very much aware that they are changed by the work they do. They know what they do is not "normal," and that others do not understand what they do. They experience a loss of innocence as a price of protecting children and helping families who live in some of the worst conditions. They experience an altered worldview because of what they encounter daily. Many state that it is hard not to look at a perfectly innocent interaction between a child and an adult and wonder if something bad is going on. They also say it is hard to maintain knowledge and awareness that there are stable and healthy families who care for their children and protect them from harm.

Trauma takes a toll on physiology and brain functioning (Scaer, 2001; Van der Kolk, 1996). Dienstbier (1989) demonstrated that levels of catecholamine and cortisol in the brains of workers in high-strain jobs with chronic stress and little control can become elevated and not return to normal levels. It is thought that chronic stress alters one's physiology and contributes to both physical and mental health problems. Child welfare workers know this all too well and are quick to tell of periods of illness they experienced during difficult cases or following difficult cases. Posttraumatic stress affects both physical and mental health in a variety of ways (Friedman & Schnurr, 1995; Schnurr, 1996; Wagner, Wolfe, Rotnitsky, Proctor, & Erickson, 2000). Posttraumatic stress increases vulnerability to heart disease and hypertension and may produce abnormalities in hormones and their ability to function normally. It produces changes in the immune system that lead to opportunistic infections, and it may produce alterations in the body's ability to identify and manage pain (Scaer, 2001). Posttraumatic stress also produces changes in brain chemistry that may lead to depression and poor coping skills. It can also lead to increased anger and hostility, which can contribute to troubled interpersonal relationships. Individuals suffering from posttraumatic stress may increase their use of substances such as alcohol, tobacco, or other drugs in an attempt to moderate the negative effects produced by such stress. In a recent study of 30,800 female veterans, Frayne and her colleagues (2004) found that women with a diagnosis of PTSD had poorer health than those without the diagnosis. Child welfare workers may be at risk for poor health because of the impact that

STS, a form of posttraumatic stress, has on their neurochemistry and physiology. Indeed, it is possible that child welfare work has the potential to make workers sick.

Trauma work also affects behavior. Child welfare workers, supervisors, and administrators have no difficulty identifying ways in which trauma alters their behavior. Participants in all the groups we have worked with have become overprotective of their own children and grandchildren. It is not uncommon for them to interrogate their children when they want to stay overnight at a friend's house. One grandmother, a child welfare supervisor, shared that before her nine-year-old granddaughter is allowed to stay overnight with a friend, the grandmother goes over how to say "no" and "good touch, bad touch." The grandmother, who related that she doesn't sleep well, asked if such anxiety is normal. Because of the nature of the work and her observations of the terrible things that are done to children, her anxiety is to be expected.

Workers often observe how their behavior is affected by work when they go to the grocery store at the end of the workday. In the store, a toddler starts crying and a mother's or father's voice gets tense and then angry as she or he responds to the child. The worker, who merely wants to get his or her groceries and go home, becomes anxious and concerned for the child and may move his or her grocery basket in the direction of the sounds just to be sure everything is all right. Other people in the store may be thinking, "That baby is tired and needs a nap," or "I'm glad I left my child at home with his dad." Because of the work they do, workers know that the tension between the parent and child may escalate and lead to verbal or physical harm. Informed by the child welfare environment, the worker's worldview is different from those of the other people in the store. Other people do not know the terrible things that children experience.

The final area the child welfare professionals frequently address is what happens in their interpersonal relationships with colleagues and significant others. Many participants share that what can be most harmful to them is the impact the work has on their personal and family life. Workers and supervisors who are regularly involved in cases of sexual abuse of children and adolescents relate that at times they have lost interest in sex and intimacy, and that has taken a toll on their personal relationships. Similarly, because others do not understand their work, they feel socially isolated and avoid revealing to others what they do. The reaction of people not involved in child welfare is normally, "How can you do that?" or "Let me tell you about a situation I know of." One worker shared that she tells people that she is a hairdresser and changes the subject. Another common response is that the work causes a lack of trust and loss of compassion. A common phrase that comes up is, "It's like nothing matters anymore." A seasoned worker shared that she does background checks on potential dates just to be sure they don't have a criminal record. What these child welfare professionals are saying is that their worldview has been changed. They are not the same people they were before they began working in child welfare. They will tell you that they work in a world where people do evil things to babies, children, and adolescents.

UNDERSTANDING HOW TRAUMA CHANGES THE PSYCHOLOGICAL FRAME OF REFERENCE OR WORLDVIEW

The next step to understanding STS is to understand how experience in child welfare changes the worker's psychological frame of reference or worldview. This is best explained by McCann and Pearlman's (1990) use of constructivist self-development theory. They explain that the concept of self is central to each person's worldview. Self is who we think we are, and it is through the self that we experience and interpret the world and how we define the meanings we discover in life. From the time we are born, we develop our self, and that self continues to develop across our life span. Central to self are cognitive schemata that define psychological needs related to how the self is constructed and develops. The cognitive schemata are safety, trust/dependency, independence, power, esteem, intimacy, and control (McCann & Pearlman, 1990, p. 59).

McCann and Pearlman argue that safety is a major theme throughout life. Safety is a need for all humans, and as Janoff-Bullman (1989) pointed out, the reality of the world is that it is not safe, and we engage in illusions of safety as a means to function in an unsafe world. From the time we are born, we hope to be protected from harm. If we are protected from harm in our early years, then we will most likely develop positive safety schemata. While we know that bad things happen in the world, we have not experienced them to the degree that we feel unsafe.

Similarly, we have a need for trust and dependency. As McCann and Pearlman demonstrate, we need to be able to count on others and receive support from others, and that includes self-trust. If children are cared for and their needs are met, they are likely to develop a positive trust schema, believing that they can count on being cared for. This schema will continue to develop positively through adolescence and into adulthood, provided the majority of their experiences with trust are positive.

McCann and Pearlman (1990) describe independence as "the need to control one's own rewards or punishments or to be in control of one's behavior and destiny" (p. 71). Independence schemata have to do with being in charge of, and in control of, one's self. This schema allows individuals to believe that they can make things happen through their own actions and choices.

McCann and Pearlman argue that, in contrast to independence, power is related to having control over the environment in which one lives. The degree to which a child exerts control in his or her environment contributes to the development of a positive power schema. If environmental control continues throughout adolescence and into adulthood, the power schema will be such that the individual believes that he or she exerts some control over the environment and can make things happen in that environment.

Esteem is another cognitive schema related to self. McCann and Pearlman (1990) define esteem as the "belief in one's value," which is "rooted in the need for recognition or validation" (p. 73). When we have positive self-esteem, we tend to feel positive about others and their value as humans. Like other cognitive schemata, esteem develops in childhood and grows throughout adolescence to adulthood. If life experiences, particularly interactions with family and friends, reinforce positive esteem, then an individual will develop a positive cognitive schema of self-esteem and have esteem for others.

The last cognitive schema related to psychological needs presented in McCann and Pearlman's theory is intimacy. Without connection to others and oneself, individuals become isolated. Intimacy is a combination of belonging and feeling safe in the presence of other people, as well as feelings of being connected to others. Intimacy is considered by McCann and Pearlman to be fragile and easily damaged. Like the other schemata, intimacy is developed across the life span, and with positive experiences, the developed schema will be positive.

Cognitive schemata are highly individualized and reflect the cumulative experiences of each individual across the life span. Traumatic stress changes cognitive schemata, and the traumatic experiences become integrated into the cognitive schemata. In the first chapter we used the example of the car accident to illustrate how cognitive schemata were changed by a traumatic experience. Changes in cognitive schemata contribute to changes in each individual's worldview or psychological frame of reference. Child welfare practitioners are vulnerable to changes in their cognitive schemata because of the work they do and the conditions under which they work. The consequence of these changes is an alteration in individual worldview and psychological frame of reference, which may result in the development of symptoms of posttraumatic stress, such as feeling isolated from others or having intrusive thoughts or persistent numbing. As noted in the first chapter, a practitioner may start to see the world through the lens of the client's experiences, especially those of children who have been badly hurt or killed. The practitioner may become cynical and distrustful as he or she sees the effects of trauma on children and adolescents over and over again. In addition, the work itself is dangerous, and workers may experience threats or physical harm to their bodies or to their property (Curl, 1998; Meyers & Cornille, 2002; Stanley & Goddard, 2002). Tragically, practitioners may lose their connection to their spiritual selves and feel that life has no meaning (Rogers, 2002).

Child welfare practitioners can manage the effects of posttraumatic stress. They can learn to protect their worldview. The metaphor we have used from the beginning in delivering STS education is "learning to dump your bucket." We refer to it as a pain bucket model. It was developed by one of the authors, who worked for a time with Vietnam veterans with well-developed PTSD. Getting veterans to express their feelings was often difficult, and the metaphor seemed to work. It has also worked well over the years for other helping professionals, including child welfare professionals.

DUMPING YOUR BUCKET

In the workshop, this metaphor is presented by an instructor, who sketches a bucket on a flip chart that all can see. Pleasant and unpleasant life experiences collect across the individual's life span and slowly fill the bucket. The premise is that the capacity of one's bucket is finite. The child welfare worker brings to the work his or her bucket of life experiences, certainly including personal trauma history. Child welfare practitioners use empathic engagement to facilitate relationship development with clients and to gather the information they need to provide effective help. They collect information about the traumatic experiences of their clients. Those experiences accumulate over time and add to the contents of the worker's bucket. Some of the clients' experiences may be particularly horrific.

The bucket slowly fills and ultimately spills over, interfering with the work and the practitioner's personal and professional life. The spilled contents of the bucket are contagious, as others—friends, family, colleagues—are stepping in the mess, getting it on themselves, and tracking it about. The workplace and home are all affected adversely, and relationships predictably suffer. The quality of personal and professional relationships deteriorates.

PERSONAL TRAUMA HISTORY

If the practitioner has a personal trauma history, he or she may be more vulnerable to the effects of STS, especially when a client's traumatic experience is similar to his or her own (Cunningham, 2003; Nelson-Gardell & Harris, 2003; Pearlman & Mac Ian, 1995). If the practitioner's own traumatic experience is unresolved, its effects may become exacerbated. Child welfare professionals can be taught methods of coping effectively with traumatic stress. These methods include both individual and social support strategies. These strategies allow the worker to dump his or her bucket, keeping the experiences away from the top of the bucket so that they do not spill over and contaminate the helping relationship as well as the practitioner's personal life.

COPING WITH SECONDARY TRAUMATIC STRESS AND USING SOCIAL SUPPORT

The goal of coping is to protect the child welfare practitioner's worldview and psychological frame of reference in order to reduce the impact of STS on his or her work and life. There are several intermediate objectives in learning to cope effectively: (1) to understand and accept one's vulnerability to STS; (2) to learn to balance the needs of the client, the agency, and oneself; (3) to understand the role of supervision in mitigating emotional stress; (4) to recognize when one's self-care system is not working; and (5) to recognize negative and positive coping behaviors.

SELF-ASSESSMENT

Understanding and accepting one's vulnerability to STS requires the practitioner to undertake a self-assessment. Child welfare practitioners bring a variety of ego resources, self-capacities, and personal characteristics to their work. These include both strengths and vulnerabilities. We know that many people are drawn to this work because of their own life experiences, and those experiences may include a personal trauma history. It is important to understand how a personal trauma history increases one's vulnerability to STS. Undertaking a self-assessment involves examining the way in which our personal factors influence our coping skills. There are five areas to examine: (1) physical self-care, (2) social self-care, (3) emotional self-care, (4) personal trauma history, and (5) disbelief and dismissal trauma.

PHYSICAL SELF-CARE

Physical self-care is under the control of the child welfare practitioner. Practitioners report that there are several activities that contribute to their physical well-being: sleep, rest, exercise, good nutrition, reliable transportation, massages, hot tubs, and sex are frequently mentioned. While each of these is important to physical self-care, exercise is crucial. The stress, especially traumatic stress, of child welfare work takes a toll on the body. Skovholt (2001) refers to this as living in an "ocean of stress emotions" (p. 87). Physical exercise protects the human body from heart disease, stroke, high blood pressure, obesity, back pain, osteoporosis, diabetes, and myriad other health risks. Regular exercise also contributes to a healthy immune system, promotes bone density and healthy blood sugar levels, and increases levels of HDL (good) cholesterol. Physical exercise also releases endorphins, which make us feel good. There is increasing evidence that moderate exercise, such as a brisk thirty-minute walk daily, can be beneficial. Exercise has also been shown to reduce the risk of depression and to improve mood. Duke University conducted a study of exercise and depression and found that depressed individuals who exercised for thirty minutes three times a week resolved their depression in a few months, without antidepressants (Blumenthal, Babyak, Moore, Craighead, Herman, Khatri, et al., 1999). Similar results have been found in other studies (Craft, 2005). Additional benefits of exercise include improved sleep, less anxiety, and improved sexual performance and sexual pleasure (Krucoff & Krucoff, 2000; Staten & Yeager, 2003).

Child welfare practitioners find innovative ways to exercise at work, such as taking the stairs or a brisk thirty-minute walk at lunch. Some park their cars at a distance from their office buildings to increase the distance they walk. One group obtained permission to use a large room for a thirty-minute aerobics session at the end of the workday. Many join health clubs and make exercise appointments on their calendars to ensure that they go. Others say that doing exercise in a group helps them to sustain the practice.

It is important that the practitioner have a good relationship with his or her family physician. If the family physician is aware of the traumatic stress of the work, then he or she will be in a good position to help the practitioner monitor health concerns and ensure that he or she is treated accordingly. The physician can also assess when brain chemistry has been altered and can help the worker decide on the most effective intervention. There are times when exercise is beneficial but additional interventions are needed. When exercise helps, but the practitioner still finds him- or herself depressed, the family physician may find it necessary to prescribe antidepressants.

SOCIAL SELF-CARE

Social support is a complex phenomenon, and individuals may both seek and provide it. Payne and Jones (1987) identified 192 ways to measure social support. Our interest is to discuss personal social support and what it does for the child welfare practitioner. Social support helps the practitioner maintain a balance in his or her worldview and positive cognitive schemata. Vaux (1988) maintains that social support is a transactional process subject to personal and contextual influences. Personal social support needs are defined by the practitioner as what suits him or her best. One practitioner may find having interactions and activities with friends meets his or her needs best. Another may find that quiet time with a confidant brings greater renewal than being in a crowd. Each practitioner must learn what his or her support needs are and how to best meet them.

Cohen (2002) argued that having "diverse sources of support (e.g., a spouse, children, friends, workmates, and fellow social and religious members) is associated with greater resistance to infectious agents" (p. 113). He wrote that it is possible that this diverse network of social relationships contributes to individual choices such as exercising and alcohol use. Additional benefits are the promotion of positive psychological states and the reduction of negative states. This contributes to being motivated to take care of oneself and to having multiple sources of information, which may influence well-being.

Social self-care has two aspects: intrapersonal and interpersonal. Each practitioner needs to assess how the work affects him or her personally. Once practitioners acknowledge the ways they are affected by the work, they are then in a position to enjoy the positive aspects and address the negative effects. This is individualized work and requires reflection on the part of the practitioner.

One issue that frequently comes up in discussion is making the transition from work to home or how to leave the work at the workplace. What some child welfare workers share is that they have developed rituals for making this transition. Some change clothes before they leave their office and put on exercise clothing, or what one individual called "play clothes." One worker developed a ritual with her family so that when she arrived home, she put on her walking shoes and walked a couple of miles before interacting with her family. Many say a hot shower or bath works for them. Rituals help make the transition from work to home easier. They also help the practitioner give her- or himself permission to leave work behind.

Interpersonal social self-care is having a life outside of work that involves doing what the practitioner enjoys and spending fun time with family and friends. There are a variety of ways workers make this happen. Having a supportive family and supportive friends who understand the difficulty of the practitioner's work but also appreciate the importance of confidentiality is essential.

SPIRITUALITY

Maintaining a spiritual life has been found by many workshop participants to be another essential practice. Many say that their spirituality is challenged by the evil they encounter and that staying in a relationship with God and staying in the fight are important to staying with the work. As Rogers (2002) pointed out, "A person's spiritual nature produces qualities such as compassion, forgiveness, love, faith, hope, trust, generosity, and kindness. These characteristics are affected by evil, which produces suffering, leading to the stifling or destruction of some aspect of spirit" (p. 31).

Spirituality has also been shown to lower traumatic stress (Lee & Waters, 2003). These researchers found that age and spirituality were strongly correlated with decline in trauma symptoms. They found that as spirituality increased, trauma symptoms decreased. Lee and Waters concluded that spirituality is a protective buffer for cumulative traumatic experiences. Maintaining a spiritual life helps practitioners keep their worldview balanced and their belief system intact in a world of good and evil and helps them remember that there are happy, stable, healthy people and children who are cared for and who care for each other.

EMOTIONAL SELF-CARE

Emotional self-care also involves self-reflection and has intrapersonal and interpersonal aspects as well. Each practitioner can assess how the work is affecting him or her emotionally. Periodically taking the Compassion Fatigue Self-Test is one way to monitor the ways in which one may be affected. In the times that are most difficult, practitioners benefit from having someone to talk with, whether that is a colleague or supervisor. It may also be necessary to seek professional counseling when intrusive thoughts, rumination, and an inability to leave the work at the workplace become the rule rather than the exception. Practitioners can support each other in seeking help when they recognize intrusive thoughts and rumination in each other.

Interpersonal aspects of emotional self-care involve being able to be intimately connected to significant others and friends (Tedeschi & Calhoun, 1995). This involves having an emotional life outside of work and not allowing the work to intrude into personal time. Staying present with family and friends and being close to others is pertinent to maintaining a balanced worldview, as are having hobbies and engaging in activities that bring renewal of spirit and soul.

MANAGING DISBELIEF AND DISMISSAL TRAUMA

In chapter 2, we argued that disbelief and dismissal trauma occurs when the practitioner's beliefs are violated. We also argued that this violation is what causes many workers to give up the work and leave the field. Belief violations are particularly difficult when other professionals refuse to believe that a child is being harmed when the evidence is overwhelming.

One practitioner was told by a judge to return a child to her home in spite of the evidence, which meant that she would be sexually abused by her father. She was told that she would be held in contempt of court if she refused. The worker left the courtroom then returned and, facing the judge squarely, told the judge that if it was his opinion that regardless of the evidence the child should be returned home, then he could put her in jail, and he could return the child to her home and take responsibility for what was going to happen. The judge changed his opinion.

Another example of disbelief and dismissal trauma was shared in one of the workshops provided to one state's county directors from the Department of Human Resources. After we differentiated between STS and burnout and explained the difference between direct and indirect trauma, one of the participants asked if one could be traumatized by threats from one's superiors. He went on to share that the year before, the head of the department had said that the reason children were dying was because the directors weren't doing their jobs. This resulted in a number of the directors leaving their positions to work for a different agency. We contend that the directors' knowledge, experience, and strongly held values and beliefs were violated by the head of the department.

Child welfare practitioners have to protect their beliefs in the face of frequent disbelief of the horrors of child abuse. It is important to anticipate that there will be times when they will be unable to convince other professionals of what they know to be true. Practitioners often say that it is because of this disbelief and dismissal that their spiritual practices are necessary to their work.

Trauma permeates the work of child welfare. In Meyers and Cornille's 2002 study of 203 child welfare practitioners, 82 percent had traumatic experience before they became child welfare workers. Seventy-seven percent indicated they had experienced physical assault or been threatened by a client. Having a history of trauma contributes to vulnerability of STS and to the number of symptoms experienced (Meyers & Cornille, 2002; Nelson-Gardell & Harris, 2003; Pearlman & Saakvitne, 1995). It is natural for a practitioner who is a trauma survivor to overidentify with traumatized clients, especially when there are similarities between their experiences. Managing disbelief and dismissal of abuse may be particularly difficult for a trauma survivor. The worker must respect that boundaries need to be maintained so the client receives the assistance he or she needs. It is important for the practitioner to be able to seek assistance when this issue arises, either through supervision or through professional counseling.

PROFESSIONAL COPING FACTORS

Professional factors that help child welfare professionals cope with STS in the workplace must be addressed. First and foremost, STS must be acknowledged as an occupational hazard in child welfare work that can result in an occupational stress injury. Second, certain activities can help the practitioner maintain a balanced worldview (Figley, 2002; Saakvitne & Pearlman, 1996).

One helpful activity is to start the day with a list of work to be achieved, prioritize it, and then try to organize it so that emotionally draining tasks are not piled together. Saakvitne and Pearlman (1996) suggest several activities that are essential to professional self-care. Get up and move around. You may be thinking about your work, but moving your body is important. Plan breaks in your workday that make you move around. When you find that you are at your desk all the time, your self-care system is failing. Leaving the work for a lunch break is frequently mentioned as a refreshing activity that is all too often ignored in child welfare. Another technique to reduce stress while working at a computer is to have free weights at the work station to relieve tension in neck and back muscles. Lifting and stretching reduce the tension that builds up when you do not move around. Another communication technique helpful to workers is for the worker to answer, when asked to take on a task not essential to the completion of his or her own work, "Let me think about that." This allows the worker time to evaluate whether or not this additional task needs to be taken on at all.

Colleagues are an important part of self-care (Saakvitne & Pearlman, 1996; Skovholt, 2001). They understand the work, and they are essential to professional social support. They are also the individuals to whom child welfare workers can talk about their clients (within reasonable bounds of confidentiality) and how they are affected by the work and what they are doing about it. It can be helpful for seasoned workers to validate the experiences of novice workers, especially around their natural apprehension and anxiety. Expertise and practice wisdom should be shared (Skovholt & Ronnestad, 1995). Cohesion among colleagues can help in the worst of times and can buffer the sometimes grinding ambiguity of the work. Colleagues can help us to recognize our successes with clients and to appreciate what we have done. Colleagues can also help each other to maximize the use of problem-solving coping—thinking the problem through and acting on the conclusion—rather than the use of avoidance to cope. Colleagues also understand each others' sense of humor and the need to debrief and talk about the frustrations of the work (Moran, 2002; Tedeschi & Calhoun, 1995).

THE USE OF HUMOR AS A COPING SKILL

Moran (2002) stated that "In extreme environments, especially those involving traumatic stressors, the role of humor can be covertly acknowledged while being overtly ignored" (p. 139). This is certainly the case in child welfare. Child welfare workers often use humor to cope with the horrific situations they witness or hear about from the children and families they serve. Moran (2002) discussed the theories of humor and revealed that humor can provide tension release or allow for a "reinterpretation of a given situation or event" (p. 141). He stated that a component of humor may be aggression, and this may allow the expression of feelings that a person may not be able to deal with otherwise. This type of humor, Moran claimed, can be healthy or harmful.

Moran also reported that some researchers have shown that humor, especially laughter, may be health enhancing, since humor and laughter sometimes have a relaxation effect and may have an effect on a person's immune system. Moran (2002) said, "Because humor can result in a reduction of tension and a reinterpretation of events, it can be neatly accommodated into many stress management or therapy programs with these objectives" (p. 143). He discussed how coping humor can filter out negative information and may lead a person to pay more attention to humor in the environment.

Persons outside the public child welfare agency may hear child welfare workers talk about terrible situations involving children and observe that there is a type of gallows humor that exists in child welfare. The actual situation with the child may not be the source of humor, but the worker will interject something humorous that occurred in the midst of the situation. Moran (2002) stated that in "extreme circumstances humor may be used to provide distance from events" (p. 144). This may be useful when the event is beyond human understanding. "In both humorous and non-humorous reframing, individuals may appear insensitive to outsiders, but workers within the field will frequently recognize the function such reframing serves" (Moran, 2002, p. 145).

Workers must, however, exercise caution in using humor to cope. The overuse of humor may be a form of denial or a cover-up of what is really going on with the child welfare worker. Excessive humor may be an avoidance technique (Moran, 2002). It is also a red flag if a person loses his or her sense of humor. "In the literature on traumatic stress, loss of humor may be listed as part of the symptomology" (Moran, 2002, p. 149). Moran also discussed research that claims humor may have an adverse effect on anxious individuals.

Humor is often used by child welfare workers to cope with the situations they encounter. The communication among child welfare workers often includes jargon that only they know has a humorous side. The research reveals that this is a way to cope with terrible situations. Supervisors and child welfare workers need to be aware that it can be used by the individual to work through a horrific event or to avoid dealing with such an event. Humor is a complex phenomenon, and its use as a coping mechanism in child welfare warrants further research.

PROFESSIONAL DEVELOPMENT

Professional development success and activism are crucial to child welfare workers' professional health. Professional development consists of two focused tasks (Skovholt, 2001). The first task is getting quality feedback on individual performance, reflecting on it, and gauging individual practice and professional growth. The second task is using continuing education. For example, a person can pursue formal education, attend seminars, collaborate with colleagues, and/or create a customized professional development plan.

Activism is helpful. Getting involved in some aspect of child welfare that is not the individual's own work gives the practitioner an opportunity to proactively address the challenges of the work from a different perspective. Activism may involve collaborating with colleagues to organize a self-help group to address STS in the workplace. It may involve volunteering with one of the community programs that address children from a perspective different from that of one's own agency. As Herman (1992) pointed out, "Social action can take many forms, from concrete engagement with particular individuals to abstract intellectual pursuits" (p. 208).

What these activities do for practitioners is to allow them to address child abuse from a different perspective, preferably one that allows them greater control.

ANTICIPATORY COPING

The last area that we address in our educational workshop is personal cognition, or engaging in anticipatory coping. Child welfare work takes a physical and psychological toll on the practitioner. Knowing this, the professional is in a position to make contingency plans for the traumatic events and chronic environmental strains that may occur. Building resilience through mental preparation is the goal. Skovholt (2001) identified and discussed twenty hazards of practice that we believe to be applicable to child welfare. We will discuss each and provide examples.

Clients may have a seemingly unsolvable problem that must be solved (Skovholt, 2001, p. 77). Many child welfare clients share this characteristic because there are no immediate and/or good solutions to the problem they present. An example of this would be grandparents who are old and frail and who want to parent their grandchild or grandchildren and cannot realistically undertake the responsibility. The documentary film *Big Mama* (Seretean, 2000) realistically portrays this problem.

Clients may not be "honors students" (Skovholt, 2001, p. 77). Child welfare clients often get into the system because something has gone wrong, usually between the parent and the child. In some cases, the clients' personal problems are so enormous and extensive that they simply cannot care for their children. There are also clients who are not motivated to make needed changes to turn their situation in a positive direction. It can be taxing to work with these clients.

Skovholt discussed clients who have motivational conflicts. One situation Skovholt described was a client who had four children, and the oldest child was severely disabled and had low intelligence. The client received disability payments for the child that helped the whole family survive. When the disabled child started acting out sexually, the worker encouraged the mother to put the child in a group home. In some ways, this would make caring for the other children easier, but the mother did not want to lose the disability payments and found reasons why she could not allow the child to go into the home.

Skovholt asserted that there is a frequent readiness gap between the worker and his or her clients. This is explained as person-in-environment fit. Developmentally, the client may not be ready to change or to work on solving his or her problems, even when that means having children removed from the home. Sometimes this can be a byproduct of other presenting problems. For example, a mother who is seriously depressed and finds it hard to get out of bed will have to have her depression corrected before she can care for her babies. Meanwhile, the babies have to be safe and nourished. The worker may be ready to solve the problem when the client is not.

Child welfare workers know all too well the hazard of clients projecting negative feelings onto them (Skovholt, 2001, p. 81). They know that clients often see them as a continuation of their oppression and the many negative people and social interactions they have experienced before interacting with the worker. Transference is a common occurrence. In fact, not only do workers experience the projection of negative feelings, but they also experience threats of violence and in some cases assaults. Workers will tell you that if you are going to do this work well, you have to acquire some toughness.

The sixth hazard Skovholt (2001) identified is that "sometimes we cannot help because we are not good enough" (p. 82). We refer to this as practitioner-client fit. There are instances when the practitioner is a poor match for the client and his or her problems. This can bring feelings of shame as it becomes clear that the practitioner will be limited and will not be able to help the client to the extent that he or she needs. This presents a difficulty for the practitioner, who wants to help. The worker may be well prepared to work with children but does not understand their war-veteran father's problems and interprets his behavior negatively. Workers cannot be all things to all people, regardless of how much they care about them.

Clients can have needs that are too great for the social service, educational, or health systems to meet (Skovholt, 2001, p. 82). There will never be enough resources to do the work the way practitioners want, and social services are usually at the bottom of legislators' funding concerns. There will always be clients whose needs exceed what workers can provide even if they had all the resources they wanted. There will be clients whom workers can help with what they have to offer, and these clients will be their successes.

Child welfare practitioners and social workers have difficulty saying, "No, I can't do that," leading to what Skovholt (2001) labeled "the treadmill effect" (p. 83). Saying, "No, I can't do that now," or "Let me think about that" does not mean that the worker is uncaring, but that the worker is realistic about what he or she can or cannot do. The alternative is that the worker ends up with more tasks than he or she can successfully complete and may grow resentful.

The ninth hazard, "living in an ocean of stress emotions" (Skovholt, 2001, p. 86), typifies child welfare work. Clients are most often children who have been hurt, some badly. Emotional distress is embedded in the work and cannot be avoided. Practitioners often minimize their own psychological distress when it should be expressed in a constructive way, which is important to keeping the bucket dumped.

Skovholt (2001) argued that practitioners will experience ambiguous professional loss and referred to this as "ending before the ending" (p. 88). There are times when concrete results are present, and the practitioner knows the impact they have had on a child and his or her family. But there are other times when the outcome remains unknown, and the investment of time and energy in the client is questioned. Practitioners can develop and maintain an inner belief that each investment matters regardless of the outcome. Many workers say their spiritual beliefs help them cope with this lack of closure.

Another hazard that is highly characteristic of child welfare is the covert nature of the work (Skovholt, 2001, p. 90). The covert nature and need for confidentiality means that what the practitioner does cannot be shared, and that can lead to feelings of isolation. This is why professional social support is essential and needs to be established in the workplace. Colleagues can talk with each other about cases and their feelings about their work and the satisfaction they take from it.

The constant use of empathy, interpersonal sensitivity, and one-way caring presents another hazard (Skovholt, 2001, p. 91). A hallmark feature of child welfare work is building relationships with children and adolescents and their families, and that is largely done by connecting to these clients in a meaningful way. Empathy, interpersonal sensitivity, and caring are crucial to making the needed relationship happen. While empathy is a strength, it also makes the worker vulnerable to STS. Interpersonal sensitivity helps with communication, transference, countertransference, and timing, but it can also strain workers, especially when they work with resistant, involuntary, and difficult clients. One-way caring can be a drain on the worker's energy. For these reasons, self-management and renewal are critical in child welfare work.

Elusive measures of success present yet another hazard to the work (Skovholt, 2001, p. 92). Some successes in child welfare are easily measured, and the outcomes are known. There are gray areas where the best evidenced-based practice is not as easily identified, nor are the clients' outcomes. There is always the question: Was it the intervention that made the difference, was it the relationship, or was it something else we don't know about that influenced the outcome? Who defines success, the practitioner or the client?

A related hazard is normative failure. Skovholt argued that it is important to differentiate normative failure from excessive failure. Failures do happen, and sometimes they can be analyzed to discover why they happened. There will be failures in child welfare practice along with successes. Skovholt (2001) pointed out that "practitioners must realize that they are like doctors whose patients die" (p. 95). It happens, and normative failure or the lack of success will be a part of child welfare practice. Seasoned and competent practitioners learn to become realistic about their expectations, at the same time losing some of their idealism.

Another hallmark feature of child welfare practice is the "regulation oversight and control by external, often unknowing others" (Skovholt, 2001, p. 97). Child welfare practice is heavily regulated. Often with good intentions, administrators, lawyers, and state personnel direct what the practitioner can and cannot do. State officials whom practitioners never see make decisions about their work, and often these officials draw conclusions prematurely and without full knowledge or information about the work. This causes workers tension and distress since they are constantly being asked to do more with less.

Many of the hazards described by Skovholt may be more applicable to the novice child welfare worker. The seasoned practitioner, on the other hand, faces challenges such as "cognitive deprivation and boredom" (Skovholt, 2001, p. 98). When one has been a practitioner for a good length of time, it is possible to start thinking that one has seen it all and to begin finding the work less stimulating. When this happens, the practitioner may become less attentive to his or her work and take less satisfaction from it because he or she is bored. Practitioners can avoid this if they constantly work to increase competence and continue to master skills.

The nature of child welfare practice and the environments in which it takes place can create "cynical, critical, negative colleagues and managers" (Skovholt, 2001, p. 99). Negativity can be highly contagious and spread quickly among practitioners. Cynicism in the work means there is a failure to value the successes that occur every day, which contributes to failures with clients. It leads to a belief that clients cannot grow and change. It also stifles hope, which is essential to believing in the work. Child welfare is hard enough to do even in a positive workplace. Practitioners need positive and motivated colleagues who are aware that collectively they must protect the professional environment in which they work.

Another hallmark feature of child welfare work is "legal and ethical fears" (Skovholt, 2001, p. 100). Child welfare practitioners and their supervisors are always alert to legal issues related to practice with clients. They are also concerned about ethical issues where competing values are present, and choices must be made. They are very much aware that they may be held legally liable if the outcome of a case is negative. Practitioners also know that regardless of the positive work that they do, they may not be supported by the very people asking them to do this work.

The nineteenth hazard that Skovholt (2001) identified is "practitioner emotional trauma" (p. 101), which is what this book is largely about. We know that empathic engagement and listening to the traumatic experiences of others make the practitioner vulnerable to STS, which is especially likely to occur to persons working with children who are vulnerable to the harmful acts of adults. The images of broken bones, bruised bodies, and tortured souls and the feelings that accompany these images do not recede easily. This is a reality of the work and is best acknowledged and accepted. Having done so, the practitioner can realistically assess if the successes are worth the distress of doing the work. Many workers indicate that it is worth the distress; some do not.

The final hazard identified by Skovholt (2001) is "physical trauma" (p. 102). Child welfare practitioners are well aware that the work is dangerous. Clients may be mentally unstable, angry, or under the influence of drugs or other substances. They may make threats and in some cases carry out physical attacks on workers. If the worker is affected by STS and/or burnout, he or she may not be able to assess a potentially violent situation in time to recognize what to do.

We add yet another hazard of child welfare practice—the horrific abuse and death of children. Because of the values practitioners have regarding children and the commitment they have to children's safety, abuse and death are hard to endure. Child welfare practitioners do the work because of the children and because of the changes they bring to families. Success is very powerful. Experiencing child abuse and death will change the practitioner. It is hard to acknowledge and accept that in the process of helping others recover from their wounds and heal, workers also become wounded and have to heal.

It is important to think realistically about these processes and think critically about how the practitioner can prepare to respond to them with the understanding that they are very unlikely to happen all at once. By engaging in anticipatory coping, practitioners are protecting both their personal and professional lives. This can also be a collective experience with colleagues because the phenomenon is a shared one.

In this chapter we addressed how we educate child welfare professionals on how STS differs from burnout, how it arises, and intervention options. The interventions presented here have come from the literature and from our experience with child welfare practitioners. You have to figure out what works best for you in managing the effects of the work and practice it. While there is much that individuals can do to manage STS, supervisors and administrators have important roles and responsibilities in its management also. We will address these roles and responsibilities in the next chapter.

4

Traumatic Stress and Supervision in Child Welfare

A young new child welfare supervisor entered a recent training session at 8:30 a.m. almost in tears, trembling, and totally distraught. She told the other child welfare supervisors that she did not know what to do and needed their help. The agenda for the training was postponed, and attention was focused on the recent events in the young supervisor's life. When the trainer asked what had happened, the supervisor said in exasperation, "Well, in order for you to understand, I have to go back—before last night." After a deep breath that showed everyone that she wasn't sure she could even speak without breaking down, she related the recent events. "Mary, who you know is a very young worker, on the job for less than a year, went out on a crystal methamphetamine case a few days ago. The police were with her. The front door was open and a baby was crying, but no one would respond, so they went inside. The report was that the parents were using crystal meth—not cooking it. Mary said they could not smell the meth and thought it was okay to proceed into the house. You know they [administrators and narcotics agents] have told us that. The parents were passed out and a seven-year-old girl was caring for the infant. The parents were awakened and a physical fight ensued, with the officer having to physically restrain the father. Mary called me and then contacted the judge for a verbal order to remove the children. Then the children were transported to the emergency room. While at the emergency room, Mary began having problems breathing and her skin turned bright red. We think that she has been exposed to crystal meth! Besides that, the police officer now has a staph infection from changing the infant's diaper (who had staph infection, among many other problems)."

The others in the room shook their heads in understanding and made various comments regarding the new dangers that their workers are exposed to when dealing with crystal meth. The supervisors also discussed the growing number of children coming into state custody due to the parents' use of crystal meth. They talked about the levels of irrational thought and violence that the crystal meth users are displaying and how frightened they are of persons on this drug. One said, "Well, it is worse if they are coming off it; they are more violent then." One supervisor stated that in her county, they were not getting reports about children because the neighbors and community members were too frightened of the meth users to report them.

The supervisor went on, "You haven't even heard the worst. Both of my social workers have been out night and day for months. None of us have had a decent night's sleep for weeks. We have taken seven children out of their homes due to meth alone in the last week. I am not even counting the ones we let go to other parents' homes or those we took for other reasons. I am so angry at myself because I can't even remember the children's names. We don't have the foster homes to put them in, but we can't stop doing investigations long enough to license foster homes. Mary was, at the same time she was having breathing problems, frantic about a report that came in regarding a six-year-old girl whose mom was on meth and living with a very violent boyfriend, who was also on meth, very paranoid, and had a lot of guns in the house. The child was not in school and was said to have bruises and cigarette burns on her. Mary had been searching for her for a month. Another call came in about a five-year-old boy who had an instrument of some sort inserted in his rectum by his father." The amazing thing at this point is that the group of supervisors just shook their heads. No one was surprised.

She continued, "Mary had to take this child to the trauma center ninety miles away. At this point a call came in that the six-year-old whom Mary had been looking for was in a trailer on the outskirts of the county. Susan, Mary's coworker, and Alice, the family preservation worker, said they would go see about the girl, and were accompanied by police officers. Mary had been told previously that the boyfriend in the crystal meth situation had threatened to shoot any social worker who came around, and she did not want Susan and Alice going to the home, but Mary had also been told that the mom and boyfriend were about to leave the state with the child. Susan, Alice, and the policeman stopped at the trailer they thought the child was in and were surrounded by a dozen family members and other known drug users. This was scary. You know, when a bunch of people surround you it is scary. When this situation was defused, Susan and the rest went to another more secluded trailer down in the woods. While standing at the door, knocking, Susan saw a mirror being held inside the window, and she knew someone was watching them. She knew it was possible that they were about to be in the line of fire. She shouted at the officer, who ordered both child welfare workers to get down behind the car. One officer was still in the line of fire, because they couldn't make him understand. One officer got to the car and called for backup. Then the boyfriend threatened to shoot all of them. A hostage situation ensued that lasted forty-five minutes."

She went on, "Mary heard the whole incident on the police radio while it was going on, while she was with the other police officer miles away. She was upset because she felt like it was her case, and also she could not properly attend to the abused child she had in her care, because she was worried about Susan, Alice, and the other child. The child in the hostage situation was released and the boyfriend and child's mother were arrested. The worker saw an arsenal of loaded guns in the trailer. The mom was totally unconcerned for the child. The child was covered in bruises and cigarette burns, and her teeth were rotten."

The supervisor went on to say, "Susan and Alice called me while they were hiding behind the car and scared. They did not have bulletproof vests, and they were afraid that the man had rigged explosives around the yard. I threw up after I got the call. I don't know what to do and I feel so inadequate to protect them. I can't get Mary to stop working. She is so sick with upper respiratory problems. Now she has the child at the hospital, and they think the child has been sexually abused. There are more reports coming in. What do I do? I know they are all shaken up about last night. Oh, and just on the side, we had two adults in our caseload die this week. You know, we need more workers, and we need better policy on these crystal meth cases. Something must give, or something really bad is going to happen!"

TRAUMATIC STRESS AND SUPERVISION

Something bad is going to happen? It would seem that it has already happened. Supervisors and workers are conditioned to think that these kinds of events are a normal part of their workdays. It is only because it all happened at once to a new supervisor who happened to be in a training session with other supervisors that it even got attention. Upon request, the trainer conducted a critical incident stress debriefing with workers and the supervisor that afternoon. Such debriefings were not part of regular agency policy. During the debriefing, Susan, the worker with thirteen years of experience, and a person who is often referred to as tough, broke down and cried when she told the others that her thought while hiding behind the car was that her own two-year-old daughter would not remember her. Both workers reported thinking they probably were not going to make it home that night. The two workers with children shared that they always tell their children they love them before they go out on what they think will be a bad investigation, because they know in the back of their minds that they might not see them again.

Mary, the new worker who is just twenty-three years old, reported that her parents were insisting that she quit her job. Mary said, "I don't want to quit. This is all I want to do and have ever wanted to do. I put my life, my health, and my mental health on the line for these kids. I know I do. My parents think we are put in situations that are too high risk. They insist we could be better protected. I know they are worried." Mary also reported feeling extremely guilty about not being able to attend fully to the sexually abused child because of everything else, fear, and the knowledge that if something happened to her coworkers, she would never forgive herself because it was her case.

They each reported sleep problems. The experienced worker had been taking three Tylenol PMs every night for as long as she could remember. Stomach problems, headaches, feelings of panic, tension, exhaustion, and excessive menstrual bleeding were all part of their everyday lives. The workers told their supervisor during the debriefing that they appreciated her and that they knew she was doing all she could to support them. They said they knew that she gave them everything she could. The workers were worried about the supervisor's health due to the stress she was experiencing.

When the supervisor originally told her story during the staff meeting, all the supervisors in the room expressed the same frustrations that they are not able to protect and support their workers at the level they should be able to. The supervisors stated that too few workers and too many cases, along with the ever-increasing danger level of the cases, keep the supervisors from fulfilling their educational and supportive roles. Supervisors reported that their workers and they themselves were having heart problems, stomach problems, menstrual distress, depression, anxiety, panic attacks, trouble sleeping, and high blood pressure problems. They wondered how many of them and their workers were on antidepressants, antianxiety medications, and sleeping pills. They also expressed concern at the number of staff members who were drinking, overeating, and smoking to relieve the stress. They reported workers calling in sick on a regular basis and discussed the high turnover rates among child welfare workers in each of their offices.

They expressed the belief that apparently child welfare staff safety and emotional well-being do not matter to legislators, agency administrators, or the community. One supervisor said, "Everyone knows that the state does not care about us. The legislators and governor and our own administrators have ignored child welfare forever. We are used to that, but it is just that it has gotten to the point that we can't protect the children from abuse and neglect because of the high caseloads and the severity of the cases. That is what is getting to us." Another person said, "What I would give for an old-fashioned butt-whipping case."

They questioned why the human services office in one state's capital had security guards, metal detectors, and bulletproof glass while many of the rural offices had no security at all. Many rural agencies were open to anyone walking in at any time. One supervisor said that she had asked for bulletproof glass to be installed and was told it was too expensive. The response was, "Guess we know now that one of our lives isn't worth the price of a bulletproof window." The supervisors stated that this sent the message that only the office that might be seen by state officials deserves the protection that should be offered to everyone working for the public child welfare agency.

The workers in the state where these incidents occurred do not have mobile phones issued by the agency. If they have one, it is because they pay for it themselves. The state has no employee assistance program to address mental health issues in the child welfare workforce. Critical incident stress debriefings are not part of child welfare policy or practice. The message from top levels of management is, "Do whatever it takes," "Do more with less," and "My way or the highway." The supervisors expressed anger and frustration that they are not given the staff, resources, training, and tools they need to enable the workers to protect children and preserve families. They are also angry that their own lives and the lives of their workers and staff members are not valued by the state agency or by the politicians who provide the funding and resources.

THE CRITICAL ROLE OF THE SUPERVISOR IN CHILD WELFARE

This information was received as the result of one supervisor asking for help from her colleagues, but the same types of situations have been frequently described to us as we work with child welfare professionals across the country. The literature clearly states that supervision is the key to keeping child welfare workers on the job and functioning (APHSA, 2005; Child Welfare League of America, 2001; Dickinson & Perry, 2002; Ellett & Millar, 2001; Landsman, 2001; Nissly et al., 2005; Reagh, 1994; Russel, 1987; Rycraft, 1994; Samantrai, 1992; Smith, 2004). Even though the need for effective and supportive supervision has been discussed in the research regarding child welfare worker turnover and retention, and it is the only consistent factor in keeping workers on the job, little attention has been given to the specific practice and functions of the child welfare supervisor.

Collins-Camargo (2002) pointed out that child welfare casework supervision is an important but infrequently researched aspect of practice. In a needs assessment conducted in ten southern states for the University of Kentucky Southern Regional Quality Improvement Center for Child Protection regarding needs in child welfare, Collins-Camargo discovered a significant need for improved child welfare supervision. She found that the literature confirmed her findings that administrative aspects of child protection supervision may impede the effective provision of clinical casework supervision. Targeted strategies are needed regarding child welfare supervision, as there is a lack of empirical evidence regarding techniques and supervisory practice appropriate for the child welfare setting. Collins-Camargo stated there is a need in the child welfare field for a more structured approach to casework supervision that is developed out of a learning environment that promotes evidence-based practice.

CHARACTERISTICS OF SOCIAL WORK SUPERVISION

Harkness and Poertner (1989) determined that circular definitions of social work supervision, which set forth supervisor roles and functions, have not linked supervision to client outcomes. Harkness and Poertner stated that appropriate research questions, such as "What supervisory behavior produces what outcomes with workers, clients, and problems?" have not been asked (p. 116). They called for researchers to study different models of supervision in "the context of intervening and environmental variables: the characteristics of supervisors, workers, and caseloads; client problems and goals; and the context and culture of agency practice" (Harkness & Poertner, 1989, p. 118). It is plausible that such studies would take place in the context of different cultures in the United States as well as other countries.

Kadushin's *Supervision in Social Work* (1985) proposed three functions of a social work supervisor—the administrative function, the educational function, and the supportive function. He outlined the specific skills and behaviors a supervisor exhibits regarding each of these functions and discussed the supervisor's responsibility to conduct ongoing evaluations regarding the supervisee's functioning on the job and the stressors associated with supervision. Kadushin also discussed the use of group work in supervising social workers. Kadushin, like other authors, focused on generic social work supervision.

Munson (1993) addressed clinical social work supervision and defined this type of supervision as "an interactional process in which a supervisor has been assigned or designated to assist in and direct the practice of supervisees in the areas of teaching, administration, and helping" (p. 10). He described supervisees as "graduates of accredited schools of social work who are engaged in practice that assists people to overcome physical, financial, social, or psychological disruptions in functioning through individual, group, or family intervention methods" (Munson, 1993, p. 10).

Shulman (1993) dealt with the social work supervisor's interactions with the supervisee. He drew upon William Schwartz's (1961) practice theory to discuss an interactional approach to supervision. Shulman divided the supervisory process into phases of work and also discussed the educational and evaluative functions of supervision. He emphasized the importance of working with staff groups and mediating conflicts between the social worker and the system. Shulman also discussed the need for the supervisor to help staff cope with trauma.

Each of these authors has added to the body of knowledge regarding social work supervision, but more still needs to be known about the particular needs of child welfare supervision. The child welfare field is a subculture of social work. Kadushin (1980) described child welfare social work as "a circumscribed social institution within a larger community and child welfare social workers as an identifiable organized subgroup in society" (p. 674). Kadushin (1980) also said that child welfare social workers have special interests, shared values, social interchange, in-group gossip, and a specialized language and humor that lead to practitioners developing a "distinctive way of thinking about problems and the people that are so much a part of their activities" (p. 674). The same thing can be said regarding child welfare supervisors.

UNIQUE CHARACTERISTICS OF CHILD WELFARE SUPERVISION

The knowledge base and skills discussed in general social work supervision books are useful to the child welfare supervisor, but special circumstances exist that make this type of supervision unique in the field of social work. One factor is that, unlike the worker described in Munson's book, many child welfare workers are not graduates of social work education programs. Child welfare supervisors may supervise bachelors- and masters-level social work graduates, or they might supervise a variety of bachelors- and masters-level graduates from numerous fields of study. Sometimes the field of study is not applicable to a human services profession. The supervisor may or may not be a graduate of an accredited school of social work and may or may not have a master's degree. The varied skill levels of child welfare workers make the educational function a special challenge for child welfare supervisors.

Child welfare supervisors are most often promoted from the position of child welfare worker and often supervise a staff of previous coworkers. This adds to the difficulty, as others have applied for the same job and may harbor resentment as a result of not being selected. The supervisor who was previously a friend and colleague of the workers must undergo a significant role change. Both of these situations create immediate stress upon a new supervisor, and sometimes the stressors remain unresolved in the work setting.

In many states, child welfare supervisors do not receive special training for the job of supervisor. If training exists at all, it is usually training for the supervisor on the procedure or administrative functions of the agency. Little peer support exists for supervisors, especially in the more rural, isolated areas of the country. In urban areas there is often more than one supervisor in an office, and peer support may be present in an informal context. Mentoring is not often structured into the training of child welfare supervisors. The training the supervisor receives regarding the educational, supportive, and clinical casework supervision aspects of the job is usually modeled after the practices of previous supervisors in the agency. Bad as well as good supervisory practice is passed on through such a process.

Many child welfare supervisors are appointed to the position because they were effective child welfare workers. Some of the skills needed to be a good child welfare worker can be used in supervision, but many more skills are needed for one to be a good supervisor. Many supervisors state that they were coerced into taking the job when their hearts remained in direct-line social work. These child welfare supervisors report that they loved working with children and families and only applied for the supervisory position due to pressure from administrators coupled with the fact that it was the only way to receive a promotion or pay raise. Some view supervision as a way to effect more change for families but become frustrated when they cannot effectively transfer their own practice methods to the practice of their supervisees.

Jayaratne and Chess (1984) showed that child welfare workers are under more stress than their colleagues. The nature of the work and the organizational structure of child welfare create supervisory challenges that are not present in other types of social work supervision. The heavy caseloads of child welfare workers create even higher numbers of cases to supervise, and the ratio of supervisors to workers can also be higher than it is in other fields. The decisions made by the supervisor are often life-and-death decisions involving children, and these may occur on a daily basis. Worker safety is always a concern, as well as keeping up with which worker is out of the office visiting which family on his or her caseload. A worker's safe return to the office is always on the mind of a child welfare supervisor. The supervisor is also on call twenty-four hours a day, seven days a week, because every supervisee on call for after-hours work must call the supervisor regarding major casework decisions.

The child welfare supervisor is constantly aware of the high turnover rates and difficulty retaining workers, and this sometimes affects decisions regarding disciplinary action or terminations of employment. Supervisors often must manage caseloads that are left unattended when workers leave the agency. This creates situations in which supervisors are often doing the job of a caseworker by managing vacant position caseloads and trying to supervise other workers at the same time.

Child welfare supervisors not only supervise but are responsible for the development of resources in the community and networking with other agencies. They must have skills in public relations in order to work with the courts, media, politicians, foster parents, school officials, and other agencies. Sometimes this requires mediation skills to resolve worker conflict with other persons in the community or brokering skills to obtain needed services for clients. The job involves educating the public regarding the needs of abused and neglected children. Sometimes the skill of begging for the needs of families and children to be met is required. Prevention-of-abuse-and-neglect programs are needed in the community, and these are usually initiated and promoted by child welfare supervisors. Supervisors are often expected to develop budgets and request funds from various sources other than the state. We have been in offices where the supervisor was expected to be the bookkeeper, secretary, and even janitor because these positions were vacant for long lengths of time.

The supervisor must possess a knowledge base in child abuse and neglect, family systems, and factors that place children at risk for harm, all of which require extensive knowledge of human development and appropriate social work practice. Interviewing, assessment, conflict resolution, problem solving, communication, group work, teaching, time management, administration, and the ability to motivate others are all required skills for effective child welfare supervision. In addition to all this, law, ethics, and policy must be thoroughly understood, and changes in law and policy must be monitored continuously. Intervention methods for working with families that have proved to produce desired outcomes are a part of the continual learning process for child welfare supervisors.

THE NEED FOR EFFECTIVE CHILD WELFARE SUPERVISION METHODS

The different conditions of supervisory work, the nature of the work, and the organizational structure create the need for a distinct supervision model that is based on supervisory practice that leads to desired worker and client outcomes in child welfare. The literature reveals the need for positive and effective supervision methods.

Bernotavicz (1997) stated that the role of supervisor in the child welfare agency is critical, as supervisors can create settings in which workers can accomplish their work, or they can assign work unfairly and fail to help set priorities. Supervisors can be mentors for workers and help them through crisis periods, especially when they are contemplating leaving the agency. Bernotavicz was told by over half of the respondents in her study that lack of supervisory/administrative support and poor or lack of supervision was their primary reason for leaving the child welfare agency. Several of the respondents stated that they might have considered staying if their supervisor had been more supportive. Dickinson and Perry (2002) found that levels of social support received from coworkers and supervisors positively influenced the retention rate of public child welfare workers. "With respect to supervisory support, the greater the extent to which workers perceived their supervisor as being very concerned about their welfare, the greater the likelihood respondents would remain in child welfare" (Dickinson & Perry, 2002, p. 99).

Ellett (2005) discussed the special skills required by supervisors who are supervising new caseworkers. With the high turnover rates in child welfare, it is foreseeable that a supervisor will constantly have new workers to supervise. Ellett suggested that close task and clinical supervision are needed, along with supervisory skills that will build a worker's self-efficacy. Using social cognitive theory developed by Bandura (1997), Ellett described the supervisory skills needed to increase workers' self-efficacy. One such skill is allowing learning to take place through vicarious experiences, such as modeling for the worker how to engage or interview a client. Another skill is using verbal persuasion to convince workers that they can be successful when performing difficult tasks. Enactive mastery experience or successful task completion also increases self-efficacy. This requires the supervisor to set the stage for worker success by giving the worker a case and direction in working the case that will prove successful. Ellett promoted assignment of cases commensurate with worker skill and ability in order to allow for a sense of accomplishment and the fulfillment of the desire to make a difference in the client's life. Ellett (2005) provided the following example: "If, for example, a new worker is assigned tasks that are far too difficult (enactive mastery experiences), has few opportunities to observe successful practices by colleagues and supervisors (vicarious experiences), receives little feedback, praise and encouragement (verbal persuasion), the affective components of self-efficacy beliefs will be predictably weak (physiological/affective states), and the employee may then choose to leave employment in child welfare" (p. 20).

Nissly, Mor Barak, and Levin (2005) studied stress, social support, and workers' intent to leave their jobs in child welfare. Their study revealed that a supportive network that included coworker and supervisor support could reduce a worker's intention to leave child welfare. They suggested that organizations "provide greater and more systematic supervisor training, reduce supervisor [to] employee ratios, reduce the rotation of supervisors to promote stability, and redistribute work tasks so that supervisors can spend more time with their workers" (Nissly et al., 2005, p. 96).

Reagh (1994) studied child welfare worker retention and found workers reporting that front-line supervisors were crucial in both challenging the worker to achieve at a high level and in providing encouragement and support. Rycraft found when studying child welfare worker retention that supportive supervision was a main factor in retention. Rycraft found that workers wanted supervisors who were accessible, knowledgeable of the system and casework practice, and skillful in management and leadership. Rycraft (1994) quoted a child welfare worker as saying, "A good supervisor makes a big difference. A not-so-good supervisor can break you" (p. 80).

Samantrai learned in her study of factors in workers' decisions to leave or stay in child welfare that a poor relationship with the immediate supervisor was one of two factors that led to workers leaving. Samantrai (1992) found that "workers who experienced their supervisors as sympathetic and supportive had positive attitudes about their jobs, regardless of their caseloads and other conditions" (p. 57). She also pointed out that when workers did not feel supported by their supervisors, other conditions such as workspace and physical danger became larger problems. In addition, Smith (2004) found that one of three factors influencing retention of child welfare workers was having a supportive and competent supervisor.

Landsman conducted a study in Missouri regarding worker commitment to child welfare. Missouri is a typical state child welfare system in that it is a state-administered system with a mix of urban and rural areas. Landsman (2001) found that "strong supervisory support and internal career ladders contribute to a satisfied workforce" (p. 408). She stated that it is to be expected that when caseloads are excessive and supervisor-to-worker ratios are too high, job satisfaction will decline. According to Landsman (2001), "The unique role that the supervisor plays in mentoring and supporting staff is usually one for which he or she receives little, if any, formal training. Yet strong supervision may be one of the most important elements in staff retention. Career ladders can be used creatively simultaneously to support stronger mentoring roles for supervisors and to enhance skills of personnel at all levels" (p. 408).

Supervision in child welfare requires a multitude of skills and abilities. Supervisors must be knowledgeable in child welfare practice and policy. Training regarding supervision in the child welfare setting is needed, and specific models of supervision appropriate and conducive to the child welfare setting must be determined. One important aspect of these models should be education and skills training regarding supervision in the midst of trauma.

SUPERVISION IN THE CONTEXT OF TRAUMA

The supervisor quoted at the beginning of the chapter talked about needing help in how to supervise in the context of trauma. She knew that on some level this was affecting her and her workers, and she did not know how to handle the trauma to her workers, or how to deal with their resulting stress. Some supervisors do not understand the importance of supervision in traumatic situations or, due to ignorance regarding the effects of trauma, or lack of skills in this area, choose to believe that if left alone, the worker will learn to deal with it. Many supervisors are not taking responsibility for helping their workers deal with traumatic stress appropriately, and therefore workers continue to suffer from the traumatic stress they experience in the workplace.

Kadushin (1985) defined social work supervision thus:

> A social work supervisor is an agency administrative staff member to whom authority is delegated to direct, coordinate, enhance, and evaluate on-the-job performance of the supervisee for whose work he is held accountable. In implementing this responsibility the supervisor performs administrative, educational, and supportive functions in interaction with the supervisee in the context of a positive relationship. The supervisor's ultimate objective is to deliver to the agency clients the best possible services, both quantitatively and qualitatively, in accordance with agency policies and procedures. (p. 24)

Kadushin discussed positive relationships between supervisor and worker and also stated that it was important that the supervisor enhance the work of the supervisee and be supportive of the worker in order to provide the best possible services to the client.

When supervising workers in the midst of traumatic situations, it is important that the supervisor have positive, supportive relationships with all his or her workers, or workers will not be able to trust the supervisor enough to share their thoughts and feelings concerning traumatic events. A worker may have witnessed a supervisor's lack of ability or willingness to deal with other workers' past trauma. The worker may have been told by the supervisor or other workers that you just get used to it all and from that may assume that no one talks about the feelings that come up from the situations dealt with on a daily basis. The relationship between supervisor and supervisees may not be positive or supportive. It may be evident that the supervisor does not want to hear about workers' personal feelings or reactions to their work. A previously trusting and positive relationship can be harmed if the supervisor does not pay attention to the trauma and help the worker cope with an experience. Not only can it harm the worker's relationship with the supervisor, but it may prevent positive relationships with other supervisees from developing. Both the traumatic event and the supervisor's response affect the worker's response to traumatic stress.

Shulman asserted that a parallel process occurs as supervisors demonstrate helping relationships with workers. This demonstration influences the way workers relate to clients. The supervisor can use the skills learned in direct practice to be a supportive supervisor; however, Shulman also warned that the staff member is not the supervisor's client. Shulman (1993) said that it is not appropriate to counsel a worker about a personal problem, but if the worker's personal problem is interfering with work, it is appropriate to "listen, understand and try to help the staff member obtain any necessary assistance from another source" (p. 36).

Shulman (1993) also suggested that one of the skills needed in supervision was what Schwartz (1976) described as "tuning in." Preparatory empathy is an important skill for supervisors to practice when supervising in traumatic situations in the child welfare agency. Shulman discussed the risk involved when one is honest with people in authority and how this interferes with communication between supervisors and workers. Shulman (1993) stated that for supervisors trying to put themselves in the place of their worker, "the goal is to sensitize oneself to the concerns, feelings, and issues that may be present" (p. 36). The supervisor must also tune in to his or her own feelings. After examining their own feelings, supervisors must be aware and willing to ask the worker if he or she is experiencing any problems or wants to talk about a traumatic experience at work. The supervisor's awareness of the worker's distress must be deliberate and focused. The supervisor must be the one to broach the subject and let the worker know it is acceptable to talk about the event and any resulting problems. Sometimes it takes gentle nudging by the supervisor for the worker not just to dismiss the supervisor with comments like, "I'm okay," or "It's not bothering me." The discussion must occur in a safe environment in which the worker is not afraid of repercussions. The supervisor's focused and deliberate alertness for problematic symptoms comes from his or her knowledge of the nature of the work and the symptoms of posttraumatic stress.

Avoiding discussion concerning the traumatic event or effects of trauma on the worker is a maladaptive coping behavior on the part of the supervisor and allows for maladaptive coping behavior on the part of the worker. Shulman (1993) pointed out the importance of open discussion as a mechanism for dealing with traumatic stress. The absence of such an effective mechanism can result in what Shulman described as a spread effect. The spread effect occurs when a traumatic event in "one case influences a worker's practice across the caseload" (Shulman, 1993, p. 260). This spread can be contagious to other workers and their caseloads also. Shulman observed that workers and supervisors under high stress become hyperactive. They begin to work harder and faster, as if to go fast enough not to have to think or feel the pain.

Shulman's parallel processes need to be discussed in child welfare supervisory training sessions. Supervisors who do not allow or encourage feelings and the effects of trauma to be discussed model for the workers that feelings and thoughts are not important, and people should just move on by using denial as a way to cope. In these supervisory units, workers often do not spend time talking to clients about their feelings and thoughts about what has happened to them. Workers may be viewed as uncaring and unfeeling, just collecting a paycheck without any true concern or care for the client. The workers are going through the motions of casework but have shut themselves off from understanding the client's pain and suffering.

The supervisor can offer support and encourage discussion without intruding on the worker's personal issues. Supervisory boundaries need to be kept intact. If the worker is experiencing psychological problems or the response to trauma is related to other personal history issues, the supervisor is responsible for referring the worker to appropriate resources for help.

One of the most important functions of a supervisor is to watch for the worker's ability to maintain an appropriate balance between work and personal life. The supervisor can insist the worker take time off, especially if the worker has been working overtime on nights and weekends, or can insist that a worker go home on time and not be on call for a while. The supervisor can promote and set the stage for peer support opportunities. Education regarding traumatic stress symptoms can be offered. Mentoring and monitoring are important supervisory functions. Supervisors can use group practice skills to build a team in their unit to monitor each other regarding problematic issues in the workplace. The supervisor's modeling of coping skills that involve confronting the problems and working through them will aid workers in helping their clients learn positive coping strategies.

Smith (2000) interviewed sixty-one employees of social services departments regarding times they had experienced fear in their work. Smith reported the following: "One of the questions they were asked was 'What responses would you like from an ideal supervisor to whom you took an experience of fear?' The workers reported that they would want the supervisor to be there for them, have time for them, and listen to what they have to say without criticism. Understanding, acknowledgement, recognition, validation, affirmation, and confirmation of the supervisee were also thought to be important" (p. 17).

Smith interviewed two workers in depth concerning their experiences. One worker described being attacked while on a home visit. He stated that he remembered thinking that he "needed to get back" (Smith, 2000, p. 20). Smith commented that more than needing to get back to his office, the worker was stating that he needed to get back to his pretraumatized self. The workers described being changed by traumatic experiences at work. One of the workers stated that it was "like being in a society, 'The Dead Social Workers Society,' 'The Fraternity of Fear.' We have secret meetings where you come and ball your eyes out. You're a statistic now" (Smith, 2000, p. 21). This describes more trauma than anyone wants to acknowledge. The article that Smith wrote is hard to read due to the raw emotion that is expressed in the interview process. One worker talked about her "professional invulnerability being breached" (Smith, 2000, p. 22).

Smith (2000) stated that supervision is of crucial importance in social work practice and that his research showed the need for supervisors to "help the supervisee reflect upon the experience and to explore its possible meanings and implications in a non-threatening manner" (p. 23). In the midst of helping supervisees work through directly or indirectly experienced traumatic events, supervisors also have reactions to the events.

SUPERVISORS' TRAUMATIC-STRESS ISSUES AND SELF-CARE

Supervisors have their own issues and feelings requiring their own peer support group (Shulman, 1993). The supervisor discussed in the scenario at the beginning of this chapter needed to problem solve with and be heard by her peers. Supervisors must be able to manage themselves as they feel the pain of their workers, just as the workers feel the pain of their clients. They need a peer support group to vent emotions and discuss painful cases. Public child welfare agency administrators and middle managers can allow supervisors time to be together to discuss supervisory issues and practice. Feelings about supervision, strengths, weaknesses, and the need for guidance and information can be topics of discussion. Leadership quality development and management techniques can also be discussed.

Often, supervisors are only brought together for policy discussion in staff meetings in which directives are given and problems with numbers (i.e., adoption numbers are down, length of time in foster care is up, reunification with parents is down, abuse in foster care is up, foster children have not been seen in a month, children are lingering too long in emergency shelters, or investigations have not been timely) are discussed. These types of meetings are necessary but often lead to supervisors feeling defeated and alone. If supervisors have each other to talk with about difficult issues with staff and cases, then they may be less likely to talk with supervisees in a peerlike manner. Thus, supervisory peer support might also help with boundary maintenance with supervisees.

BOUNDARY MAINTENANCE

We are always in a state of heightened emotion in child welfare. As a supervisor, I feel like I need to dig in and be there for the workers when they need me. There are no taboos regarding what we talk about in the workplace. We are always talking about how we feel about the cases and it spills over to talk about feelings about a lot of things. We talk about sexual activities constantly because of dealing with child sexual abuse. We know each other very well, inside and out. We know each other's moods and reactions to certain situations. I can tell if one of my workers comes in with problems outside of work on their mind. I have to know because it can affect their work with clients. We know each other's opinions. Sex, religion, and politics are even discussed. We are very close to each other. Only we know about our work and we can't talk to anyone else about it. We trust each other. We have to trust each other. Some of us have actually saved a coworker's life or had our own life saved by a coworker. We have to trust each other that much. We are a team. I have to be aware of how the work is affecting my workers and that involves knowing what is going on in their homes. It is how I gauge how the work is affecting them. (Child welfare supervisor, personal communication, 2002)

The above comment was related to one of the authors immediately after a workshop on supervisor vicarious liability and professional boundaries was presented. The supervisor was concerned that professional boundaries were blurred in her unit. This was an older female supervisor, and most of her workers were very young and inexperienced. She talked about feeling like a mother to them and knew that she had allowed dual relationships to develop between herself and her supervisees. She pointed out that in this type of situation in which emotions are regularly dealt with in a supervisory role, it is difficult to keep them from spilling over into areas that the supervisor should not be discussing with a supervisee. This supervisor is not alone in her struggles with boundary maintenance. The nature of the work in child welfare creates a need for special precautions in keeping boundaries intact and dual relationships to a minimum.

The National Association of Social Workers' *Code of Ethics* (1996) states the following in Section 3.01 regarding a social worker's ethical responsibility in practice settings and supervision and consultation:

(a) Social workers who provide supervision or consultation should have the necessary knowledge and skill to supervise or consult appropriately and should do so only within their areas of knowledge and competence.

(b) Social workers who provide supervision or consultation are responsible for setting clear, appropriate, and culturally sensitive boundaries.

(c) Social workers should not engage in any dual or multiple relationships with supervisees in which there is a risk of exploitation of or potential harm to the supervisee.

(d) Social workers who provide supervision should evaluate supervisees' performance in a manner that is fair and respectful. (p. 19)

The NASW *Code of Ethics* clearly states the need for clear, appropriate, and culturally sensitive boundaries and the avoidance of dual relationships with supervisees, in which there is a potential for harm to the supervisee.

Russell and Peterson (1998) wrote about the management of personal and professional boundaries in marriage and family therapy programs. Their work is applicable to child welfare workers and supervisors. Russell and Peterson stated that dual relationships occur when a person has two or more roles with the same person. It is inevitable that this will occur for a supervisor at different points in his or her career. It is especially common in small towns and rural areas in which supervisors and supervisees attend the same church or belong to the same clubs or school and community organizations. Some may actually be part of the same family. Some dual relationships are unavoidable but must be recognized and kept at the forefront of awareness in order for the potential for harm to be lessened.

Russell and Peterson explained that when dual relationships exist it is important to take precautions to be sure that the supervisor's judgment is not impaired and that the supervisor does not use the dual relationship to exploit the supervisee. These authors remind us that these boundaries exist for several reasons. Russell and Peterson pointed out that the boundaries protect a person's private life from his or her professional, more public life. They stated that if boundaries become blurred then it is possible that the supervisor and supervisee could lose perspective, and that this is even more problematic if the blurring of boundaries is unrecognized or covert. This creates confusion regarding the supervisor-supervisee relationship.

Supervisors are more powerful than their supervisees. The power differential can lead to situations in which the supervisee may find it "difficult to comment on boundary infringement, confusing agendas, or the inappropriateness of the invitation to a dual relationship" (Russell & Peterson, 1998, p. 459). Russell and Peterson stated that, if confronted, the supervisor is placed in a poor position to defend him- or herself. This may lead to both the supervisor and the supervisee feeling more vulnerable.

Peterson (1992) presented four characteristics of boundary violations: role reversal, secrecy, abuse of professional privilege, and the presence of a double bind. Gabbard and Pope (1989) discussed what they call a "slippery slope." This involves not one big mistake but a series of small inappropriate actions or flawed decisions that lead to a fall. It is easy to fall down the slope and commit boundary violations in clinical social work supervision, and especially in the child welfare setting.

Many case discussions are held behind closed doors. Supervisors and supervisees spend private time together discussing emotional situations. Child welfare supervisors are as stressed as the workers. The level of stress can lead to the outpouring of emotions regarding many situations, not just the particular case being discussed. The potential for case discussions to slide into discussions of personal issues is very real. This is often what occurs when supervisors find themselves knowing much about the worker's personal life and when the supervisor has shared intimate details regarding his or her own personal life with the supervisee. Personal intimacy creates a relationship in which one is more a friend than a supervisor, and thus a dual relationship has begun.

Often, child welfare supervisors have established friendships with supervisees from when they were coworkers. It is very difficult to stop being someone's friend because of the new supervisor role. Also, coworkers and supervisors spend time away from home at conferences and training sessions. It is quite common for workers and supervisors to have lunches and dinners together. These seemingly innocent situations also create a climate for slippery slopes.

Supervisory sessions that involve the sharing of personal life details may evolve into the sharing of personal problems. One supervisor related the following:

> One of the workers I supervise told everyone at the office that her husband is involved with another woman. He is having an affair. Everyone also knows that he drinks heavily and does not work regularly. The worker has also disclosed that he had hit her and

is emotionally abusive to her. No one can understand why she is staying with him. Everyone was upset with her for not leaving him and we are all afraid he will hurt her again. The tension in the office is thick. She is behind in her work, but how can I expect her to do her work when she is in this situation? She is emotionally over-whelmed. She is in the same situation as many of her clients. She can't be objective. I hate going to work because everyone is bickering about other things, but I know this is the reason they are all fussing with each other. My supervisor is on my case because the work in our unit is falling behind. I have tried to talk with her and I guess you could say that I have counseled her about her marriage. I just want the situation re-solved and her to get back to work. I know that it is wrong for me to counsel her, but who else does she have to talk to?

This scenario is typical of places to which the slippery slope can lead. Child wel-fare supervisors are very skilled at listening and often have much life experience or knowledge. They deal day in and day out with problematic family situations. They are empathetic and trustworthy. They have good problem-solving and counseling skills. Of course supervisees would gravitate to them for a listening ear and a shoul-der to cry on. It is important that supervisors realize this and be vigilant in not al-lowing boundary violations like this to occur.

This applies not only to personal disclosures but also to involvement in coun-seling regarding secondary traumatic stress and direct trauma resulting from the work in child welfare. Sometimes the work brings a worker's past trauma to the sur-face. The supervisor's role is to educate the worker regarding the symptoms of trau-matic stress and to alert the worker to the possibility of encountering them in this type of work. The supervisor will be the person, along with coworkers, to identify possible symptoms and can listen to the worker's reactions to a child's traumatic sit-uation. Coping skills and life and work balance can be taught. This should be regu-larly discussed with all supervisees. However, the supervisor cannot be the super-visee's counselor. Russell and Peterson (1998) name two types of dual relationships that are prohibited. One is sexual intimacy. The other is the provision of therapy. The supervisor needs to refer the supervisee to someone who can be his or her counselor if therapy is called for.

Another child welfare supervisor spoke of a similar situation during a discus-sion on supervisory boundaries, saying, "Okay, I have slid down the mountain and have not just landed in mud, but I am covered up, drowning, and I feel like I am in quicksand. Someone throw me a rope, please. How do I get out?" It is important to realize when this has occurred and to take action to remedy the situation. As previ-ously stated, boundary violations can have an impact on the work environment. Many have learned from experience about these types of situations instead of hav-ing the foresight to see what could happen when boundaries are blurred. The situ-ation should be dealt with directly, and open and honest discussions need to occur regarding mistakes that have been made. This requires "clearing the air" between the supervisor and the supervisee.

In the previous scenario, the supervisor talked with the worker whose husband was having an affair and told her she had overstepped her boundaries and had gotten too involved in her personal issues, as had everyone in the office. She talked with each person individually about keeping personal issues and work issues separate. After time had passed, the supervisor conducted a staff training on personal boundaries with clients and with each other and discussed why it is important to keep professional boundaries and shared that she was also learning about the problems that can occur if supervisory boundaries are not respected.

When deciding where to draw the line in supervision, especially when supervising in a trauma-laden environment, the supervisor needs to ask, "Does this issue exist because of work? Is the issue directly related to the work? As I deal with this, am I strictly discussing how the issue affects the work of the supervisee? Am I crossing the line into becoming the worker's counselor? Am I relying on my supervisees for friendships?" Another red flag that the relationship with the supervisee has become problematic is that the relationship with the supervisee is causing problems with a significant other. Another situation described involved a child welfare worker's past trauma. The supervisor reported the following:

> One of my workers came to me visibly shaken and upset. She was on the verge of tears and trembling. She said she needed to talk. I closed the office door, and she told me that she had just interviewed an eight-year-old child regarding sexual abuse by her stepfather. The child shared that her stepfather had been forcing her to masturbate him for several years while he fondled her genital area. The child had endured this but told her mother what was going on when her stepfather tried to get her to have oral sex with him. The child's mother did not believe her, and the child told her stepmother, who did believe her and reported the sexual abuse. The worker stated that the child described the same experience that she had had with her own stepfather, and the emotion and details were the same as what she went through. She couldn't stop the interview, as the child trusted her, and she couldn't show the child that she could not handle what the child was saying. The worker was an emotional wreck. She cried and cried. I couldn't just shut her down. I talked to her about her own experience and I couldn't help counseling her about her own abuse. Our relationship is strained now, and it doesn't feel like I am her supervisor because she keeps coming to me to talk about her own abuse. It opened a floodgate of emotions for her, and I am the only one she trusts to talk about it. She is a good worker, and I have to help her through this.

The supervisor became the therapist in this situation. The work often leads to this type of situation or other similar scenarios. Sometimes therapy is required to resolve issues related to being the child of an alcoholic, a neglected child, a foster child, or adopted; having a mentally ill, incarcerated, or drug-addicted parent; growing up around domestic violence; or having been physically or emotionally abused as a child. The nature of the work often brings up these memories, and the worker is forced to work through them. At times, therapy is needed due to the worker's depression, relationship problems, anxiety, obsessions, compulsions, alcoholism, drug addiction, eating disorders, gambling, or codependency issues.

Child welfare workers are not immune from having the same problems as their clients. They are human beings. The tendency of child welfare workers is to think that they cannot allow anyone to know about their personal problems, and certainly not other professionals in the community. Many times they fear the loss of respect of their clients and other professionals. They refer clients to other professionals such as therapists and counselors and work with them on a professional basis. In small towns and rural areas, only one or two persons may offer these services. Workers and supervisors often get caught in this trap and therefore try to counsel each other. As we have demonstrated, this is not an appropriate way to handle these issues. It is the responsibility of the supervisor to refer the worker to a professional for counseling regarding these types of problems and situations.

ENMESHMENT AS A BOUNDARY VIOLATION

Another phenomenon that sometimes occurs in child welfare settings is enmeshment. The child welfare unit might become enmeshed and take on the characteristics of some of the unhealthy families with whom they work. If the unit adopts the behavior of not talking about their feelings regarding cases, and workers therefore find themselves becoming numb to feelings and dissociating to cope with the trauma of their clients, then a climate of distrust can develop. This occurs when others discount or ignore people's feelings. Distrust may also develop when a person feels misunderstood or criticized by the supervisor or coworker. Gossip, unkind comments about others, or cliques in the child welfare unit may be present. Sometimes workers do not trust outsiders, and sometimes they do not trust each other.

Some or all of the persons in the work unit may be suffering from traumatic stress and depression. Fatigue can make these situations worse. People are irritable and can be overly emotional, or touchy. At times workers and supervisors may treat each other rudely or yell at each other. Respect for each other wanes, and boundaries are ignored. The child welfare unit can become just like many dysfunctional families in that they do not trust, feel, or talk and as a result begin to isolate from others. This may happen as individuals become alienated and feel alone or the unit as a whole closes down. This takes place especially if it is felt that others do not understand or support child welfare work. Sharing the load, working together, and networking all slow down or stop altogether, and entropy develops. The unit becomes unproductive, and even though workers appear busy and very tired and stressed, work outcomes are mediocre or unsatisfactory. Investigations of abuse and neglect are not completed, and foster children's needs are not met. Paperwork piles up, and report after report reveals undone work.

Other professionals, foster parents, and community members complain about the child welfare agency's lack of responsiveness and quality of service. Sometimes this is the state of affairs because there are not enough workers, but sometimes it occurs even when there are enough workers and caseloads are reasonable. The child welfare workers feel hopeless and helpless to make their situation any better and therefore take on the oppressed mannerisms of many of their client groups. The supervisor is critical in not allowing this to happen in the unit he or she supervises.

The research on child welfare supervision states that appropriate and positive supervision is the linchpin of a productive child welfare system. This has been discussed previously, but it is important to reiterate that the supervisor is the person who can encourage the expression of feeling and the discussion of cases, and promote a climate of trust in the unit. The boundaries that keep the supervisor from becoming involved in workers' personal issues and counseling needs should, however, be kept in order to promote a positive working environment. A mechanism for referral to counseling as needed could help keep dual relationships and blurring of boundaries to a minimum.

CHECKING FOR BOUNDARY VIOLATIONS

Russell and Peterson (1998) offer a litany of questions for supervisors to ask regarding boundary violations. The personal checkup questions include:

- What is going on in my life?
- Have there been any major losses or transitions?
- How have I been responding to these?
- Am I making progress on goals I value?
- Do I enjoy comfortable connectedness with peers, people of equal power to me? Whom do I call to share exciting news or if I need a favor or if I want to talk?
- With whom do I spend my leisure time?

Russell and Peterson also suggested asking questions regarding the care of the professional group. These are:

- Do I feel understood and supported by my colleagues?
- Do they know at least as much about what's going on with my personal and professional life as my supervisees?
- How are supervisees protected regarding misuse of power?
- Is there a mechanism in place for supervisees to address the misuse of power?
- Is there anonymous evaluation of supervision?
- Is professional behavior being modeled?

Russell and Peterson also suggested questions for supervisee and student care. They suggest that supervisors look at their behavior in relation to whom they spend time with outside of work and whether or not they are equally accessible to all. Another important question to ask is whether or not the supervisee is meeting the needs of the supervisor. Russell and Peterson asked if the supervisor has caregiver needs and propose that the supervisor watch for any secret, special relationships with supervisees that would be embarrassing if found out.

SUCCESSFUL SUPERVISION IN CHILD WELFARE

There are many successful supervisors in child welfare. The research shows how good supervision allows for children to be protected from abuse and neglect and how it leads to worker retention. Good supervisors act as role models for workers, who will fill their shoes in the future. Reamer (1989) stated that "Over time, social workers have generated a substantial pool of knowledge and conventional wisdom about the purposes and methods of supervision" (p. 445). We have worked with countless supervisors from all over the country who are very skilled at child welfare supervision. It appears that these skills are learned from modeling past supervisors and through experience, as the child welfare supervision body of knowledge has not yet been captured in the literature. These supervisors have knowledge of child welfare practice and policy and they are always learning. They are willing to try new practice methods and display flexibility. They are able to change with the many policy and law changes and keep order and stability in their supervisory units. These supervisors may or may not have a masters-level education but seem to have a good understanding of systems theory and know they must maintain equilibrium in their units while encouraging a steady state of growth in the workers they supervise.

The types of skills and knowledge needed were listed when we discussed the factors that make child welfare supervision different from other fields of social work supervision. Good supervisors in child welfare also have leadership skills. Kouzes and Posner (2002) surveyed thousands of persons and asked, "What values (personal traits or characteristics) do you look for and admire in your leaders?" (p. 24). They named the top four characteristics as being honest, forward looking, competent, and inspiring. They combined these qualities and others and asserted that "Credibility is the foundation of leadership" (Kouzes & Posner, 2002, p. 32). Kouzes and Posner found in their decades of research that persons who perceive their supervisors to be credible also feel attached and committed to the organization and have a strong team spirit. Those who view their supervisors as less than credible only produce if they are being watched, are motivated by money, and criticize the organization while feeling unsupported and unappreciated. These employees are often looking for another job, especially if the organization is experiencing any problems.

Kouzes and Posner (2002) also discussed five practices of good leaders. These include modeling, inspiring a shared vision, challenging the process, enabling others to act, and encouraging the heart. Good child welfare supervisors incorporate these practices into their own supervisory practice. Kouzes and Posner's principles can easily be applied to child welfare.

A child welfare supervisor must model professionalism and adhere to social work values and the code of ethics. The supervisor should have a vision of how the child welfare system can be and share the vision with supervisees. The child welfare unit will then behave as a team in reaching shared goals and in developing new possibilities for the services they offer children and families. There is constant steady growth in the unit and in the individual employees of the agency.

A good child welfare supervisor is also constantly looking for new ideas and encourages workers to experiment and take risks regarding new methods of practice or needed policy changes. This type of supervisor will allow for mistakes, allow others to learn from mistakes, and encourage small positive steps toward change. Supervisors following this model foster collaboration, interdependence, trust, and accountability and help workers develop competence and confidence.

The practice of encouraging the heart involves expecting the best, having standards of practice, recognizing strengths and accomplishments, and celebrating victories. The child welfare system often focuses on the failures and not the successes. However, there are many successes in the work with families and children that need constant recognition.

In child welfare, and when one is supervising in the context of trauma, there is a special quality that separates the good supervisors from the others. This is the ability to enable others to act. When workers have symptoms of STS or have been victims of direct trauma, their work falls behind or the quality of work diminishes. Sometimes the worker loses patience with clients or becomes hopeless about a client's potential for change or progress toward goals. The work becomes robotic, and the supervisor may see this reflected in generic case plans and services that are inappropriate for the identified needs of the client. Deadlines are not met, and paperwork piles up. The bare minimum is done, or the work falls below the acceptable standard required by the agency. Often these workers appear to be busy, tired, and stressed. Sometimes they seem lethargic and unorganized. Much time may be spent talking about clients and child welfare issues or on nonproductive activities. Sometimes these workers are always helping another worker with his or her clients. The worker may take time off work for personal issues, or he or she may have continuous health problems. Attempts at discussing the situation lead to a long litany of excuses for failure to do the job. The excuses may be work centered, or the blame is put on outside issues that are consuming the worker's attention and energy. In either situation, the supervisor may become frustrated and stressed when unable to motivate the worker to do the work.

The supervisor may have a desire to be rid of the worker and start over with someone new. At times the supervisor may act harshly toward the worker and encourage him or her to find another job or just quit. Many public agencies require the supervisor to put the worker on a performance improvement plan in order to document the supervisor's attempts to help the worker improve. We have seen many program improvement plans written in the heat of anger and frustration because the supervisor waited until he or she was completely aggravated to write the plan. The worker does not respond or expends minimum effort to get through this period.

Everyone in the supervisory unit is affected during this process. Other workers may react to the stress, feel as though the supervisor is being unfair, or become angry at their coworker for not doing his or her job. On occasion, other workers who are able to get their work done are asked to help the coworker get caught up on work. This can lead to resentment and mistreatment of the coworker, especially if this happens on a regular basis. The other workers may also be affected by the low level of work done by one worker in that they also begin to fall behind in their work. The entire unit can become infected with hopelessness and helplessness regarding the completion of good work.

Enabling others to act and become competent is an essential skill that is required for supervisors to create strong child welfare workers who deliver premium services to clients. Supervisors need to realize the value of the performance improvement plan and use it at the beginning of a work production problem. The supervisor must approach the issue with a positive attitude and the belief that the worker can change. The supervisor must be trusted by the worker, and the two must have a positive working relationship. The plan must be created together in the spirit of cooperativeness and collaboration. The worker must realize that there is a need for change and be willing to work toward improvement. The worker must have the ability to accomplish the steps necessary for change to occur. This means determining small steps in order to achieve success and praise and recognition in small increments. The tools to do the job must also be provided by the supervisor.

This skill of enabling involves the same belief that is required when the child welfare worker is working with a client. The worker must believe the client can change and must have a positive working relationship, which requires that the client trust the worker, in order for change to occur. The client must have a say in the plan, and the plan must be a collaborative effort on both the worker's and client's part. The client must agree that the work involved is worth the effort. The goal must be something the client wants to achieve and is capable of achieving. If the skills and tools to accomplish the task are not present, the worker's job is to help the client attain the skills and tools necessary for him or her to be successful at accomplishing the small intermediate steps in the work as well as the ultimate goal. If the supervisor can model this type of behavior in an attempt to effect change in another human being (the worker), the supervisor is actually modeling for workers what needs to happen for positive change to occur with their clients.

The supervisor must be aware of the effects of traumatic stress on the worker in order to recognize when this is affecting the work product. The loss of workers who are written off as having burnout when they are really experiencing traumatic stress symptoms is a tragic loss to the child welfare system. Supervisors who believe that people can change, know how to motivate workers for positive change, and do not give up on workers who suffer the effects of trauma from the work are precious commodities in the child welfare system.

THE UNIVERSITY OF KENTUCKY SOUTHERN QUALITY IMPROVEMENT CENTER FOR CHILD PROTECTION

The Southern Quality Improvement Center for Child Protection was started through a Department of Health and Human Services, Administration for Children and Families grant. Its purpose is to promote innovation and evidence-based practice improvements and to disseminate information on promising practices in child welfare through targeted research and demonstration projects that are evaluated on a cross-site basis. This project began in 2001 with an advisory board representing ten southeastern states. Each state had a representative from academia, public child welfare systems, or client systems. In the beginning the group came together for a two-day meeting to discuss the greatest need for improvement in the public child welfare system. An almost immediate consensus was reached. Everyone agreed that research-based improvement in the realm of child welfare supervision was needed most.

The Southern Quality Improvement Center for Child Protection provided funding for four states to develop models for clinical supervision practice that involved learning labs for the supervisors. The state projects have been in existence for three years. Crystal Collins-Camargo (personal communication, June 10, 2005), director of the project, stated that the projects have each been different in their approach and emphasis, but each has revealed the need for supervisors in the field of child welfare to use peer consultation and collaborative learning to enhance supervisor practice. The organizational culture in most child welfare agencies has not supported such a peer relationship, nor has it supported an atmosphere where collaborative learning is promoted for supervisors or their workers.

Collins-Camargo remarked that it has been evident throughout the project that the supervisors involved have been enthusiastic about learning new supervisory methods and creating their own instruments and practice methods for clinical case-work supervision. Mentoring has been welcomed by the supervisors. It has given them a sounding board and someone to talk with about issues about which they had no one to talk to before the project. A variety of topics have been addressed in the learning labs, including case review and modeling as strategies for promoting worker practice change, development and measurement of supervisor competencies, leadership and management to support organizational improvement, supervision in the context of trauma and change, learning-focused supervisee evaluation, 360-degree feedback, evidence-based performance improvement, worker motivation, and promotion of an outcomes-focused and supportive organizational culture.

The supervisors also report that the group meetings have created more teamwork among the units and allowed for peer-to-peer feedback and guidance. Collins-Camargo stated that the final evaluation of the project will involve comparison of data on the organizational culture, preventable turnover, social worker self-efficacy and practice, and case and client outcomes. She shared that the projects have each been successful in various ways, and it is hoped that the model of supervisory learning labs will be sustained and continue to be improved upon with each new supervisory group in states currently funded as well as in other child welfare systems.

5

Traumatic Stress and Child Welfare Administration

DISCUSSIONS ABOUT ORGANIZATIONAL CLIMATE AND CULTURE ARE NOT commonly found in social work or child welfare literature. These two concepts offer a means to understand the work environment and the potential for organization administrators to positively influence the motivation and behavior of workers. Osborne and Gaebler (1992) found that workplace cultures are successful when they value results over process and focus on mission instead of policies that define practice. Such organizations give workers independence to do their work and also value workers' use of their professional judgment. Glisson's (2000) review of research found evidence that supported the concepts of climate and culture as essential to organizational performance.

Glisson, citing Brown and Leigh (1996), stated that positive organizational climates empower workers both professionally and personally. Organizational climates are created through workers' shared perceptions. If workers perceive the organization to be a safe and supportive work environment, then they will perceive the organization positively. Workers regard positive climates as places were they are treated fairly, conflict is well managed, and they are challenged by their work and are given the support they need. In such climates the worker perceives that the work he or she does is valued, as is the work of colleagues. It is the workers' shared perception of the organization that creates the organizational climate (Glisson, 2000). Climate is derived from individuals' subjective appraisals and experiences in the workplace.

Organizational culture is thought of as shared assumptions, values, and beliefs that inform and guide group members' behavior, thinking, and practices (Denison, 1996; Desphandé & Webster, 1989; Rousseau, 1990). Whereas climate is derived from individual perceptions, culture is derived from the social system that reinforces the norms, values, and acceptable behaviors within the organization. Glisson (2000) argued that "organizational climate is the shared perceptions of individuals of the psychological impact that the work environment has on the employees, whereas culture is defined as a property of the collective social system that drives the way things are done in the organization" (p. 198). Expanding his understanding, he argued that "culture captures patterns of social interactions, and climate captures the personal meanings that individuals give to those interactions"

(Glisson, 2000, p. 198). This leads to the need to examine the organizational culture and climate in which child welfare work is conducted.

Ellett and Millar (2005) pointed out that professional organizational culture has not been examined in relation to staff retention in child welfare. In their study of organizational culture and child welfare retention, they found that child welfare staff knew what they needed from supervisors and administrators. This included "demonstrating a willingness to help and assist staff when problems arise; providing assistance to enhance the quality of case decisions and services to clients; demonstrating empathy and personal concern for staff as professionals; encouraging staff to fully actualize their potential and encouraging and providing support for staff to continue their social work education and to participate in continuing professional development activities" (Ellett & Millar, 2005, p. 12).

Administrators influence organizational climate and culture through leadership and management. As leaders, they have a critical role in staying abreast of developments in the field that affect child welfare staff. Secondary traumatic stress is a factor that must be attended to by administrators. STS affects both the individual perceptions of organizational climate and the norms, behaviors, and values defined by organizational culture. Administrators have a moral and legal responsibility to address STS and a duty to care that will be more fully addressed in the next chapter.

LEADERSHIP

Administrative leadership contributes greatly to organizational climate and culture. There are numerous definitions of leadership. Bennis (1982) wrote that there are more than 350 definitions of leadership, and more are developed with every passing month (p. 44). He asserted that the art form of leadership begins with the question, "How do organizations translate intention into reality and sustain it?" Bennis found that the chief executive officers he studied had common characteristics. One such characteristic is vision that communicates with clarity the organization's purpose such that it compels commitment from employees. This type of communication synergizes the various constituencies within the organization. These CEOs had persistence and tenacity to motivate even in the worst of times, and the ability to empower employees to work toward and ultimately produce positive outcomes.

In child welfare, leaders inspire practitioners to engage in some of the most difficult social work practice, and they also administer the organization in which it takes place. Public child welfare agencies and business organizations have different characteristics. Business organizations exist not only to provide a service but also to make a profit. The agency exists so that child welfare practitioners can intervene where children are at risk and bring about changes in the way families care for their children (Patti, 1987). The practitioner may also work to improve the social and environmental conditions in which the family lives (Patti, 1987). These professionals use social work interventions to bring about changes. The interventions are influenced by the workers' philosophies, values, emotions, compassion, and an array of resources to make the interventions work, often with involuntary and resistant clients. The practitioners' persistence in the face of multiple formidable barriers is essential to success.

There are several facets of leadership, according to Bargal (2000), that are relevant to child welfare work. Leaders create vision and culture. Vision is a tangible picture of children and their families being transformed from dysfunctional to functional through the work of the practitioner. Bargal (2000), citing Schein (1985, 1992), wrote that leaders are the keepers of organizational culture, values, ideology, and norms (p. 307). Leaders define how the organization will cope with problems inherent in the work, for example STS. Bargal identified three areas of personal characteristics that constitute components of leadership effectiveness.

The first set of characteristics is traits such as drive, self-confidence, flexibility, charisma, and professional worldview (Bargal, 2000). Child welfare leaders must have energy and initiative and the ability to see what needs to be done. At the root of self-confidence is knowledge of and competence in child welfare management. Without the worker's self-confidence, the initiatives will not be implemented and the vision will be lost. Child welfare is constantly changing, and leaders have to be flexible in how they think and solve problems. They must encourage adaptation on the part of the practitioner. Charisma includes a passion for the work that gives the leader the ability to get others excited and passionate about what they are being asked to do. It is an essential component of leadership. Professional worldview means having an understanding of what child welfare practice is and how it can be used to improve the lives of children and their families. And it includes a firm grounding in the professional values and ethics of social work.

The second area Bargal addressed is knowledge, and the third is skills. Both are essential to leadership in child welfare. The most desirable base for knowledge and skills in child welfare is formal education in social work and social welfare and its mission, goals, and values. Aspiring leaders must have a thorough understanding of child welfare systems. The leader must also be knowledgeable about the organization and its structure. The leader needs to understand why child welfare practitioners do what they do and the reasons for policies and procedures. Changes in policy and practice should be empirically based.

Interpersonal and managerial skills are essential. Strong interpersonal skills are necessary. These include communication, empathy, and the ability to demonstrate concern regarding the dangers inherent in the work. Another characteristic of child welfare leadership is the ability to manage the child welfare agency in a world of few resources, lack of community understanding of the work and its dangers, and many other barriers. Child welfare leaders must also be knowledgeable of and competently involved in the political context in which child welfare practice takes place.

Child welfare leaders must also realize that their greatest resources are the practitioners working in the agency, and they must make clear that they are the organization's most valuable asset. In this work, the leader must have the charisma to inspire practitioners, whose work environment is dangerous, difficult, and often unpleasant, to believe completely in what they do. They must also maintain and promote that belief in the child welfare system in a community of other professionals and community members who frequently express disbelief in the practitioners' work. Child welfare has endured a bad reputation for years that often arises from a lack of understanding, and a community mind-set of always looking for someone to blame. The leader of the child welfare organization can dispel this reputation by helping to educate the public and praising the work of the practitioners. Leaders must also support practitioners in their willingness to put themselves in danger in their efforts to protect and save children from harm and even death. By doing so, the leader will increase the practitioner's commitment to the work and the profession.

THE ABSENCE OF LEADERSHIP

Leadership is sometimes absent in some child welfare agencies. As pointed out earlier, in many states political appointees are the departmental directors of public child welfare organizations. Politics sometimes creates a system where directors often change. Sometimes these political appointees have no knowledge of human services in general and child welfare in particular. When political appointees who have no background or training in child welfare or social work obtain positions in the child welfare system, practitioners' work may be compromised, as are outcomes for children and families. While appointees may have some relevant knowledge or skill, if they don't know the field of child welfare, then they don't have the expertise to be in the position.

It is important to note that some directors who have been appointed have educated themselves about the field of child welfare. This group of political appointees is open and receptive to learning from experienced child welfare supervisors and middle managers. This can be a positive experience for the system. However, it seems logical that someone who knows child welfare and has leadership skills would be better suited for the job. When the senior administrator remains ignorant of child welfare, the situation can become truly problematic.

There are serious consequences when this happens. First and foremost, the needs of child welfare practitioners may not be met. For example, the need for safety procedures and bulletproof vests or other body armor when the potential for assault is high may go unrecognized. The need to debrief traumatic events may not be considered the norm and may not be practiced within the agency. The need to monitor for STS may not be understood. Leaders with no knowledge of STS cannot grasp the implications for the agency and for clients when workers have developed STS symptoms.

Due to directors' lack of expertise, policies may be developed that are unreasonable and impractical because their implications are not understood. One simple example is the imposition of unrealistic dress codes for child protection investigators. More than once, new directors have required male field workers to wear ties and females to wear nice professional clothes and nylon stockings, and no tennis shoes. These policies are a danger to workers and also decrease the probability that they will build successful relationships with clients. Ties can be used to choke a person, and nylons and heels were not designed to facilitate rapid departure from a dangerous situation. Workers often complain that dressing up creates a feeling of "I am better than you" with the client. It is easier for some clients to relate to workers if the dress is professional but casual. Clients' homes are not the cleanest at times, and workers must sit on couches and chairs that are not clean. Workers are often heard discussing unrealistic dress codes mandated by new directors. Usually, they roll their eyes and comment, "Here we go again."

Procedures may be so "by the book" that there is little room for innovation and creativity where and when it would be possible. The need for professional development and continuing education may not be supported and may be interpreted as a luxury and sacrificed because the link between building competencies and best practice with children and families is not understood. Continuing education may not be seen as an investment in the stated goals for children and families. The appointee without child welfare expertise may not see the value of professional peer support groups for supervisors and practitioners or how that support may increase commitment to the profession, work, and agency. The absence of leadership with the requisite vision, knowledge, and skill leads to demoralization of the people working within the agency.

One of the most serious consequences of the appointment of directors who do not have child welfare experience is that they may not understand the organization well enough to protect it, thereby contributing to its decline. Faced with limited resources, the appointee may be persuaded to do more with less by the governor or legislature. Political appointees are easily replaced if they do not fall in line with the desires of the appointing authority. In light of the fact that most state child welfare agencies seldom have the resources they need to begin with, there is no way to do more with less. This puts children and families at risk and means that the state is failing in its duty to care for and protect one of its most vulnerable populations.

SECONDARY TRAUMATIC STRESS AND THE ORGANIZATION

Both forms of posttraumatic stress, primary and secondary, are present in child welfare organizational culture. We specifically postulate and have provided evidence that secondary traumatic stress is an occupational hazard in the child welfare field that can produce occupational stress injuries. As an occupational hazard, it must be addressed along with other risks of the work. Catherall (1995) pointed out that "All institutions that are exposed to STS will find it exacts a toll on the functioning of the staff unless deliberate steps are taken to prevent, or at least limit, its pernicious effects" (p. 232). Catherall stated that there are three steps in addressing STS: (1) psychoeducation, (2) preparedness, and (3) planning. We believe there is also a need to have an appropriate and effective fit between Catherall's steps and agency culture.

Agency administrators must accept responsibility for managing STS and make it a part of the organizational culture so that the organizational climate is perceived by the worker as positive and supportive. There are a number of strategies and activities that can become part of the child welfare agency's administration, culture, and organization to achieve that fit. It is important that administrators undertake these activities with the understanding that they are in the best interests of the agency, the staff, and the families they service. When workers perceive the administration's negative attitude toward STS intervention, even if the intervention is being implemented, the effort will probably not succeed. Usually practitioners are highly sensitive to their own well-being and know when others are not sensitive.

PROBLEMS IN NORMALIZING STS

First and foremost, STS must be addressed as an occupational hazard for child welfare workers; their supervisors; and, under extreme circumstances, such as when a child's death occurs, the whole agency staff. While some authors consider normalizing STS to be part of the work, we think this practice can be problematic. To make something "normal" is to make it usual and not abnormal. Thus STS may be considered the total responsibility of the worker, and not the agency and administrators, because STS affects everybody.

This approach allows administrators and supervisors to engage in the silencing response and thus avoid the problem (Baranowsky, 2002; Danieli, 1984). Baranowsky (2002) identified sixteen ways that avoidance and silencing take place:

> changing the subject; avoiding the topic; providing pat answers; minimizing worker distress; wishing or suggesting that the worker would "just get over it"; boredom; being angry or sarcastic with workers; using humor to change or minimize the subject; faking interest or listening; fearing what the worker has to say; fearing that you will not be able to help; blaming the worker for his or her experiences; not believing the worker; feeling numb or avoidant prior to meeting with the worker; not being able to pay attention to the worker; and constantly being reminded of personal traumatic experiences when working with certain workers. (p. 162)

While she discussed these as pertaining to clients, they are equally applicable to workers. Just as clients can be silenced by our inattention, so can workers in the face of administrative inattention. Some of these responses are also a form of workplace bullying, as described in chapter 2.

ADMINISTRATION AND TRAUMATIC STRESS

Child welfare workers experience abnormal traumatic stress that is outside the realm of what other helping professionals encounter, and it is often beyond their control. This hazard is an unavoidable risk that may or may not be foreseeable. To understand that STS is an occupational risk of the work is to begin to prepare to recognize and manage it with the knowledge that it is inevitable for the majority of people working in the child welfare field. This requires administrators to accept responsibility for the agency's response to the effects of STS on staff (Catherall, 1995; Tehrani, 2004). It also requires planning for the trauma that may arise from a variety of sources. An atmosphere of cohesion and support regarding pervasive traumatic stress should not be avoided. The culture should not subscribe to the belief that persons who suffer from traumatic stress are viewed as not having the "right stuff." Comments like, "You make a mistake in my agency and you're gone," or "You'll get used to it," are not used in a supportive environment. When these attitudes are expressed frequently, they might be a form of workplace bullying (Tehrani, 2004) and we think they are related to disbelief and dismissal trauma.

Correspondingly, the culture must convey that the work that goes on in the agency is important and meaningful in the lives of children and families, regardless of the lack of public support or understanding. Administrators must convey to workers that they understand the cognitive, emotional, and physical risks workers take every day on behalf of children and families. Workers know what administrators think of them by how they are treated within the organization. Workers' perceptions of their work environments, or organizational climates, are directly linked to successful social service outcomes for children and families (Glisson & Hemmelgarn, 1998).

Administrators who understand the effects of STS on the agency's practitioners will prevent its deleterious impact on practitioners' work with clients. Administrators can greatly influence the management of STS by putting in place organizational and structural constructs and changes that send a clear message regarding concern for and support of workers and their supervisors. Failure to take responsibility for addressing traumatic stress sends a clear message that staff understands: "You don't matter, and you are expendable." The ongoing crisis in child welfare worker retention can hardly be surprising in work environments where this is the norm.

SELECTIVE HIRING PRACTICES

It is essential to identify recruits, preferably social workers, who want a career working with children and families to fill child welfare positions. Agency supervisors should be trained to screen for workers who plan to stay long-term with the agency, instead of accepting any qualified person who applies (Fryer et al., 1989). Child welfare practice is not just a job. A mismatch between the work and the prospective practitioner can result in a lack of commitment to the work and early separation (Wanous, 1992). For example, someone who wants nine-to-five work is not a good fit for a child welfare agency where being on call and having to go out at night are common. According to McElroy (2001), selective hiring sends a clear message to practitioners who do the work that they must be committed to child welfare. Administrators should convey the message that what child welfare workers do matters and is valued. Practitioners who are new to the environment should have characteristics similar to those of the effective practitioners already working there. Individuals bring with them traits that contribute greatly to the organizational culture. If individuals have a high dedication to child welfare and to quality practice, as well as the ability to be creative, then the organizational culture will reflect those same features (Glisson, 2000).

At the same time, potential employees must be told about the reality of the work, both the good features and the more difficult challenges, including specific information about traumatic stress. The agency has an ethical and legal responsibility (which is the topic of the next chapter) to do so and might best achieve this by having seasoned workers share the continuum of their experiences, the pain and the rewards, with potential employees. Seasoned workers and supervisors might also share why they remain committed to the work despite the physical dangers and the potential for experiencing traumatic stress. This would allow the potential worker to realistically assess whether or not he or she wants to commit to the work and the organization.

PROFESSIONAL DEVELOPMENT AND EDUCATION ABOUT STS

Primary and secondary traumatic stress must be addressed in the professional development and education of all child welfare workers. It should be recognized as a hazard that the agency is committed to managing. For example, practitioners report that education about the sexual abuse of children enhanced their ability to cope, especially when they are confronted with difficult cases (Follette, Polusny, & Milbeck, 1994). Workers need to know what their personal and professional responsibilities are in relation to traumatic stress and how they will likely be affected. Through education, workers can learn to recognize STS when it happens to them and when it happens to colleagues and know how to respond. They will also be able to differentiate it from burnout. Workers also need to be informed as to what their supervisors' and administrators' responsibilities are in relation to STS and what support they can expect from both of them.

Through education, practitioners can also learn of the importance of professional support groups. They can come to understand the importance of both receiving and providing support. It is especially important for practitioners who are new to the organization to hear seasoned practitioners talk about how they have come to cope with STS. As Catherall (1995) stated, "The institution has the responsibility to identify the potential for its occurrence and estimating the degree and frequency of exposure" (p. 233). It is the agency's duty to care (Tehrani, 2004).

ADMINISTRATORS' SUPPORT FOR SUPERVISORS

Administrators have a clear responsibility to support supervisors. Failure to do so sends the message that supervisors, and thus workers and clients, are unimportant. As noted earlier, Shulman (1993) described a parallel process that occurs between the supervisor and the worker. The process applies to the relationship between administrators and supervisors as well and requires that administrators provide supportive supervision and guidance to the supervisor. This is particularly relevant to preparedness as described by Catherall (1995), and it includes emotional support, the sharing of information, tangible support, and establishment of relationships that allow full and open communication (Flannery, 1990). Administrators need the skills that Figley described as social supportiveness skills, which are skills needed by practitioners working with traumatized families. "These include clarifying insights, correcting distortions (placing blame and credit more objectively), and offering or supporting, new and more generous or accurate perspectives on traumatic events" (Figley, 1989, p. 16).

Administrators using social supportiveness skills with supervisors help supervisors to rethink traumatic events and share clarifying insights. The administrator must listen carefully to the supervisor's telling of such events and be able to restate not just the facts of the event but the feelings attached to it. In doing so, the administrator reassures the supervisor that he or she understands what the supervisor has experienced. The administrator can help the supervisor elaborate and expand his or her understanding of the trauma by using clarifying insights so that some parts of the experience do not go unattended. And, as Figley pointed out, these interactions should be nonjudgmental and supportive and caring. These interactions help supervisors work through trauma and gain knowledge that will be applied to future events.

Another activity that administrators may use when supporting supervisors work through a traumatic experience is correcting distortions (Figley, 1989). It is in the retelling that memory disorganization and disruptions may be discovered and the understanding of what happened may be more fully known and felt. This allows for credit and blame to be assigned more objectively and without prejudice. This also contributes to as full a recovery as is possible.

Administrators also provide supportive reframes. This provides the supervisor a different or more generous perspective of the traumatic event and allows him or her to find the positive in what has happened, especially what has been learned.

Just as the administrator assists the supervisor in managing a trauma, the supervisor is then able to help workers manage the trauma that is inevitable in their work. This parallel process prepares the worker to become more skilled at helping clients recall and manage the traumas they have experienced. Administrators with these skills create an organizational culture that maintains a balanced worldview and psychological frame of reference, thus reducing the negative effects of traumatic stress.

CRITICAL INCIDENT STRESS DEBRIEFING

Critical incident stress debriefing (CISD) was previously identified as one important way to intervene with primary or secondary traumatic stress. CISD is defined as structured psychological debriefing that follows a traumatic incident. It is usually conducted in small groups within twenty-four to seventy-two hours following the traumatic event (Mitchell & Everly, 1996). While it was originally used for disaster responders, emergency service workers, and military personnel, it is now applied across a wide range of critical incidents usually involving trauma. One of the authors has performed CISD in child welfare settings, particularly following children's deaths and other extremely stressful events, with positive results. CISD is a psychoeducational process that provides a formal structure for discussion of what happened during a crisis. CISD may be conducted by one individual trained to de-brief crisis situations or by a team of persons trained to conduct CISD for groups. The goal of CISD is for participants involved in the critical incident to share their experience and to proceed toward integration of the experience and recovery (Lewis, 1994).

There are several phases in CISD. They are

◆ Introductory remarks and group rules
◆ Facts of what happened
◆ Thoughts experienced during the event
◆ Reactions
◆ Distress symptoms experienced
◆ Suggestions for harm reduction
◆ Reentry to the work environment (Dyregrov, 1989, 1997; Mitchell & Everly, 1996)

Based upon crisis intervention and group process, CISD can be an effective way to address traumatic events and ensure that staff have an opportunity to address what happened; how each person was affected by it; ways to manage, cope, and support each other; and what the events portend for the future. Having CISD as part of the agency's standard operating procedures also assures staff that administrators are concerned about mitigating the stress experienced during traumatic events. There is some controversy regarding CISD because some research demonstrates it may produce mixed results (Robbins, 2002). CISD should not be used indiscriminately, nor should attendance be compulsory. CISD teams, particularly supervisors, should be thoroughly trained and should follow the CISD structure that Mitchell and Everly propose. This method has provided consistent, positive results. CISD can become part of the culture in such a way that the positive effects are talked about among workers, and they participate voluntarily.

EMPLOYMENT ASSISTANCE PROGRAMS

Employment assistance programs (EAPs) are another way child welfare agencies can support their staff. EAPs provide services that are intended to promote productivity, contribute to quality performance, reduce absenteeism, and increase morale (Farkas, 1989; Minnesota, 2004a). EAPs usually consist of internal and external professionals who are available to work within agencies or are available to staff at other locations. A hallmark feature of EAPs is confidentiality. Supervisors can make referrals to the program when workers are in need of services (Minnesota, 2004b). EAP staff can also conduct CISD when traumatic events occur and can provide ongoing counseling for STS.

PROFESSIONAL SUPPORT GROUPS

Professional support groups for workers and for supervisors provide forums where participants can address the traumatic stress aspects of the work. Workers and supervisors need to be in separate groups because authority roles of workers and supervisors are different, and participants need to be able to speak freely. Administrators establish the groups on the basis that the work has a continuum of outcomes from significant successes to extreme traumatic stress. They also make it clear, in establishing the groups as part of the work, that their agenda is to create a supportive work environment for staff and in so doing acknowledge the distress that the work can cause (Nissly et al., 2005; Reagh, 1994). The groups provide a mechanism through which individuals can address how they are being affected by the work, maintain connections to fellow workers who are also affected, and share coping strategies (Catherall, 1995). Peer groups have been found to help workers and supervisors maintain empathy and compassion, reframe events objectively, and reduce isolation (Lyon, 1993).

SOCIALIZATION AND MENTORING

Socializing a new employee is much like offering hospitality to a stranger. New employees are strangers and need assistance becoming effective employees within the organization. Citing Bachelder and Braddock's 1994 study of practitioners new to direct-service work, Hewitt, Larson, O'Nell, and Sauer (2005) identified several ways in which coworkers assist a new practitioner's entry into the work and influence his or her decision to stay. Coworkers help new employees to adjust and find their way around. This may be as simple as showing new workers where forms are kept and how to organize a file drawer. New practitioners learn to do the work from their observations of seasoned practitioners. In a good work environment, experienced practitioners assume it is their responsibility to advise and train new practitioners about how to carry out the work. In a positive organizational climate, seasoned practitioners can be supportive of new workers and help them begin to learn about the traumatic stress of the work, how to recognize its effects, and how to manage it. In addition, as part of socialization, seasoned practitioners can teach newer workers how to take safety precautions.

When agency leaders and supervisors become aware of how practitioners collectively help newer workers into an organization through socialization, the need for more individualized mentoring will be acknowledged and addressed. Hewitt, LaLiberte, Kougl-Lindstron, and Larson point out that there are many kinds of mentoring and different reasons to have mentors. Specifically, mentors "support and socialize an employee to have a successful employment experience and to move toward certain career goals and to support an employee in developing certain skills." (Hewitt et al., 2005, p. 179). A seasoned practitioner guides the new worker, in a one-on-one relationship, through the work. This includes both day-to-day activities as well as the traumatic aspects of the work. The mentor relationship is a safe place for the new worker to share concerns, questions, anxieties, discomforts, and how he or she is being changed by the work. Mentors can also impress upon new practitioners the need to protect themselves when they are in the field and to recognize their professional growth and successes.

Administrators underestimate the value of successful socialization and mentoring. The promotion and support of these activities sends a message that the administration is concerned about the practitioner's well-being as well as retaining the practitioner in the organization.

PHYSICAL AND PSYCHOLOGICAL SAFETY

Staff need a pleasant workspace that provides a physical and psychologically safe environment. A pleasant workspace should be a space that staff organize and decorate as they choose. With administrators' encouragement, staff can individualize their work area to reflect their interests both professionally and personally. For example, pictures of family, friends, pets, or vacations are positive visual images of the worker's personal life that can serve as reminders to maintain balance between work and home to protect his or her worldview. Positive motivational statements posted around the workspace can help the practitioner remain grounded and stay in touch with the larger vision of child welfare practice. Workspace utilities should be maintained. It is demoralizing working in a building where the roof leaks or the basement smells of sewage because the plumbing leaks.

SECURITY

Child welfare work is dangerous. Workers cannot avoid going into hostile and unsafe environments. Having police protection when the threat level is high is essential. Sometimes agency policy requires workers to wear bulletproof vests in some neighborhoods. It is necessary to have policies in place to protect staff from physical assaults and to establish effective standard operating procedures for safety. All buildings must be secure, and procedures for going in and out of buildings must be followed by everyone in the agency. Metal detectors can prevent people from bringing weapons into the building. Offices need to be arranged so that clients cannot block the door. The worker needs to be able to get up and get out easily should a hostile situation arise. Another protective device is having code words that practitioners can use to alert others to an unsafe situation. When such words are used, those in hearing range need to know exactly how to respond. Workers must always be alert in the building's parking lot as well.

Finally, psychological safety is also an important issue for child welfare professionals. Child welfare staff often work in fear of their own agency. They are very much aware of how others are treated when something goes wrong, especially in instances where the worker could do nothing to change the situation. Often these types of situations occur when a child dies of abuse or neglect. This often comes from upper administrators who are removed from the situation and make premature judgments and decisions that are harmful to the worker. This is akin to what we have previously described as disbelief and dismissal trauma. One worker we spoke with said of her workplace, "This place is a catch-22; first, it is dangerous in the field, and then when I come back to the office, I never know if there is going to be some big blowup and I am going to be put in the hot seat. It's not safe anywhere."

She clearly felt unsupported by her agency and felt that she could be verbally attacked at any time by her own agency administrators. Those same administrators are responsible for the organizational culture and the safety of the work environment. A physically and psychologically safe environment lets staff know that they are valued and that their protection is important.

INNOVATIONS IN SPITE OF CONSTRAINTS

There is room in child welfare practice for innovation in how the work is organized and carried out. Innovations do not need to be extreme or costly but should represent a deliberate change from old practices to new practices that are in the best interests of workers, supervisors, the agency, and the families and children they serve. Innovations may also serve to reduce worker turnover. Some of the previously discussed factors related to worker turnover are associated with issues that organizations could change through structural adjustments within the agency. Some of these changes might require legislative action. The needed changes may require communities and workers to become politically active to influence politicians to fund child welfare, because many times the political climate, budget cuts, and spending limitations do not permit agencies even to attempt to foster a better working environment for their workers. Additional staff could reduce heavy caseloads and the amount of time individual workers spend on call after hours. The amount and type of paperwork can also be improved with thought and attention to the problem by management. Career ladders and professional development activities would also create a better organizational climate. In child welfare organizations that have been innovative in creating a better work environment, workers and supervisors report a high level of satisfaction with child welfare work.

SOCIALIZATION TO CHILD WELFARE: ADMINISTRATIVE RESPONSIBILITY

Socializing new workers requires developing a thoughtful and meaningful orientation to the work. As Jaskyte (1999) pointed out, there is considerable literature in other fields regarding socialization to employment, but this process has not been addressed in social work. She also makes the point that as professionals, social workers must interact with a variety of other professionals who may not appreciate or understand social work or its contribution to the interdisciplinary setting.

Effective socialization to the agency is related to organizational commitment (Wanous, 1992). It is also how the individual learns policy, procedures, and practice and becomes acclimated to the organizational culture. Careful consideration of new worker training should be an ongoing task of administrators. It is in the administration's interest to have new workers socialized and trained so that practice excels and quality supervision exists. Mentors or experienced coaches should be available to help the new worker transition into child welfare work.

It is also in the interest of administrators for new workers to be given caseloads that are reasonable and balanced in terms of the extent of trauma involved. For example, it is unreasonable for the new worker to be handed twenty of the worst sexual abuse cases that more experienced workers are more than eager to pass on to someone else. Giving a new worker cases that are considered the worst or toughest, or too many cases, is a way of setting the worker up for failure. At times, new workers have been expected to take on a full caseload and high numbers of investigations before they have even attended the first training session. This practice promotes anxiety in novice workers. Administrators who allow such practices are not acting constructively or in the agency's best interests, and certainly not in the best interests of the families and children whom they serve.

Administration must pay attention to individual workers' work flows and be flexible in shifting responsibilities as is needed. Why do child welfare agencies insist on creating situations in which the same worker who worked an emotionally exhausting ten-hour day is also the worker who is on call that night and the following weekend? Some child welfare workers are "one-person units" and are on call twenty-four hours a day, seven days a week, fifty-two weeks a year, except when they leave their homes for vacation. Based on personal experience, we feel it is safe to say that many workers receive phone calls pertaining to work even while they are on vacation. The overwhelming influx of mobile phones (paid for by the worker, not the agency) means that workers can be reached anywhere and at any time. Having experienced child welfare work prior to the era of mobile phones, we find it hard to imagine having to be more accessible. There is little time for private life. Turning one's private mobile phone off is an option, but the worker risks a guilt trip if something happens to a child on her caseload and she can't be contacted.

Creating shift work, hiring other child welfare workers for on-call duty, or having enough workers to allow the worker who worked the night before on an emergency call to take the next day off would lessen the number of workers leaving the agency due to after-hours work, unpredictable work schedules, and on-call duty requirements.

It would also be advisable never to have "one-person units" in the structure of the agency. Job duties can be made flexible. For example, no one should remain a sexual abuse investigator for years at a time. Because of the intensity of traumatic exposure, workers need a break from this type of work and should be allowed to work in adoptions or another less trauma-laden area for a period of time. Ideally, the work should be done in teams where workers have a triaged caseload. This would redistribute the exposure the worker has to trauma and allow all workers to have caseloads that include cases with high probability of success to balance the effects of the more trauma-laden cases.

ADVANCEMENT AND COMPENSATION

Another innovation would be to have career ladders put in place for advancement and promotion. A career ladder would have clearly designated norms for advancement and specific qualifications for promotion. Experienced workers might act as career development mentors to new workers. These coaches would facilitate maturation into child welfare practice. Career ladders should be put in place and should not be dependent on funding. Child welfare staff members who have worked hard to achieve a promotion or salary increase should not be told that the advancement cannot and will not happen in the near future due to budget cuts. This is totally demoralizing and disappointing to staff members. It also conveys the message that the worker's longevity, experience, and work toward a higher degree of education or professional development are not valued in the organizational climate.

Salaries need to be commensurate with advancement and promotion and at a level that keeps skilled workers from seeking other higher-paying jobs that are not as demanding (Chrestman, 1995). Salaries should start at a point that is reasonable for the type of work and pay appropriate amounts for the skills needed to work in child welfare. Jayaratne and Chess (1984) claimed that "The stresses inherent in the job are hard enough, the agency should do its utmost to define the job clearly and to increase comfort in the physical environment. Such minimal changes in the child welfare and community mental health settings could conceivably result in appreciable differences in performance and turnover" (p. 450). Jayaratne and Chess also stated that addressing the issue of financial rewards may result in less turnover among workers. Hazard pay would be one compensation that might help to retain workers doing child protection investigations.

MANAGING FOR WORKPLACE EXCELLENCE

In 1995, the General Accounting Office conducted a symposium addressing organizational transformations that contribute to the workforce of the future (Struebing, 1996). Presenters had all received awards for excellence and innovations in the workplace. Several principles were identified by participants as essential to staff management for workplace excellence. These are relevant to child welfare.

- ◆ People must be valued as assets rather than costs, with the understanding that the organization's success depends on each individual and the group.
- ◆ Organizations should develop a clear mission, vision, values, and organizational culture that require high standards of performance and personal behavior for all in the workplace.
- ◆ Administrators need the authority to be flexible in managing workers and free to innovate where there is the opportunity. Get away from doing everything by the book, with the exception of procedures that are required by law.
- ◆ The agency should be organized to meet the mission with input from workers who carry out the mission in the field.
- ◆ The goal of management should be to achieve results and not to rigidly impose the book on workers. This includes listening to workers with new ideas regarding what is best practice in specific situations.
- ◆ Professional development for staff should be considered an investment and not a cost. Learning by staff is an investment in the organization and its clients' needs and contributes to building competencies.
- ◆ Administrators need to reward staff frequently and visibly for excellence in performance.

◆ Finally, organizations must view change as constant rather than crisis induced. Adaptation is a requirement of constant change and should be a philosophy for effective organizations.

Retention of child welfare workers depends on many factors. One factor we know adversely affects workers is the traumatic stress of the work. Ellett and Millar (2005) found that the main reason workers intended to remain working in child welfare was their dedication to a positive organizational culture and the availability of administrative support. Interventions in STS and administrative support must be improved if we want to stem the outgoing tide of child welfare workers and create a culture that promotes positive coping skills for the workers who remain committed to the profession.

Administrators and supervisors create the organizational climate and culture in which child welfare work takes place. There are many relatively inexpensive interventions that can help organizations build a community that is supportive and promotes cohesion in the workplace. Workers who are valued and respected are less likely to seek employment elsewhere. STS permeates child welfare work, and there is much that can be done to manage it and protect the worker and the agency.

6

Child Welfare Work and Traumatic Stress: An Occupational Hazard

A machete-wielding father was fatally shot yesterday after he attacked a veteran Child Protective Services (CPS) worker in the worst known case of on-the-job violence at the state welfare agency. The CPS worker, accompanied by a co-worker and a Ferry County sheriff's deputy, was investigating a complaint that three children were living in a home . . . without running water or electricity when the children's father attacked her. (The father) pummeled one of the social workers with a machete and a 2-by-4 as she lay on the ground before the sheriff's deputy shot and killed him. The worker, whose name was not released, suffered cuts, a broken arm and wrist and a possible skull fracture. She was admitted to Deaconess Medical center in Spokane for a CAT scan. . . . Governor Christine Gregoire, who represented CPS workers as an assistant attorney general, commended the injured worker for her 13 years of CPS work. "This incident reminds us all of the dangers that many state workers face every day," Gregoire said. (Martin, 2005)

This chapter addresses the nature of child welfare work and identifies secondary traumatic stress as an occupational hazard. It further proposes remedies in worker compensation law for when occupational stress injuries do occur in the child welfare workforce.

PROTECTING CHILDREN IN AMERICA: THE EARLY YEARS

Child welfare has its roots in the social justice reform movements of the mid- to late 1800s. New York passed the first state legislation to safeguard the rights of children in 1874, and the American Society for the Prevention of Cruelty to Animals, organized many years before, was a prime actor in establishing state authority to protect children. New York's Society for the Prevention of Cruelty to Children was established in 1875 and was the first organization devoted to child welfare in the United States (McDaniel & Lescher, 2004).

In 1912, the federal government became involved with child welfare with the creation of the Children's Bureau, but its actual participation was limited. Working with the courts, private nonprofit humane societies took the lead in protecting maltreated children. The New Deal era saw the emergence of the federal government as the premier authority in child welfare. Part of the Social Security Act of 1935 was the Aid to Families with Dependent Children (AFDC), a program designed to prevent child welfare authorities from removing children from their families for financial reasons (McDaniel & Lescher, 2004). With modifications, the AFDC program remained in effect until 1996, when the Temporary Assistance for Needy Families (TANF) program replaced it. TANF is a block grant program based on time-limited benefits and strict work participation requirements. Most of the families and children served by child welfare workers have been served at one time or another by AFDC or TANF.

In 1974, the federal government established a model statute for state child welfare agencies in an effort to standardize policy, programs, and practice. All fifty states have since enacted the model statute. The National Center for Child Abuse and Neglect within the Department of Health and Human Services is able to track trends in child maltreatment and the steadily rising demand for more protective services. Child abuse and neglect remains a major social problem; unfortunately, programs combating child maltreatment are inadequately funded, and the lack of funding constitutes one of the many occupational stressors experienced by child welfare professionals.

CHILD PROTECTION TODAY: THE CASEWORK METHOD

McDaniel and Lescher (2004) presented a concise list of the unique characteristics of child welfare casework that distinguish it from other publicly provided social services. Child welfare casework

- ◆ Emphasizes reaching out to children and families involved in child maltreatment
- ◆ Gives critical safety and risk assessment responsibilities
- ◆ Gives authority to protect children
- ◆ Requires knowledge of the law and the skillful use of the court
- ◆ May necessitate an immediate response
- ◆ Requires a careful balancing of the rights of involved parents, children, and society at large (p. 45)

Child welfare services are defined as specialized supports and interventions for neglected, abused, or exploited children and their families. Child welfare workers focus on rehabilitating the family and home through interventions and services that address the specific situations and conditions that lead to child maltreatment (Comstock & McDaniel, 2004, p. 50).

Comstock and McDaniel (2004) reported in their 1999 *Guidelines for a Model System for Abused and Neglected Children and Their Families* that the National Association of Public Child Welfare Administrators established the following mission of child welfare agencies: "To assess the safety of children, intervene to protect children from harm, strengthen the ability of families to protect their children, or provide an alternative safe family for the child. Child protective services (CPS) are provided to children and families by CPS agencies in collaboration with communities in order to protect children from abuse or neglect within their families" (p. 12).

Upon receiving a referral, the child welfare agency goes through the seven basic steps required by the casework process: (1) intake, (2) investigation, (3) family assessment, (4) service planning, (5) service provision, (6) monitoring of family progress and evaluation of case plan, and (7) case closure (Comstock & McDaniel, 2004, pp. 54–56).

Throughout the casework process, the child welfare worker strives to develop trust and a relationship with the family being helped. This collaborative helping relationship is based on the following principles, to which workers must adhere:

- An individual has the right to determine his or her own destiny, to make his or her own choices and decisions, and to deal with any resulting consequences of his or her action or inaction.
- An individual has the right to be treated with respect, regardless of weaknesses, faults, or conditions.
- An individual has the right to be accepted as a human being of worth, despite certain actions.
- An individual has the right to have personal information maintained in professional confidence. (Comstock & McDaniel, 2004, p. 56)

The child welfare worker has considerable authority concerning the protection of children and support of families. The family in need of assistance is well aware of the power that the worker possesses. Balancing the use of that authority within the helping relationship is an important and never-ending challenge for the worker. Use of collaboration with the family is always preferable to the power option, which is applied only after collaborative efforts have failed.

DANGER AND THE POTENTIAL FOR INJURY IN CHILD WELFARE WORK

As early as 1990, J. Donald Millar, director of the National Institute for Occupational Safety and Health, identified psychological disorders "as one of the 10 leading work-related diseases and injuries in the country today" (Dilworth, 1991b, p. 11; Millar, 1990). American psychologists and NIOSH agree that "stress-related disorders will be the most pervasive occupational diseases of the 21st century" (Dilworth, 1991a, p. 14).

Few occupations offer the high level of emotionally charged human engagement of child welfare work. Parents and other family members naturally harbor intense feelings about their children, regardless of the quality or skill of their familial interactions. In our training sessions with child welfare professionals, we have heard countless tales of violence aimed at these workers. Examples of such incidents run the gamut from verbal abuse and stalking to threatened, attempted, and sometimes completed physical assault. These are direct threats that produce occupational stress injuries that may result in symptoms of posttraumatic stress. Confronting the death of a child is another traumatic event that is all too common and produces the normal human responses to traumatic stress. Then there is work that produces similar reactions, which we have described as secondary traumatic stress. We know that STS affects other helping professionals who work with traumatized populations as well. For example, Horowitz, Wilner, and Alvarez's 1979 study (cited in Paton & Smith, 1996) showed that firefighters and social service workers were exposed to the same amount of traumatic events over a six-month period. However, the social service sample reported higher levels of symptoms of trauma than the firefighters (Paton & Smith, 1996, pp. 23–24).

Paton and Smith (1996) provided insight into the possible role of professional and/or personal preparation for traumatic events in professionals' development of symptoms related to trauma: "It could be inferred that, despite similar levels of exposure to traumatic events, the fire fighters' training and expectations increased their preparedness for at least some of the demands made upon them and reduced their risk status (in terms of symptom incidence). The higher risk status of the social services group, following this line of argument, could be attributed to a lack of preparedness for traumatic demands and this increased the level of threat to their professional and/or personal integrity that manifest itself in the observed symptomology" (p. 24). Paton and Smith (1996) argued that emergency response professions are not the only occupations in which workers are affected by traumatic stress and recommended that "the research and intervention net be cast wider to encompass these other groups" (p. 224). They are making the case for helping professionals, a group to which the child welfare occupation belongs, to be included in this type of research.

Peters (2001) presented a strong case for lawyers who regularly represent children to recognize and accept the fact that they are vulnerable to vicarious traumatization as a result of their work. She emphasized that "Indeed, it is the intensity of their compassion and empathy that creates tremendous strain on the lawyer's daily functioning" (Peters, 2001, p. 425). Compassion and empathy are the essential tools of the frontline child welfare professional. Surely, if lawyers representing traumatized children are in need of help, the workers who interact most closely with such children deserve attention as well.

The empirical connection we make with child welfare professionals and STS is a recent addition to the literature on both child welfare and traumatology and leads us to conclude that traumatic stress is an occupational hazard inherent to child welfare work. In chapter 3, we outlined personal strategies for the prevention of STS, and coping strategies should it occur. Chapter 4 presented proactive actions that organizations can take to minimize the likelihood of STS among its personnel and to help them cope when it occurs. What legal options do child welfare personnel have when STS occurs anyway?

WORKERS' COMPENSATION AS RELIEF: BACKGROUND

Before the mid-1800s, employers could not be held liable for injuries suffered by employees, because the employer had no duty to care for his employees. With the Industrial Revolution, laborers moved from the farms to the industrialized cities in order to find work. They were forced into hazardous jobs with long hours and unsafe working conditions. As a result, work-related injuries and illnesses became common.

Laws were enacted that were intended to redress injured laborers or their survivors. Duties to care were imposed on employers for the protection of the labor force. However, employers were able to defeat most of the tort actions brought against them. As a result, states enacted laws to protect workers. By the 1920s, all but eight states had adopted such laws, and by 1949 all states had workers' compensation laws. These "workers' compensation laws were enacted to mitigate litigation expenses for both sides and to eliminate the need for injured workers to prove their injuries were the employer's fault" ("Workers' Comp Injury Settlement," 2004).

Today, all states and the federal government have workers' compensation laws that address injuries and illnesses that happen in the course of employment. Workers' compensation awards are based on one's inability to earn a wage due to a job-related disability and are intended to be drawn upon only until the worker is able to resume a productive role in the workforce. An employee who accepts an award relinquishes the right to pursue any common-law claims against the employer regarding the injury for which he or she is being compensated.

It should be noted here that there is considerable precedent for compensation for posttraumatic stress disorder, of which STS is a form. Pensions were available for World War I veterans suffering from shell shock, the label for PTSD at that time (Pitman et al., 1994). Posttraumatic stress disorder became a recognized diagnosis in 1980 with the publication of the third edition of the *Diagnostic and Statistical Manual of Mental Disorders* (American Psychiatric Association, 1980). Sparr, White, Friedman, and Wiles (1994) stated that "Given the severely traumatic events associated with combat, PTSD logically represents the most compensable of mental disorders under veterans' disability benefits, a form of workers' compensation" (cited in Pitman, Sparr, Saunders, & McFarlane, 1996, p. 381). Members of the armed forces, police officers, firefighters, and child welfare workers share two things in common: they frequently encounter traumatic situations, and they are all government employees.

The Occupational Safety and Health Act of 1970 created the Occupational Safety and Health Administration (OSHA), which establishes standards for job safety and compliance. It also appointed the National Commission on State Workmen's Compensation Laws, a temporary organization representing the interests of federal and state governments, business, labor, and the general public. In 1972, the commission recommended a set of standards for state compensation that included these essential elements: "Compulsory coverage in all acts; elimination of all numerical and occupational exemptions to coverage, including domestic and farm labor; full coverage of work-related diseases; full medical and physical rehabilitation services without arbitrary limits; a broad extra-territoriality provision; elimination of arbitrary limits on duration and total sum of benefits; and a weekly benefit maximum that rises from an immediate 66⅔ percent to an ultimate 200 percent of average weekly wage in the state" (Larson & Larson, 2000, p. 27). During the ten years that followed, state workers' compensation laws were dramatically liberalized. It is noteworthy that the federal government left the workers' compensation systems in the hands of the states and has continued to do so to the present day.

Workers' compensation laws do not cover employees of state and local governments unless they are in a state with an OSHA-approved safety and health plan. Since the vast majority of child welfare work is done under the purview of state and local government, this could be a problem for states with no OSHA-approved plan. Fortunately, the vast majority of states do have approved plans.

State legislatures and courts administer workers' compensation programs within their separate jurisdictions. They are by no means standardized throughout the nation. Therefore a claim for workers' compensation in one state might be upheld, while the claim would be denied in a neighboring state. Three trends have developed since the mid-1980s. First, more and more states have written mediation and other forms of dispute resolution such as arbitration and the use of ombudsmen into their workers' compensation systems. Second, as federal legislation such as the Americans with Disabilities Act of 1990 has been enacted, attorneys have been working to discern the proper relationship and interaction between federal law and state-administered workers' compensation law. The third and most important trend is the move by several states to address such concerns as spiraling medical care costs, the increased complexity of contest administrative proceedings, and the widespread perception that claimant fraud is rampant. As a result, the vast majority of states have enacted laws to reduce employer costs (Larson & Larson, 2000, pp. 27–28). Such laws can involve "(1) Restrictions on the right of the claimant to choose his or her medical provider, (2) utilization of managed care, (3) anti-fraud provisions, (4) measures designed to reduce attorney involvement at the administrative level, (5) measures to encourage early resolution of claims, and (6) measures to reduce duplicate recovery among different reimbursement systems. Also, some of these measures have made it more difficult for claimants to prevail in cases involving preexisting conditions, 'mental-mental' or stress cases" (Larson & Larson, 2000, p. 28).

It is far beyond the scope of this book to examine the policies and practices of each state regarding workers' compensation. We will, however, attempt to provide an overview of how the system typically works as well as current trends and important developments.

WORKERS' COMPENSATION: GENERAL POLICY AND PRACTICE

In order to establish causal connection between the workplace and the injury or disease, almost all states have adopted the phrase "arising out of or in the course of employment" (Larson & Larson, 2000, p. 32). And most have adopted what is called the positional-risk doctrine. The full implications of the positional-risk test are explained by Larson and Larson (2000): "An injury arises out of the employment if it would not have occurred but for the fact that the conditions of the employment placed claimant in the position where he or she was injured" (p. 34). Under the positional-risk doctrine, we can find no reasonable excuse for denying a claim for post-traumatic stress disorder (either direct or indirect) in a situation in which the state has clearly placed the child welfare worker in harm's way by sending him or her to a run-down house in a drug-infested, crime-ridden neighborhood to remove a child and the worker sustains an occupational stress injury in the process.

Three categories of risk exist in workers' compensation law. Only one is universally compensable; this is the category on which we focus. "Risks distinctly associated with the employment" are clearly addressed by Larson and Larson (2000):

> This group comprises all the obvious kinds of injury that one thinks of as industrial injury. All the things that can go wrong around a modern factory, . . . machinery breaking, objects falling, . . . fingers getting caught in gears. . . . Equally obviously associated with employment, however, are also the occupational diseases, which as the very name implies, are produced by the . . . conditions inherent in the environment of the employment. As far as the "arising" test is concerned, this group causes no trouble, since all these risks fall readily within the increased-risk test and are considered work-connected in all jurisdictions. (p. 34)

WORKERS' COMPENSATION: FRAUD

We noted earlier that a widespread perception of welfare fraud has developed, and that most states have enacted laws to address this issue (Larson & Larson, 2000, p. 28). Most states require the posting of certain labor law information in a prominent place in the agency or business. These postings usually provide information on workers' compensation and warnings about fraud. The Alabama Labor Law Poster Service (Alabama, 2005) offers the following information about its workers' compensation program:

> STATE OF ALABAMA WORKERS' COMPENSATION INFORMATION If you are injured on the job, or contract an occupational disease, notify your employer immediately. Your employer will advise you of the physician to see for authorized treatment. WORKERS' COMP INSURANCE CARRIER: _____. TELEPHONE NUMBER _____ .

> Assistance is available under the Alabama workers' compensation law including mediation service. For information call: 1-800-_____. Department of Industrial Relations, Workers' Compensation Division, (Mailing Address). Code of Alabama, 1975, #25-5-290(d), requires that this notice be posted in one or more conspicuous places in your business.

> WORKERS' COMPENSATION FRAUD: It could be a ticket to jail! The Alabama Attorney General and the Alabama Department of Industrial Relations are working together to find and prosecute Workers' Compensation Fraud. Workers' Compensation Fraud is

STEALING! WANTED: Information Leading to the Discovery and or Conviction of Workers' Compensation Fraud. Making a false statement to obtain workers' compensation benefits (Ala. Criminal Code 13A-11-124) is a Class C Felony under Alabama law. False statements are punishable by up to $5,000 and up to 10 years in prison. Felony theft statutes may also apply. FIVE TYPES OF WORKERS' COMPENSATION FRAUD:

Agent————Employer————Employee————Medical————Legal

WORKERS' COMPENSATION FRAUD CAN BE:

- Reporting an off the job accident as an on the job accident.
- Reporting an accident that never happened.
- Complaints of accident injury symptoms that are exaggerated or non-existent.
- Malingering—to avoid work when injury is healed.
- Not reporting outside income from other work-related activities while drawing workers' compensation benefits from another employer.
- Making false or fraudulent statements for the purpose of obtaining workers' compensation benefits.

To Report Workers' Compensation Fraud: Call 800-____-_____ or 334-_____.

Both employees and employers can be guilty of workers' compensation fraud. The Alabama poster lists employer fraud as one of the five types of workers' compensation fraud. Interestingly, however, the specific actions constituting such fraud listed on the poster involve only employee misconduct. Larson and Larson devote an entire chapter to employer misconduct. Nonphysical injury to an employee caused by the employer can involve actual fraud and conspiracy. For example, if an employer "knowingly orders an employee to work in an unsafe environment, concealing the risk from him, and, after the employee had contracted an industrial disease, deliberately failing to notify the state, the employee, or doctors retained to treat him, of the disease and its connectivity with the employment, thereby aggravating the consequences of the disease" (Larson & Larson, 2000, p. 522). Larson and Larson offer as an example a case involving asbestos exposure. The employer knew that asbestos was dangerous. Still, he assured the employee that it was safe, and he failed to provide the employee with adequate protective equipment. In this case, the employer was sued by the employee.

It is easy to apply the logic of this asbestos case to child protection. Asbestos exposure is a threat to the industrial worker's health just as exposure to trauma is a threat to the health of the child welfare worker. Are agency administrators liable when they fail to protect their workers from exposure to trauma? We think so.

Sexual harassment is also a form of employer misconduct. Since the child welfare field overwhelmingly comprises women, this also needs attention. Sexual harassment is a form of gender discrimination, and there are two types. The first involves unwanted sexual advances. The second type is the creation of a hostile work environment because of an employee's gender. This type of hostile work environment has nothing to do with overt sexual activity but is a form of gender discrimination. It has to do with an employer intimidating (bullying) an employee (Larson

& Larson, 2000, p. 531) and treating employees differently according to their sex. This different treatment may extend to salary, discipline, feedback, and the assignment of work duties and workspace. It may take the form of verbal abuse. Employees may elect to sue in sexual harassment cases in most states.

Dangerous conditions—whether in the form of a direct physical threat to the worker or an indirect one created by the cumulative effect of empathically engaging with traumatized clients—exist in child protection throughout this country. It is time that public child welfare agencies acknowledge that these are risks distinctly associated with the work and take appropriate actions to address those risks and when necessary be prepared to mitigate the effects of traumatic stress within the workforce.

EMPLOYERS' DUTY TO CARE

Statutory provisions and common sense require employers, including public child welfare agencies, to ensure the health and safety of their employees at work. Employers are required to provide a safe workplace, as well as such information, training, and supervision necessary to minimize health and safety hazards in the work environment.

In order to perform their duty to care, employers must conduct thorough assessments to determine the specific risks to the physical and mental health of their employees. Then, on the basis of what is discovered in the risk assessment, they must develop and implement policies and practices to avert personal injury, either physical, mental, or both. Child welfare employers must consider stress a threat to their employees' mental as well as physical health.

Having identified health and safety risks, employers must introduce health surveillance when

- there is an identifiable disease or adverse health condition related to the work concerned;
- there are valid techniques available to detect indication of the disease or condition;
- there is a reasonable likelihood that the disease or condition may occur under the particular conditions of work; and
- surveillance is likely to further the protection of the health of the employees to be covered. ("Stress at Work," 1995, p. 4)

Surveillance may include medical examinations of employees' physical and mental health by qualified clinicians.

All four requirements indicating a need for health surveillance exist in the child welfare work environment. Posttraumatic stress, either primary, secondary, or both, is an identifiable adverse health condition related to the work. Adequate and effective techniques are readily available to detect the condition. We have shown empirically that traumatic stress is inherent to child welfare work. Medical examinations and such procedures as the Compassion Fatigue Self-Test (Figley,

1995) may result in early detection, early treatment, and therefore a better chance of recovery.

The employer fails in his or her duty to care when he or she fails to "take reasonable care to prevent *reasonably foreseeable risks*. It follows that an employer will be regarded as negligent if it does not take reasonable steps to eliminate a risk which it knows or *ought to know* is a real risk, and not merely a possibility which would not influence the mind of a reasonable employer in the circumstances" ("Stress at Work," 1995, p. 6).

Just as a prudent military commander would not send troops into battle without the means to fight and win, the child welfare administrator or supervisor should never send his or her workers into the field without the means to defend and protect themselves.

WORKERS' COMPENSATION: DEFINING INJURY

While workers' compensation laws vary by state, some generalizations can be made. The role of physical injury is important to understand. The laws concerning workers' compensation were first drafted to deal with physical injury, and these are quite easy to deal with judicially. An industrial worker who suffers a broken arm from a fall off a ladder is likely to be compensated for that injury until he heals and is able to return to the workforce. Purely physical situations are usually clear cut, but when mental injuries are added to the laws, as has happened in recent years, the matter becomes much more complex.

Three broad categories should be considered when mental or emotional stimulus or injury is in play. The late Professor Arthur Larson, a renowned expert in the field of workers' compensation, analyzed these three categories of "psychic injury" at some length (Larson & Larson, 2000, p. 262).

The first is when a physical stimulus causes a mental injury—the physical-mental category. For example, a child welfare worker who is attacked by a machete-wielding father and suffers cuts and bruises before a sheriff's deputy kills the attacker with a handgun may develop PTSD symptoms. She may be unable to work due to the severity of those symptoms and may need treatment for PTSD as well as for her physical wounds. A court would have little difficulty awarding in her favor because of the physical stimulus.

The second category involves a mental stimulus that causes a physical injury—the mental-physical category. For example, a child welfare worker is notified that an angry foster father is holding a child on her caseload hostage in the family's home. The father has fired on police officers who are trying to defuse the situation. In driving home from the scene, the traumatized worker drives too fast and has a serious accident, wrecking the county automobile she is driving. She sustains serious head and chest injuries and requires hospitalization. The court in this case might take her mental state into consideration in deciding whether or not to find in her favor on her workers' compensation claim.

The third category, and by far the most complex, occurs when mental stimuli cause mental injury—the mental-mental category. State legislatures and courts have developed different tests for determining whether or not to award compensation for such injuries. While most states have awarded compensation for mental-mental claims under some circumstances, some states still flatly refuse to do so under any circumstances. However, more and more states are recognizing and accepting stress-related claims (Dilworth, 1991b). Some states require the mental injury to have been caused by a sudden traumatic shock. Others recognize that psychological disabilities can also be caused by gradual, protracted, and/or cumulative emotional stress (Gelman, 1989). In child welfare work, where both primary and secondary traumatic stressors are all too common, either type of causation could be applicable.

WORKERS' COMPENSATION AND PTSD: A PSYCHIATRIST'S PERSPECTIVE

Any workers' compensation claim for the effects of either primary or secondary traumatic stress must meet the diagnostic criteria for PTSD in the latest edition of the *Diagnostic and Statistical Manual of Mental Disorders,* published by the American Psychiatric Association. Assessing PTSD in a claimant is often problematic for mental health professionals called in to make diagnostic determinations. James O'Brien, M.D., a forensic psychiatrist practicing in Southern California, observed that PTSD is one of the most common conditions in workers' compensation claims relating to stress. His opinion is that the principal problem is overdiagnosis by applicant-appointed clinicians.

O'Brien pointed out that conflicts with supervisors and chronic illness normally do not meet the strict diagnostic criteria in the *DSM,* but sometimes clinicians try to include these things in the PTSD assessment. He pointed out that a less common problem for clinicians is when the claimant has a history of past trauma unrelated to the work environment and has apparently resolved that issue with no impairment. The claimant may then confuse past trauma with an unpleasant interaction in the workplace. The clinician must sort out what is work related and what is not.

O'Brian (n.d.) observed from his experience that there are "four conditions necessary for the successful resolution of a workers' compensation claim for PTSD" (p. 2). These conditions are "(1) a motivated patient, (2) a motivated or at least facilitative employer who can accommodate reasonable recommended work restrictions (such as day duty only), (3) the relative absence of complicating pre-existent psychological factors, such as drug abuse, alcoholism, job dissatisfaction or severe personality disorder, and (4) a therapist who will encourage the patient to re-acclimate to the workplace and not allow the patient's condition to worsen by endlessly extending disability" (p. 2).

O'Brien pointed out the possibility of claimant malingering and offered some suggestions for clinicians to determine whether or not that is occurring. He stated that early diagnosis is important, and that aggressive treatment should begin as soon as possible. He cited, as have we, the importance of critical incident debriefing as an early intervention for all victims. He closed with an admonishment for management that we think quite pertinent for the child welfare environment: "Even under the best of conditions, treatment is often difficult. Being a workers' compensation claimant often creates its own stress. If a patient is the victim of multiple crimes in a site with lax security and the employer does not aggressively address employee safety problems, the resentment and feelings of abandonment by the employee can lead to irreconcilable hatred and dissolution of the employee-employer relationship" (O'Brien, n.d., p. 2).

WORKERS' COMPENSATION: STRESS CLAIMS AND STATES' REACTIONS

During the 1970s, state courts and legislatures began developing standards for dealing with mental-mental or stress claims. As a result, a variety of processes developed throughout the country. California's experience is documented by Larson and Larson (2000): "In 1982, the California Court of Appeals let stand an award for mental stress caused by the claimant's 'honest misperception of job harassment which interact[ed] with [her] preexisting psychiatric condition.' The breadth of coverage implied by the court's holding is hard to overstate: Compensability was judged purely on the claimant's subjective perception of work stressors, not objective reality. In addition, the claimant's susceptibility to mental stress, due to a preexisting psychiatric condition, was not considered an alternative cause of her injury" (p. 255).

As a result, California's reported workers' compensation stress claims rose from 1,282 in 1980 to 4,236 in 1984 and to 6,812 in 1986. Larson and Larson speculated that the actual number of claims may have been ten times as high as reported. These claims were very costly, causing worry about the cost of doing business in California and concern about what was believed to be widespread fraud in mental-mental cases.

The California legislature acted to address these concerns. Between 1989 and 1993, the following statutory measures were put in place to limit stress claims:

> (1) A claim must be based on "actual" employment conditions, which must be shown to be a "predominant cause" of the mental injury; whereas exposure to a violent act need only be a "substantial cause" thereof; (2) claims must be proved by a preponderance of the evidence; (3) mental illnesses are evaluated according the diagnostic standards developed by the American Psychiatric Association; (4) no mental injury claims may be filed until the employee has worked for the employer for six months; (5) no mental injury claim may be founded on a good faith personnel action such as discharge or demotion; and (6) the post-employment filing of claims is sharply limited. (Larson & Larson, 2000, p. 256)

Several other states have amended their laws to more strictly limit stress claims. Some states refuse to award stress claims unless the stress is caused by a physical injury. Essentially, Larson and Larson saw state legislature restrictions as falling into five broad categories: (1) those requiring a certain level of stress, (2) those raising the standard of causation, (3) those increasing the burden of proof,

(4) those imposing specific diagnostic guidelines, and (5) those limiting benefits. A few states award benefits for stress claims under occupational disease standards without differentiating between mental and physical injuries.

"OCCUPATIONAL DISEASE": THE CASE OF *FAIRFAX COUNTY V. MOTTRAM*

The Virginia Supreme Court's decision in *Fairfax County Fire and Rescue Department v. Mottram* (2002) was an important development regarding workers' compensation claims for PTSD. Although the case involved emergency services personnel, one can reasonably postulate that the findings of the court create a precedent that might apply to child welfare workers as well.

Before *Fairfax County v. Mottram,* Virginia law limited claims for PTSD to cases arising from a single critical incident. In this case, however, as summarized by Lindahl (2004), "The court held that PTSD resulting from multiple traumatic stressors may be considered a compensable occupational disease analogous to dermatitis developed by a flower shop employee with chronic exposure to irritating stimuli. The decision, which constitutes legal recognition of work-related cumulative PTSD in rescue workers, provides benefits for treatment and encourages earlier treatment of traumatic stress in this group" (p. 543).

The Virginia code defines "occupational disease" as "a disease out of and in the course of employment, but not an ordinary disease of life to which the general public is exposed outside of employment" (*Fairfax County v. Mottram,* 2002, p. 374). Six factors are necessary in order to establish that a disease arose out of employment. Lindahl (2004) summarized the six as those "(1) involving a 'direct causal connection between the conditions under which work is performed and the occupational disease'; (2) occurring 'as a result of the exposure occasioned by the nature of the employment'; (3) 'fairly traced to the employment as the proximate cause'; (4) not resulting from 'exposure outside of the employment'; (5) 'incidental to the character of the business'; and (6) having 'its origin in a risk connected with the employment and flowing from that source as a natural consequence'" (p. 545).

Fairfax County v. Mottram is a major contribution to laws regarding PTSD and workers' compensation, at least in Virginia. Child welfare professionals and the attorneys who represent them will do well to carefully monitor developments in their respective states.

CHILD WELFARE, PTSD, AND WORKERS' COMPENSATION: ELEMENTS OF A CLAIM

We believe that we have made the case that posttraumatic stress, the causation of which may be either primary, secondary, or a combination of both, is a major occupational strain that may result in stress injury for child welfare personnel. While the individual and the agency can do much to mitigate the effects of such stress, it cannot be prevented from occurring from time to time. When that happens to the extent that a worker can no longer perform the tasks required of the job, and when the cause clearly arises out of and in the course of employment, the injured worker is entitled to workers' compensation. We believe that such compensation means salary replacement while a worker is temporarily disabled; monetary compensation in the event of permanent disability; access to health care and medication; and, if the worker cannot return to child welfare work, retraining for employment in another field.

As previously emphasized, workers' compensation laws vary from state to state, but it is logical to postulate that a claim should meet certain standards if the claimant's case is to be made. First, the claimant must have suffered a personal injury by either a sudden traumatic event or the accumulation of a number of traumatic events over time. The trauma may be derived from either primary or secondary causes. This is crucial in claims based on PTSD, because symptoms may not appear for months or even years after the traumatic events. Of course, the injury must have occurred during the course of employment, and it must have arisen due to the employment.

Second, the injury must be defined as a diagnosable mental disorder recognized by the most current edition of the *Diagnostic and Statistical Manual of Mental Disorders*. Personality disorders are excluded because they are preexisting conditions and therefore cannot arise out of the employment.

Third, at least one medical professional with expert knowledge of the conditions claimed as injury must examine and verify the condition via competent diagnosis in accordance with the *DSM*. Since the burden of proof rests with the claimant in workers' compensation cases, the more experts who agree on the diagnosis, the better. Any preexisting conditions must be considered during this examination phase. Finally, this expert testimony must attribute the cause of the injury to the claimant's exposure to trauma within the course of and arising out of the conditions of employment.

One final note of singular importance: there can be no time limits from the occurrence of the traumatic events to notice of claim to the employer in PTSD cases as long as the specifier "with delayed onset" appears in the *DSM*'s discussion of the condition. It has been thoroughly demonstrated by war veterans and others that PTSD symptoms frequently do not manifest themselves until months or years after the trauma. Politicians who have written restrictions into workers' compensation law in an effort to limit such claims in spite of the *DSM* do a disservice to the child welfare workforce.

Traumatic Stress, Social Work Education, Child Welfare, and Research

SOCIAL WORK PROFESSIONALS WORK WITH PEOPLE WHO HAVE EXPERI-enced trauma and victimization. The traumatic events may include the sexual or physical abuse of children, rape, domestic and familial abuse and violence, crime, genocide, and wars. And as recent events have shown, environmental and natural disasters such as floods, storms, and fires also result in trauma. McCann, Sakheim, and Abrahamson (1988) reviewed prevalence studies that indicate the world is full of human suffering. Child welfare practitioners intervene daily in situations in which children and adults are suffering from traumatic experiences. In many different client populations, workers encounter burns, broken bones, cuts, and bruises on people who have experienced powerful and potentially destructive emotions such as despair, terror, and feelings of worthlessness.

A rapidly expanding body of knowledge has enabled social work education and training to address psychological trauma and to teach students how to help their clients heal. However, despite two decades of growth in the field of traumatology, little attention has been given to educating social workers to recognize their vulnerability to secondary traumatic stress and to cope with its effects. Therefore, social workers may develop STS, and it may go untreated or they may mistake it for burnout and leave the profession (Pryce & Knox, 1999).

As the social worker develops STS, the worker's empathy and hope for the client's healing may give way to cynicism and doubt that the client will grow and change. The social worker's introspective questioning of his or her level of competence affects the worker-client relationship from assessment through intervention to termination. If the worker draws negative conclusions about his or her abilities, the worker's ability to help the client heal may be undermined. Over time, STS can challenge the social worker's idealism and optimism and then may cause the worker to have doubts about what the profession is supposed to accomplish. It may also be internalized in such a way as to affect the social worker's psychological and physical health, behavior, and interpersonal relationships.

Traumatology, as a field, has grown exponentially as traumatologists have learned more about the effects of traumatic stress on individuals, families, groups, organizations, and communities (Morrissette, 2004). With the development of the PTSD diagnosis in 1980, many helping professions became interested in working with trauma victims, long a tradition in the social work profession. In social work, we have not been attentive to the social worker and his or her needs beyond concerns about factors influencing therapeutic effectiveness such as transference, countertransference, general stress, and the catchall category "burnout." The subjective experience of the social worker, student or practitioner, who works with trauma victims has not been adequately addressed. Hence, social workers who work with traumatized client populations, such as child welfare workers, often have minimal knowledge about STS and how it may affect them. This is not surprising, as STS is not commonly discussed in social work textbooks (Pryce & Knox, 1999).

Studies have shown secondary traumatic stress to be harmful to social workers and other trauma workers, and researchers have proclaimed that social workers must be educated regarding how to recognize the symptoms and understand the process of vicarious traumatization and how to cope with the effects of indirect trauma as they become involved with traumatized clients (Bell, Kulkarni, & Dalton, 2003; Cunningham, 2003, 2004; Dane, 2000; Figley, 1995; Fournier, 2002; Maidment, 2003; Nelson-Gardell & Harris, 2003; Pearlman & Saakvitne, 1995). This learning must take place at both the baccalaureate and graduate levels of social work education.

In the first known study of the inclusion of indirect trauma in the undergraduate social work curricula, Shackelford (2006) explored whether or not social work programs are teaching the information and skills needed to recognize, understand, and cope with the effects of indirect trauma. The main objective of the study was to determine if BSW students are learning about the effects that working with victims of trauma could have on them and if they are learning how to cope with secondary traumatic stress, vicarious traumatization, and compassion fatigue. Shackelford's findings showed that recently graduated BSW social workers in the United States do not have adequate knowledge of indirect trauma. A survey distributed to these graduates explored their knowledge of vicarious traumatization, secondary traumatic stress, and compassion fatigue, as well as burnout, countertransference, and posttraumatic stress disorder. Every respondent recognized the term "posttraumatic stress disorder," and 99 percent of the respondents recognized "burnout." Only 37 to 60 percent of the respondents to this survey recognized the various terms associated with indirect trauma. Recognition of a term is one of the lowest levels of intellectual skills (Bloom, 1956). On average, respondents answered half of the questions regarding indirect trauma, its effects on the worker, and the coping skills needed to manage the effects correctly. This showed a lack of knowledge of the possible effects of working with traumatized clients and a lack of knowledge regarding coping strategies that mitigate the negative effects of this work. The recently graduated BSW students responding to this survey had fewer sources of information concerning indirect trauma than they had for posttraumatic stress disorder, countertransference, and burnout. They also reported that the trauma-related topics mentioned most frequently in the classroom were burnout and posttraumatic stress disorder in clients. Most often, the effects of indirect trauma were discussed in lectures concerning social worker self-care. Recently graduated BSW students were found to lack the knowledge and understanding of indirect trauma that is needed to protect them from harm that might occur professionally and personally as a result of their work with traumatized clients.

Social workers need to be educated about STS. Social work education has not kept pace with the rapidly expanding body of knowledge on traumatic stress and its effects on social workers. Many social workers enter the field with little or no knowledge of the phenomenon, and their supervisors are ill prepared to deal with adversely affected workers, whom they must support and manage (Shulman, 1993). Social workers need education regarding effective self-care and coping skills, and how to make discriminating decisions when seeking social support in the work environment versus support from family and friends. Social work educators must incorporate this body of knowledge into the curriculum to ensure that practitioners enter the field both aware and capable of dealing effectively with STS as an occupational hazard (Shulman, 1993; Stamm, 1995). STS cannot be prevented since it is a normal human and universal response to secondhand exposure to violence, disasters, and other types of trauma. The adverse effects of STS can be prevented from developing into a disorder (Figley, 1995).

Students who have taken one of the author's university courses on STS have returned to report that when they started to be affected by the work, they knew what was happening and what to do about it. Practitioners exposed to STS education in agency training sessions and in undergraduate and graduate child welfare courses that included a training module on STS have reported similar experiences. Management of STS is essential to mitigating its negative effects. Students and practitioners can learn to cope with and manage STS.

LESSONS LEARNED FROM TEACHING TRAUMATIC STRESS

We have learned several lessons as we have worked to integrate primary and secondary traumatic stress into the social work curriculum. Our experiences are similar to those of other authors such as Cunningham (2004) and McCammon (1999). A fully developed university-level course on STS and social work has been included as an appendix to this volume. One of the issues that educators should prepare for and address is that many social work students have personal trauma histories. In some cases the traumatic experience has been resolved, and the student has gained meaning from it. When a student has not resolved the experience, he or she may want to use the class and/or the professor for therapy. In developing the syllabus and in introducing the course, it is important for the professor to establish that the course may bring up past issues for students and that the best place for students to work through those issues is the counseling center. It is important to advise the director of the counseling center or other appropriate person that you may be making student referrals to them.

Sometimes students will come in for a meeting about academic matters and the conversation will turn to personal traumatic experiences that are similar to what is being discussed in class. This is a boundary alert! It is important for the professor to maintain boundaries. When it is appropriate, the professor may offer to walk the student to the counseling center after it is made clear to the student why the professor cannot act as his or her therapist. Even if the professor is fully qualified to perform trauma counseling, to do so would be to enter into a dual relationship with the student. The professor who embarks on teaching a course on traumatic stress must always be alert so that boundaries are not crossed.

One of the ways we prepare students for traumatic content is to encourage them to stay in a cognitive and learning mode. In training sessions we have urged them to think about their feelings. We want to keep the student from becoming overwhelmed by his or her emotional reactions to traumatic content. We have been told that this is helpful, but it is sometimes difficult not to become emotional. This is also a way of teaching anticipatory coping for when the social worker has powerful and negative feelings toward clients but must maintain appropriate professional behavior. It is important to validate strong responses to trauma and also to teach how those reactions can be managed. This approach is also a method of building resilience in the student.

Students need to be taught early in the class how a personal trauma history can affect their work with clients, especially if it is unresolved and the student is still struggling with it. Students can be encouraged to learn from the class content. They can assess where they think they are developmentally with their experience and if they have derived personal meaning from it. They can be encouraged to determine how their cognitive schemata have been affected by the traumatic experience. This may be done privately, or the student, if comfortable, may want to share his or her experience with the class. This is different from the student using the class as a medium for obtaining counseling. This technique requires the professor's professional judgment in determining what disclosure is appropriate for class discussion. The line between learning from each other and counseling each other should not be crossed. The professor needs to include content that provides empirical evidence of what is known about STS and about how personal experience of trauma makes a practitioner vulnerable.

Students, with guidance from the professor, will need to develop rules for the class. First students should be taught that traumatic experience is highly individualized and everyone must agree to respect this in the sharing of experiences and reactions to case examples. Students must know that without this agreement, it is possible to further traumatize another person by disbelieving or dismissing his or her experience. The professor can also help students understand that it is through diversity, or sharing our differences, that we learn much about ourselves. The professor should also discuss what is and what is not appropriate to share in class. Before sharing personal experience, the student should be instructed to ask him- or herself what the purpose of sharing is. For example, Is sharing this adding to the learning of fellow classmates, or is it fulfilling my own needs? What reaction am I looking for from the other students and the professor? If sympathy or counseling is the answer, then the student should see a therapist.

When the professor is lecturing and using videos or other materials, it is important to be explicit about what the content is and the impact it may have. If the content or experience of the visual imagery is disturbing, then a student may choose to leave the class. It is important for the student to reflect on why it was important to distance him- or herself from that specific content.

One professor used a film from Walter Reed Medical Center as an introduction to traumatic experience. The film shows graphic scenes of actual combat, wounds, and the injured being cared for in the hospital. The gunfire and emergency room scenes are very loud and disturbing. The professor explained this to the class and said that anyone could leave temporarily if it was overwhelming. After the beginning of the video, a few students chose to leave, while others did not. After viewing the five-minute film, the class talked about their feelings, thoughts, and other reactions to being a witness to such traumatic experiences.

At the end of the class, an older student followed the professor back to the office and explained that he was angry with the professor for showing the film. The result of the ensuing discussion was that the student remained angry. The professor reminded the student that he had had the option to leave if the content was too disturbing. This is an example of how students may project unresolved issues onto the professor. This does not mean that media displaying traumatic content should not be shown. Educators are responsible for preparing students for the real life experiences they will find themselves in upon becoming social workers. It does mean that educators should prepare themselves for students' emotional responses.

In classes and courses dealing with traumatic stress, it is wise to have two instructors or at least a teaching assistant. There may be times when a student loses his or her composure and needs immediate assistance. That can be done outside the classroom so that the class is not disrupted, the individual's privacy is protected, and his or her needs are met.

Student presentations should take place after students have learned the course content. This prepares them to learn how to share traumatic content and how to listen or be a witness to another human being's experience. The student presentations may involve students' own traumatic experiences, their experience of secondary trauma, or a fictional but realistic story that they tell. In organizing the presentations it is helpful to be sure that students are not all presenting the same type of experience in the same class period. It also helps for students to compare and contrast the experiences shared in facilitated discussion.

As we know, traumatic stress can be contagious. As students make their presentations, members of the class may become affected by what they hear. At the end of presentations, and before the students leave, it is important to have some time to debrief what has been said and what has been learned. Students often arrive at powerful insights following presentations about themselves and their peers.

Finally, the professor needs to have an understanding of his or her own philosophies and spiritual beliefs and how he or she arrived at them. The content of a traumatic stress course can raise important existential questions and questions about spirituality. Often students want to put their experiences into a philosophical and/or spiritual context. Traumatic experiences can raise questions about why the experience happened (Calhoun & Tedeschi, 1999): "Why did this happen to me?" "Am I a bad person?" "Am I being punished for something I did?" If the professor can provide the student the means to constructively examine his or her experience in the context of his or her beliefs, the professor may help students to better understand traumatic experiences. Clients may want their social workers to discuss spiritual issues related to traumatic experiences, and they should be prepared to do so. Students can learn not to impose their own beliefs on their clients but share them in appropriate ways.

Calhoun and Tedeschi (1999) provided an excellent description of what a good spiritual outcome from traumatic experience might be: "The ultimate arbiter of posttraumatic growth in spiritual and religious matters is the client. If the individual's struggle with trauma leads him or her to experience a better understanding of spiritual or existential matters, if the individual experiences a strengthening of freely chosen spiritual commitments, if the individual undergoes an increased sense of purpose and meaning, or if the individual selects a new and better life course, then there has been a good outcome. We are making the assumption that the choices and changes are good" (p. 121).

Social workers have long believed that human beings can grow and find meaning in the face of adversity (McMillen, 1999). Students can be educated to understand the role that hope plays for people when traumatic events happen to them. Without hope, there is no future, and no belief that something good can develop from something bad. McMillen (1999) pointed out that "perceptions of benefit appear to be more that just a Pollyannaish denial of negative consequences" (p. 457). Traumatic events are harmful, but people can and do grow from them and discover their own resilience. McMillen (1999) proposed that "adverse events can lead to changes in life structure, views of self and others, and in interpretation about meaning and purpose in life" (p. 458). Hope is part of what social work brings to the people with whom we work.

INCLUSION OF TRAUMATIC STRESS IN THE SOCIAL WORK CURRICULUM

We think that, given the extent of human suffering, traumatic stress needs to be both taught in independent courses devoted to the subject and integrated into standard courses. Students should be prepared to manage themselves concerning the traumatic events in their clients' lives. If they can be given knowledge about traumatic stress and how it can affect them through their work, they will be better protected and so will their work with clients. In chapter 6, we noted that the number of mental-stress workers' compensation claims is projected to rise sharply in the future. Students need to be prepared for work with traumatized clients so that they do not become one of those projected statistics.

THE IMPORTANCE OF TRAUMATIC STRESS TO CHILD WELFARE EDUCATION

There is no question for us that students committed to child welfare need to be educated about traumatic stress and the impact that empathic engagement can have on their well-being. Future child welfare workers need to know about self-care from a personal and professional perspective. With educational preparation, students can begin anticipatory coping, developing self-care plans, and understanding their own trauma histories and how these may affect their work with clients. In addition, each student's goal is to build resilience and understand that just as clients grow and prosper through adversity, so will they.

HOW TO INTEGRATE TRAUMATIC STRESS INTO THE CURRICULUM

One of the authors of this book teaches Human Behavior in the Social Environment to graduate students. The students are required write a paper analyzing their own development, including any traumatic experiences they have had. The paper is written under a fictitious name known only to the professor. The student is required to use the course content to analyze his or her own development from childhood to the present. The student also analyzes any traumatic experiences he or she has had and puts these experiences in the context of theory, changed cognitive schemata, and what meaning the experiences have come to have for the student. The student also reflects on how these experiences may come up in the context of future social work practice and how the student will manage and cope. An alternative assignment is for the student to create a fictitious character and develop the paper in the same manner. This allows students who may be reluctant to write about their personal histories to participate meaningfully in the learning experience.

Policy courses are another part of the curriculum into which trauma can be integrated. Students should understand that as social workers they are responsible for self-care and that they need to advocate for it in their agencies. Nowhere is this advocacy more important than in the child welfare agency. Students can be given case scenarios in which trauma work is taking place in the agency. The students, in the role of administrators, are to develop policies for the organization that will mitigate the effects of both primary and secondary traumatic stress. Students should analyze their policies by examining them in terms of four criteria: (1) effectiveness, (2) efficiency, (3) administrative feasibility, and (4) political feasibility (Rudolph & Stamm, 1999, p. 281). Students discuss their policies in light of each criterion and answer the following questions, explaining how they arrived at the answers. They should also explain how they will implement the STS policy and evaluate it. The first question could be, How will the proposed strategy mitigate primary and secondary traumatic stress in the organization? The answer to this question is found in evidence-based research.

The next question might be, Are these policies efficient? The students then evaluate the possible positive and negative effects, outcomes, and potentially unintended outcomes the policies may have. Students have to think through potential financial costs to the agency. Then they must identify one benefit that counters each cost (Rudolph & Stamm, 1999, p. 282). For example, dollars spent on prevention, safety, and psychoeducation for STS may contribute to reductions in child welfare worker turnover.

The third set of questions addresses administrative feasibility (Rudolph & Stamm, 1999, p. 283). What organizational structures will be changed to implement the policy? What will the total fiscal cost be to the organization? What activities will it take to implement and maintain the policy change? Will there be a burden on workers when the policy is implemented?

Finally, there are questions involving internal and external political feasibility (Rudolph & Stamm, 1999, p. 283). What impact will the implementation of the policy change have on other policies, procedures, and practices? Also, does the organization have to have commitment to the proposed policies from external agencies? The professor can use another policy analysis model to explore the issue if it seems more appropriate.

RESEARCH ISSUES: HOW WE CAN BE CHANGED BY WHAT WE STUDY

In the process of writing this book, and in past years, we have found ourselves experiencing dreams, sometimes nightmares, intrusive thoughts, and sleep disturbances. Clearly, we have been affected by teaching about traumatic stress, as well as the research we have conducted. Listening to the experiences of child welfare workers was essential to understanding their experience, but it has changed us also. We believe that our reactions have contributed to this research. By studying our own reactions, we were able to gain a stronger understanding of the impact traumatic stress has on child welfare workers.

Students can also be affected by what they study when they do research on traumatic stress. They may also be affected when trauma is revealed unexpectedly. This happened recently when a student was interviewing homeless women and discovered that many of them were homeless due to domestic violence. Upon listening to the details of the violence, the student became distressed. She reported that she continued to think about the trauma the women experienced throughout the semester.

In studying traumatic stress, the researcher needs to practice the same self-care strategies that we would teach child welfare practitioners. Self-care needs to be both personal and professional. Staying present for family members is just as important to a researcher studying traumatic stress as it is for the child welfare practitioner. Similarly, the memories of and reactions to the researcher's own traumatic experiences may be triggered by the research. It is critical for researchers not to let their own experiences bias the work they do. If the trauma is particularly horrible, the researcher may want to process the content with a counselor to help manage the effects.

A RESEARCH AGENDA: WHAT WE NEED TO KNOW

There is much we need to know. Our review of empirical literature does not produce a consistent pattern of findings, and perhaps that is because the field is relatively new. From our perspective, social work researchers have much to contribute to this field of study.

We need to know more about personal characteristics that make child welfare workers vulnerable to STS. It appears that there may be a correlation regarding at least one variable, and that is the age of the worker. Younger people appear to be more affected than older people. Considering that the older a person is, the more coping resources he or she brings to child welfare, it seems logical that younger people are more likely to be affected by STS. We need more data to know if this relationship is constant. If it is, the policy implications are clear. Younger workers do not need to be managing the most traumatic cases when they enter the child welfare system. There is evidence that it takes two to three years to become competent in all aspects of the job.

Once the practitioner understands the work, then slowly giving him or her more traumatic cases may keep the practitioner from becoming overwhelmed. During this time, supervision should be intensive because the worker lacks experience working in the more serious, high-risk cases. The supervisor and mentor can work with the practitioner to monitor his or her reactions to the work and the way he or she may be affected. This practice should be evaluated to determine if it contributes to worker retention.

We are in a good position to determine if education about STS in schools of social work makes a difference to retention in child welfare. It would be an interesting and useful research project to identify students entering child welfare who have received education about STS and to determine what impact, if any, that knowledge and resultant self-care practices have on them in their roles as practitioners. Education may make a difference.

Child welfare practitioners who are already in the field need education in STS as well. We have seen an overwhelmingly positive response from those who have attended our STS workshops. However, this educational process needs a more intensive evaluation. Is a onetime introduction to STS sufficient, or do child welfare practitioners need ongoing education? Given the turnover in child welfare, it appears that an ongoing program of STS education would be useful.

In a similar vein, we have argued that peer support in the workplace is extremely important to supervisors and caseworkers. Both groups should have opportunities to talk about the work and how it affects them. The benefit is that supervisors and caseworkers are not all likely to be adversely affected by the work at the same time. This means that individuals who need to process difficult cases can do so while other members of the group can be supportive and offer advice if it is requested. Such groups reduce the isolating effects of STS. It should be noted that it is also an opportunity to share success stories and discuss why those cases were successful. We need further evaluation of peer support groups such as these, and what impact they have on workers, supervisors, and client outcomes. The evaluation should include any potential negative outcomes the group may have. Both the process and formation of the group as well as the outcome can be studied.

We also need to understand the impact this work has on workers' family members. There have been studies of how the family members of other professionals are affected by the work they do. We need to know how family members perceive child welfare work and how the family supports the practitioner. Is there a need to intervene with family members so that the family can be more supportive of the practitioner and better understand his or her work? Clearly, spouses of soldiers need to understand combat stress and PTSD and how it may affect them and their children. Is there any reason to think that this need is somehow different for child welfare practitioners' families? We tend to think not.

PERSONAL CHARACTERISTICS AND STS

We still need to deepen our understanding of how social work and child welfare practitioners are affected by STS and what the best-practice response to it is. Bride (2004) asserted that we need a better understanding of academic and professional roles in relation to STS. We also need to understand the relationships among age, gender, ethnicity, spirituality or existential beliefs, educational degree, level of degree, length of professional experience, childhood trauma and other personal trauma history, personal and professional social support, positive and negative coping strategies, and the use of empathy in relation to STS. While some research has been done, we need more, and we need longitudinal studies on these areas of focus. Along with correlations, we need to use statistical modeling to determine the individual contribution each variable makes to STS as well as the shared variance. We also need to know what, if any, interactions exist between the variables and their relationship to STS.

Child welfare workers will readily share how their interpersonal relations with significant others are affected by the work they do. They will also share that their sex lives are often compromised because of cases involving sexual abuse. Intimacy, a cognitive schema, is altered because of what the child welfare practitioner experiences in his or her work. We don't know how to intervene in this problem. We have argued, along with others, that people who do trauma work should not be harmed by the work they do. One of the most important facets of human experience should not be lost because of this work. We need to know more about how to protect workers' most intimate relationships and what keeps them from being damaged.

Another area in which we want to deepen our understanding is the nature of the relationship between STS and burnout in child welfare. When does the combination become compassion fatigue? Does STS precede burnout, or do they develop simultaneously? Can we identify the nature of the trauma in child welfare cases that is most predictive of the development of STS? Does compassion satisfaction buffer either STS or burnout? Are there differences in how STS and burnout affect different areas of child welfare practice such as child protective services and foster care? These questions and others need to be researched so that we may achieve a better understanding of these phenomena.

Clearly, we are concerned about the mental health of child welfare workers. We are also concerned about their physical health. It has been demonstrated that posttraumatic stress is highly correlated with women's general health problems. Child welfare workers are quick to relate physical health problems to the work. Is it possible that STS compromises the immune system? We need to know if STS produces physiological problems and neurochemical changes similar to those caused by primary traumatic stress. If so, then similar interventions can be studied to determine if they are effective and if they hasten recovery from STS.

Coping, social support, resiliency, and their relationship to STS need thorough examination. All three are complex variables, and it has been argued that positive coping strategies such as anticipatory coping and social support contribute to resiliency in child welfare workers and to the management of STS. Is resiliency the ability to recover from STS, or does it protect the worker from experiencing STS? We need to know more about these variables in relation to STS and resiliency.

ORGANIZATIONAL FACTORS AND STS

Workplace bullying has been introduced as an important concept related to the development of STS. The child welfare field needs to examine this problem in depth and determine if it is contributing to workers' social, psychological, and/or physical health problems. If bullying is taking place in an organization, then intervention is required. Workplace bullying is a form of harassment and may contribute to worker turnover.

A related construct that needs investigation is disbelief and dismissal trauma. Just as STS is thought to arise out of empathic engagement, we believe disbelief and dismissal trauma comes from violations of strongly held and highly valued belief systems. When child welfare practitioners work intensively to investigate evidence of child abuse, particularly sexual abuse, and other professionals refuse to believe that the evidence proves what happened to the child, the disbelief and dismissal produce traumatic stress. Understandably, professionals who do not do this work find the abuse hard to believe. When these doubting persons cannot allow themselves to believe what child welfare workers are telling them about an abused child, the worker naturally reacts. This disbelief and rejection of the evidence they present is traumatizing. It is not unlike the trauma that sexual abuse victims experience when they are not believed. The practitioner experiences the additional trauma of not being able to protect the child and knowing that the abuse will continue. Another aspect of disbelief and dismissal trauma is that its cumulative effect may well prompt practitioners to leave child welfare. This concept needs further research.

We do not have a clear understanding of who goes into child welfare. The information that is available as to why people are attracted to the work is mostly anecdotal. We need a profile of these professionals and an understanding of the goodness of fit between the practitioner and the work. This knowledge would contribute to improving hiring practices and identifying the most suitable people to do this often traumatic work. Also, we need to better understand who is successful, as well as who stays and why they stay. In light of the difficulties of the work, it is important to know what promotes retention. We also need to understand if practitioners, supervisors, and administrators are all equally affected by STS or if direct-service work is the variable most strongly related to STS. This information would clarify what interventions are needed.

Lee and Waters (2003) have identified spirituality and age as buffers to the cumulative effects of trauma. This relationship needs further exploration. If in fact spirituality is found to alleviate STS, potential candidates for child welfare work can be told of the important role that spirituality plays in helping people cope with the trauma of the work. We have been told this repeatedly by child welfare workers, but little empirical evidence exists to support this hypothesis.

Moran (2002) suggested a means of monitoring and evaluating the role of humor in organizational climate, as humor is part of child welfare work. Learning more about how child welfare practitioners use humor to alleviate and manage distress may help us to understand when it is more indicative of problems in the organization and working environment. This is a future research need.

Harkness and Poertner (1989) asked, "What supervisory behavior produces what outcomes with workers, clients, and problems?" (p. 116). They also called for researchers to study "different models in the context of intervening and environmental variables: the characteristics of supervision, workers, and workloads; clients' problems and goals; and the context of the culture of agency practice" (p. 118). Traumatic stress should be evaluated along with these variables.

We have argued that child welfare agencies should use critical incident stress debriefings to reduce the negative effects of traumatic events experienced in the agency. The use of CISD needs evaluation. For whom does it work best, and when is it best applied? If it is done on a voluntary basis, as we suggest, then what happens to individuals who do not participate? What are the long-term effects of CISD? Does it contribute to resiliency and retention?

Our final thought is that further research on international child welfare is needed. Are there common themes for all international practitioners regarding STS? In the context of international cultures, what can we learn about how different groups of people think about this phenomenon?

In deepening our understanding of the relationship between STS and child welfare, we may discover the best-practice interventions to use and policies to implement. It is urgent that this research be conducted and that we find answers to these questions. Child welfare is in crisis, and these questions must be answered if the field is to be strengthened and workers retained. Ultimately, it is the children and families we serve who are affected most by our knowledge—or lack thereof.

Epilogue

In 1957, Ner Littner, M.D., a psychiatric consultant, published a monograph entitled *The Strains and Stresses on the Child Welfare Worker*. Littner wrote: "Basically the child welfare worker enjoys her job and accepts as part of it the various tensions I have attempted to detail. The many satisfactions she derives from her work more than make up for any of the frustrations. Otherwise it would be completely intolerable for any period of time" (p. 20). The strains and stressors the child welfare worker experiences have not changed in the forty-eight years since Littner's work was published. We found the same strains and stresses described by Littner in our research. Clearly the crisis in worker retention suggests that the work is intolerable for many. We have argued that the trauma of the work contributes to this situation. Much can be done within the child welfare field itself to manage the traumatic stress that is an inevitable part of the work. STS is an occupational hazard for child welfare practitioners, but it is manageable when the worker is supported by supervisors, administrators, and colleagues.

The following statements were made by child welfare workers in a follow-up survey to a workshop on STS.

◆ "I recently dealt with a child fatality. Though this was not my first experience, I was able to anticipate some of my feelings rather than minimizing them."
◆ "This workshop has made me more aware of the need to take care of my health when the negatives arise."
◆ "I've started exercising regularly, eating right, taking vitamins (especially B vitamins), and participating in more spiritual activities. Since doing these things, I've noticed my ability to handle stressful situations has improved drastically!! I'm friendlier at home and at work. I have a more positive outlook on things. I just hope I can keep it up. I've had no desire for a cigarette or alcohol."
◆ "The training helped me to become less stressed when hearing the awful reasons or situations why these children were in custody. Thanks to the training, I came back home without the stomach pains and headaches that I have had in the past."
◆ "A coworker was having intimacy problems with her boyfriend and had begun to think of sex as repulsive. Back in February, she had removed two young females from their home due to sexual abuse. She had to testify at the perpetrator's trial in early July. I believe her attitude toward sex is secondary

traumatic stress related to her close involvement with these girls and their revelations of graphic details of the sexual abuse."

◆ "I have not had problems with my ulcer since the training."

◆ "The trainers reminded me that it is important to take care of myself physically, emotionally, and mentally if I am going to provide quality services to my clients. When I am confronted with stressful situations, I remind myself to take a mental break."

◆ "The workers continue to talk about the training and remind each other of what they learned in the training."

◆ "Work has been unbearable for a month or two and my home life has suffered as well. With the information from the workshop, I am better able to understand what is happening around me so that I can do something to help myself. My home life has improved."

◆ "Workers appear to better understand their own vulnerability."

◆ "We are lucky that we have a very caring office and we work together very closely. We have always given each other support. Now we know what it is we have been doing all these years."

We have learned much about what makes the work tolerable and satisfying over the past ten years. We hope that our work contributes to the child welfare community in general, to the retention of workers specifically, and most important to better outcomes for the children and families they serve and protect. We also hope that it can be used by social work educators and others to better prepare students for the challenges they will face in the helping professions.

We have shown the depth and scope of the problems traumatic stress currently pose for the child welfare community. The choice for the child welfare professional is clear. Recognize and accept the inevitability of traumatic stress inherent in the work, and learn to prevent it where possible and reduce its negative effects when it does occur. Or continue to face the personal consequences and the consequences for family, friends, colleagues, and, last but certainly not least, clients. The choice for the child welfare agency is also clear. Proactively seek and implement deliberate effective programs that provide buffers between traumatic stress and the workforce. Do that, and watch retention, morale, and positive client outcomes rise. Ignore the problem or do nothing, and worker attitude, competence, and psychological health will continue to decline, as will retention. It will cost far more in terms of productivity and client outcomes to ignore the problem than to face it squarely.

Empirical Evidence of Secondary Traumatic Stress in Child Welfare Workers

A GROWING BODY OF KNOWLEDGE IS DEVELOPING REGARDING SECONDARY traumatic stress. In 1995, when Charles Figley's book *Compassion Fatigue* was published, the content appeared to be highly applicable to child welfare work. Child welfare workers' clients are most often children and families in which trauma is occurring or has occurred. A committee of Department of Human Resource trainers, academics, child welfare workers, and supervisors was formed to discuss how this information might best be provided to child welfare workers. Using the knowledge available on STS and the process of vicarious traumatization, the committee developed a workshop explicitly for child welfare workers. The workshop was limited to six hours due to the limited time available to child welfare workers for continuing education. One of the challenges of developing the workshop content was the novelty of educational material focusing on the well-being and mental health of child welfare workers. The committee solved this problem by having workshop participants focus on themselves and how the work might be affecting them and by collecting data to determine if workers were being affected by STS and what its relationship with personal characteristics and burnout might be.

METHODOLOGY

At the beginning of the workshop, each participant was given a large envelope containing a human subject consent form to participate in research, and the Compassion Fatigue Self-Test, a demographic questionnaire, and a post-workshop evaluation satisfaction survey. Participants were asked to read the human subject consent form and, if they chose to contribute to data collection, to fill out the Compassion Fatigue Scale and demographic questionnaire. Figley gave permission for the Compassion Fatigue Self-Test to be altered for child welfare workers. The term "psychotherapists" was dropped in the instrument title, and in item 38, "psychotherapists" was changed to "child welfare worker," and the word "therapy" in items 28 and 29 was dropped. The original Compassion Fatigue Self-Test has two dimensions (Figley, 1995). Twenty-three of the items cover the STS dimension, while the remaining seventeen items constitute the burnout dimension. A Likert scale is used for each item (1 = rarely/never, 2 = at times, 3 = not sure, 4 = often, and 5 = very often). Higher scores on both dimensions indicate higher risk for STS and burnout. Risk categories are indicated for both dimensions of the scale. Risk for compassion fatigue or STS is extremely low for scores of 26 and lower, while scores of 27–30 indicate low risk; 31–35, moderate risk; 36–40, high risk; and 41 or higher, extremely high risk. Risk for burnout is extremely low for scores of 36 and lower, moderate for 37–50, high for 51–75, and extremely high for 76–85.

The evaluation of participants' satisfaction with the workshop consisted of eleven questions regarding the content, the trainers, and subsequent use of the information. Two open-ended questions were asked of participants. Participants were asked to share what was most useful in the workshop and how the workshop might be improved. Workshop participants were asked to read the items on the Compassion Fatigue Self-Test and reflect on the questions and their own reactions to the questions. Reading the instrument helped workshop participants to think about their own compassion fatigue and provided the means for data collection on STS among child welfare workers, supervisors, and administrators to begin.

DATA ANALYSIS

Data collected in each state were analyzed independently. This allows us to descriptively compare the states to determine if there are similarities and differences among the variables. It also allows us the opportunity to conduct an item analysis and determine how child welfare workers are experiencing STS. Using the results of these analyses, we then determine if statistical modeling would be appropriate in the future.

State 1

The workshop was piloted in two counties in a state in the southeast. Twenty-six participants participated in the data collection. The mean age of the participants was 43.5 with a standard deviation of 8.3. The youngest person was twenty-five, and the oldest was fifty-five. One participant (4.2%) listed current job function as intake, three (12.5%) as investigations, three (12.5%) as ongoing, five (20.8%) as in-home services, two (8.3%) as adoptions, and ten (41.7%) as "other." Twenty-four of twenty-six participants responded to the questions. There was a range of educational experience. One participant (3.8%) was a high school graduate. Eight of the participants (33.3%) had non–social work bachelor's degrees, and five (20.8%) had non–social work master's degrees. Five individuals (20.8%) had BSW degrees, and four (16.7%) had MSW degrees. One individual (4.2%) reported "other" for degree. Two individuals did not share this information. Ten participants (41.7%) were caseworkers, five (20.8%) were supervisors, and nine (37.5%) indicated "other" for their current child welfare position. Two individuals did not respond to this question. The mean number of years working in child welfare was 9.9 with a standard deviation of 6.1. The range of years was one through twenty-three. The majority of respondents (78.3%) were female. Three individuals chose not to share their gender.

Scores on the STS scale ranged from 27 to 73. The mean score was 43.7 with a standard deviation of 10.7. The burnout scale scores ranged from 21 to 62. The mean score was 40.4 with a standard deviation of 9.7. Skewness and kurtosis were divided by their standard errors, producing low values indicating that the two scales had relatively normal distributions. Reliability analyses produced a .82 alpha of the STS scale and .84 alpha for burnout. The strength of these alphas suggests that the items in each scale have good internal consistency. Other studies have found that younger workers are more affected by STS than older workers. In this sample, while this difference was not statistically significant at the .05 level, younger workers were more affected by STS than older workers, as determined by Pearson correlation ($r = -.37$; $p = .09$). Similarly, participants with fewer years of experience were more affected by STS than were individuals with more experience ($r = -.36$; $p = .08$). STS and burnout were highly correlated ($r = .85$; $p = .01$) with 72 percent of shared variance. There was no statistically significant difference between individuals with experiences with childhood traumas and those who did not have such experiences, although it should be noted that individuals with traumatic childhood experiences had a higher mean than did the other group. The sample was too small to compare education, current position, gender, and STS.

Both STS and burnout scales were recoded into two risk categories, low risk and high risk. Low risk for burnout was the same as the STS risk category. For STS, extremely low risk and low risk were combined into one category of low risk. For STS and burnout moderate, high risk and extremely high risk were combined into high risk. This procedure was followed for all states.

As risk for STS increased, risk for burnout increased, although the relationship was not statistically significant at the .05 level ($p = .13$). Two individuals were in the low-STS category. Both of them were also in the low-burnout category. Of the remaining twenty-two individuals at high risk for STS, seven (31.8%) were in the low-burnout cell and fifteen individuals (68.2%) were in the high-burnout cell. The results, although not statistically significant, indicate that one can experience high STS without being affected by burnout and that one can experience both high STS and high burnout.

An item analysis was conducted to determine in what ways participants experienced STS. Participants responded either no or yes for each item. The response of "not sure" was not included in the analysis. In this sample, sixteen participants (66.7%) felt estranged from others, startled easily, and had firsthand experience of trauma in childhood. Seventeen participants (70.9%) had difficulty sleeping and had experienced firsthand trauma as adults. Sixteen participants (62.5%) felt the need to work through a traumatic experience, and fifteen (62.4%) were preoccupied with more than one client. Nineteen participants (79.2%) felt trapped by their child welfare work. Twenty-one individuals (87.5%) experienced a sense of hopelessness working with clients, and 54.2 percent reported being in danger with their clients.

Participants gave the workshop high evaluation marks. Twenty-two participants (88%) strongly agreed that the workshop was relevant to child welfare work.
Twenty-four (96%) found the trainers knowledgeable. Twenty-one (84%) strongly
agreed that they were encouraged to participate and that the presentation was interesting. Twenty-one (80%) indicated that the workshop would help them improve
their methods of self-care. Nineteen participants (75%) strongly agreed, and five
(20%) agreed, that the workshop content would help them manage STS. Twenty-
five participants (100%) indicated they would use the information in their work,
that the workshop was a good investment of their time, and that they would recommend the workshop to colleagues. Twenty-four (96%) of the participants believed that the handouts would be a good reference for them.

State 1 Summary
The data collected at the beginning of the workshop provided results indicating
that this sample of child welfare workers was being affected by STS and less so by
burnout based on the risk categories of both variables. The results were also consistent with other studies showing that younger workers and those new to the work,
regardless of age, are more affected by STS than are older and more experienced workers. The results also demonstrated a strong correlation between burnout and STS.

There were concerns regarding the results of the data. The small sample limits
any generalizability, as does the self-selection of the sample. It is possible that the
workshop topic attracted a group of individuals most affected at that time by their
work and not indicative of the impact of STS in general. These concerns led to a commitment to replicate the data collection until confidence in the results was ensured.

State 2

The director of training for child welfare for this southeastern state obtained a
grant to fund training on STS for all child welfare personnel in the state. Fifteen
workshops were provided to approximately 360 child welfare aides, workers, supervisors, and administrators. The workshop participants were given a human subjects
consent form and the same pre-workshop instruments and post-evaluation survey
used for State 1. The results presented here are from 356 individuals who completed
both the pre-workshop instruments and the evaluation. The mean age of the participants was 37.5 with a standard deviation of 10.2. The youngest person was
twenty-three and the oldest was eighty. The sample consisted of 6 case aids (1.7%),
3 homemakers (.9%), 270 social workers (77.1%), 54 supervisors (15.4%), and 5 administrators (1.4%). Twelve (3.4%) listed their job as "other." The majority of participants were social workers and supervisors. A little more than half of the participants had social work degrees. There were 162 BSWs (46.3%) and 39 MSWs (11.1%).
Of the remaining participants, 6 (1.7%) had high school diplomas, 111 (31.7%) had
non–social work undergraduate degrees, and 21 (6%) had non–social work master's
degrees. Eleven (3.1%) reported having "other" degrees. Six individuals did not respond to the question. The mean number of years working in child welfare was 8.6

with a standard deviation of 7.9 and a range of one month to forty years. The majority of participants were female (89.8%). Fourteen individuals chose not to share their gender.

Scores on the STS scale ranged from 23 to 95. The mean score was 43.6 with a standard deviation of 11.5. The burnout scale scores ranged from 17 to 75. The mean score was 38.7 with a standard deviation of 11.2. Skewness and kurtosis were divided by their standard errors. The STS scale was slightly skewed, with kurtosis low in value. The measures produced relatively normal distributions. Reliability analyses of the STS scale produced a .85 alpha and a .82 alpha for burnout. In this sample, younger workers had higher STS scores than did older workers ($r = -.18; p < .001$). Years of experience was inversely related to STS ($r = -.13; p < .01$); with greater child welfare experience, there is less STS. These are weak correlations with minimal shared variance. STS and burnout were highly correlated ($r = .72; p < .001$) with 52 percent of shared variance. There was no significant difference on gender. An analysis of variance by education and STS was statistically significant ($F = 5.5; p = .001$). Individuals with a bachelor's degree in social work had a higher mean score (46.3) compared to individuals with other degrees (41.0). Current position was analyzed by combining case aide, homemaker, administration, and "other," and keeping social workers and supervisors as they were. There was a significant difference between social workers and supervisors ($F = 6.42; p = .002$). Social workers (mean = 44.79; SD = 12.02) were 5.7 points higher in their mean STS scores than supervisors (mean = 39.09; SD = 8.83). A statistically significant relationship was found between childhood trauma and STS. Individuals who experienced childhood trauma had higher means than those who did not ($t = -6.87; p < .001$). The mean for individuals who had childhood trauma was 46.7 with a standard deviation of 12.0; in contrast, individuals without childhood trauma had a mean of 38.8 with a standard deviation of 9.0.

Secondary traumatic stress and burnout were recoded into two risk categories, low risk and high risk. Thirty-one participants had low STS scores. All of them also had low burnout scores. Of the 325 with high STS scores, 143 (44.0%) had low risk for burnout, and 182 individuals (56.0%) had high burnout scores. The chi-square analysis was statistically significant ($X^2 = 35.52; p = .001$).

An item analysis was conducted to determine in what ways participants were experiencing STS. Participants responded either no or yes for each item. The response of "not sure" was dropped from the analysis. Two hundred eighteen participants (61.3%) avoided thoughts and feelings of a frightening experience, 173 (48.5%) felt compelled to avoid certain activities and situations that reminded them of a frightening experience, and 170 (47.7%) reported feeling estranged from others, while 192 (54%) indicated they had difficult sleeping, and 170 (47.8%) had outbursts of anger and irritability with little provocation. Two hundred fifty-two (70.9%) had had firsthand experience with traumatic events as an adult, and 168 (47.2%) had experience with traumatic events in their childhood. Two hundred seventy participants (75.9%) reported being preoccupied with more than one client, and 281 (78.9%) felt trapped by their work as a child welfare practitioner. The majority of respondents (83.7%) had a sense of hopelessness working with some clients, and 253 (71.1%) had been in danger when working with clients, while 181 participants (50.8%) reported startling easily.

The workshop received positive feedback from 331 (93%) of the participants; 317 (95.7%) agreed that the content was relevant to child welfare work. Of these participants, 206 (62.2%) strongly agreed that the content was relevant to their work, and 321 (96.7%) found the trainers knowledgeable. Most workshop participants (96%) felt they were encouraged to participate. Three hundred (91%) found the content interesting and felt that the workshop held their attention, 296 participants (89.4%) felt the information would improve their own self-care, and 298 (89.8%) felt that what they learned would help them manage STS. The majority of participants (91%) indicated that they would use the information in their work, and 299 (90.3%) felt that the handouts would be useful. The majority (94.3%) responded that their knowledge of STS was increased, and 300 (90.1%) said that the workshop was a good investment of their time. The majority of participants (91.2%) would recommend the workshop to colleagues.

State 2 Summary

The results from this sample indicate that child welfare workers are being affected by STS and less so by burnout. The alpha reliability coefficients were strong, supporting the two scales' internal consistency. In this sample, younger workers had higher STS scores than did older workers, and years of experience had an inverse correlation with STS. The longer the worker had stayed in child welfare work, the less he or she was affected by STS. Secondary traumatic stress and burnout were highly correlated. As STS scores increased, burnout tended to increase also. The item analysis descriptions are consistent with development of STS. Workers reported avoiding feelings and thoughts, feeling estranged, having sleeping problems, and having outbursts. Many respondents had had experience with trauma both in adulthood and as children. Unfortunately, many individuals felt trapped by their work, had a sense of hopelessness, and had been in danger while working with clients. The results also indicate that participants were overwhelmingly satisfied with the workshop and its content.

State 3

This southern state offered the workshop to child welfare workers, supervisors, and administrators. Three workshops were provided to eighty-seven child welfare staff over a three-day period. Approximately thirty individuals attended one of the three days. The workshop was delivered the same way it had been done in the two other states. There was one difference in the measures.

The authors of the Compassion Fatigue Scale had developed a new revision of that instrument and had added compassion satisfaction as a new dimension on the measure (Figley & Stamm, 1996). Alpha reliability for the STS scale was .84, and burnout was .83. Twenty-six items had been added to the scale to measure compassion satisfaction. The three scales' Likert responses had also been changed to 0 = never, 1 = rarely, 2 = a few times, 3 = somewhat often, 4 = often, and 5 = very often. The scale reliability alpha was .87. Higher scores on the scale indicated greater satisfaction with caregiving. The scales' range was 0 to 130. Potential for compassion satisfaction also had categories. Scores of 118 and higher indicated extremely high potential, 100–117 indicated high potential, 82–99 indicated good potential, 64–81 indicated modest potential, and below 63 indicated low potential. The average score based on a sample of 370 individuals was 92.1 with a standard deviation of 16.0. The Compassion Satisfaction and Fatigue Self-Test has sixty-six items.

The results presented here are from eighty individuals. The mean age of the child welfare participants was 41.2 with a standard deviation of 8.0. The range of age was twenty-seven to fifty-nine. Thirty-two participants (41%) listed their current job functions as social worker, nine (11.5%) as social worker (advanced), eleven (14.1%) as social worker (advanced) supervisor, fourteen (17.9%) area social work supervisor, and two (2.6%) as regional director; four (5.1%) worked in the state office and six (7.7%) listed their position as "other." Two individuals did not respond to the question. Twenty-six respondents (32.9%) had non–social work bachelor's degrees. Nine individuals (11.4%) had BSW degrees. Similarly, there were eight participants with non–social work master's degrees (10.1%) in the sample. In contrast, thirty-five (44.3%) had an MSW. One individual (1.3%) responded "other" for degree held. One individual did not respond. The mean number of years working in child welfare was 13.3 with a standard deviation of 8.4. The years ranged from one to thirty. The group was predominately (85.7%) female. Three individuals did not indicate their gender.

Scores on the STS scale ranged from 6 to 67. The mean score was 33.3 with a standard deviation of 11.1. The burnout scale scores ranged from 15 to 58. The mean score was 32.5 with a standard deviation of 9.1. The satisfaction scale ranged from 47 to 122. The mean score was 90.2 with a standard deviation of 13.2. Skewness and kurtosis for all three measures were divided by their standard errors to test for normalcy. The three variables had relatively normal distributions. Reliability analyses of the STS scale produced an alpha of .84 and an alpha of .83 for burnout. The alpha for the satisfaction scale was .87. There was no relationship between age and STS. There was a significant relationship between childhood trauma and STS ($t = -2.77$; $p < .001$). Respondents who had experienced childhood trauma had a higher mean of 36.0 with a standard deviation of 10.5. In comparison, individuals with no childhood trauma had a mean of 29.1 with a standard deviation of 11.0. There was an insignificant negative correlation between years of experience and STS. Secondary traumatic stress and satisfaction had a modest negative relationship, ($r = -.23$; $p = .04$). Burnout and satisfaction also had a negative correlation ($r = -.27$; $p = .02$). Interestingly, satisfaction and years of experience had a positive correlation ($r = .33$; $p = .003$). Secondary traumatic stress and burnout were highly correlated ($r = .73$; $p < .001$) with 53 percent of shared variance. There were no relationships with gender, education, and current position.

Secondary traumatic stress, burnout, and compassion satisfaction were recoded into the two risk categories, high and low, and two potential-for-satisfaction categories, high and low. Of the eighty participants, thirty-three were in the low-risk category for STS. Thirty-one of them (93.9%) were in the low-burnout category. Two individuals (6.1%) had low STS scores and high burnout scores. In contrast to those participants, forty-seven had high STS scores. Twenty-six (55.3%) had low burnout scores, and twenty-one (44.7%) had high burnout scores. The chi-square analysis was statistically significant ($X^2 = 14.12$; $p = .000$). The analysis indicates that STS is affecting child welfare workers more than burnout. No association was found between STS and satisfaction.

An item analysis was conducted to determine in what ways participants were experiencing STS. Participants responded either no (never and rarely) or yes (a few times, somewhat often, often, and very often) to each item to be consistent with the prior two-item analyses. Sixty-eight participants (85%) had had firsthand experience with trauma as an adult, and fifty-one (63.8%) had had firsthand experience with trauma as a child. Fifty-four (68.4%) felt trapped by their work as a child welfare practitioner. A similar number, fifty-six (70.9%), had been in danger while working with clients. Forty-four (55%) felt estranged from others; forty-five (56%) avoided certain thoughts and feelings that reminded them of a frightening experience, and forty-three (54.5%) had a sense of hopelessness working with their clients. Forty-nine participants (61.4%) reported having difficulty sleeping, while forty (50%) avoided certain situations because they reminded them of a frightening experience. Forty-two participants (52.6%) experienced outbursts of anger and irritability for no reason. Forty participants (50.2%) reported being infected by clients' traumatic stress. Interestingly, thirty-six of the participants (45%) reported needing to work through a traumatic experience.

The workshop received positive feedback from the majority of the participants. Unfortunately, seventeen participants (21%) responded to the questions on the front of the evaluation survey but did not turn the evaluation form over and consequently did not fill out the satisfaction part of the questionnaire. The remaining sixty-three participants did fill out both sides of the workshop evaluation survey. Sixty-two (98%) reported that the workshop was relevant to child welfare work. The same number found the presenters knowledgeable. Sixty (95%) participants felt encouraged to participate, and sixty-one (97%) thought the presentation was interesting. Sixty-one (97%) thought the information would help them improve their self-care, and sixty-two participants (98%) thought the content would help them manage STS. The majority of participants (98%) indicated they would use the information in their work, and sixty (95%) reported that the handouts would be a good reference for the future. The majority (97%) also thought their knowledge of STS had increased, and sixty-one participants (97%) thought that attending the workshop was a good investment of their time. Sixty-one participants (97%) would recommend the workshop to colleagues.

State 3 Summary

Consistent with prior findings, child welfare participants in this sample are being affected by STS. They were less affected by burnout, as demonstrated by the chi-square analysis. The alpha reliability coefficients for the three dimensions were good, supporting the three scales' internal consistency. This was an older group and had a smaller range of ages than did the prior two samples. The majority of child welfare workers had non–social work degrees. In contrast, the majority of supervisors had master's degrees in social work. The practitioners in this group were experienced in child welfare; more than half had twelve to thirty years in child welfare. The workers were predominately female, like the other two groups. In contrast with the other groups, there was no relationship between age and STS. While insignificant, the negative correlation between years of experience and STS is consistent with the other data sets. Both results must be put in the context of the age of the group. As expected, both STS and burnout had negative relationships with compassion satisfaction. Of interest is the positive correlation between satisfaction and years of experience. Individuals who had had childhood experiences of trauma were more affected by STS than those who did not. Consistent with the first two groups in this study, STS and burnout were highly correlated. As STS scores increased, burnout scores did also. The item analysis found that the child welfare practitioners were being affected by STS in a variety of ways. The majority had firsthand experience with trauma as an adult and in their childhood. Two-thirds felt trapped in this work and reported having been in danger when working with clients. The remaining responses indicated that these practitioners were having symptoms of STS, felt estranged, avoided thoughts, had feelings of hopelessness, had difficulty sleeping, avoided situations related to prior frightening experiences, had outbursts and irritability for no reason, and felt the need to work through a traumatic experience. Once again the evaluation of satisfaction with the workshop indicated a positive response.

State 4

This state, also in the southeast, offered the workshop to two of the state's largest counties. Two hundred child welfare workers, supervisors, and administrators participated in the training. The training proceeded as it had in other states. Prior to beginning, participants were asked to volunteer to fill out the Compassion Satisfaction and Fatigue Test. In this sample, 179 agreed to do so, creating a strong response rate. Eight workshops were offered, and approximately 25–30 participants attended each. Four individuals failed to fill in the first page of the Compassion Satisfaction and Fatigue measure. Consequently, the mean STS, burnout, and compassion satisfaction scores were used for their scores on each variable. In addition, several individuals failed to complete all items, leaving one or two items blank. For each occurrence, the mean of the items was calculated and substituted for the missing item.

The mean age of the participants was 36.8 with a standard deviation of 9.8. The youngest participant was twenty-three, and the oldest was sixty. Seventeen individuals chose not to report their age. One hundred twenty participants (70.2%) listed their current job function as social worker, fifteen (8.8%) as social worker (advanced), thirteen (7.6%) as social worker (advanced) supervisor, and ten (5.8%) as area social work supervisor; two (1.2%) worked in the state office, and eleven (6.4%) listed "other." Eight participants chose not to share their position. The majority were direct-service workers and supervisors. The majority of participants had non–social work degrees. Eighty (46.2%) had a bachelor's degree. Thirty-nine (22.5%) had BSWs. Twenty-two individuals (12.7%) had non–social work master's degrees. Twenty-seven individuals (15.6%) had MSWs. Five individuals (2.9%) indicated "other" for education. Six participants chose to not respond to the questions re-garding education. The mean number of years working in child welfare was 6.0 with a standard deviation of 7.3. The range of years in child welfare was less than a month to twenty-seven years. More than half of the sample had four to twenty-seven years of experience. The majority (84.9%) of participants were female. Six individuals chose to not report their gender.

Scores on STS scale ranged from 6 to 75. The mean score was 36.5 with a stan-dard deviation of 13.3. The burnout scale had a range of scores from 6 to 71. The mean score was 34.7 with a standard deviation of 12.1. The satisfaction scale ranged from 43 to 117. The mean score was 82.6 with a standard deviation of 16.0. Skew-ness and kurtosis for all three scales were divided by their standard errors to test for normalcy. All three scales had relatively normal distributions. Reliability analysis for the STS scale produced an alpha of .84, and .86 for the burnout scale. The anal-ysis produced an alpha of .90 for compassion satisfaction. STS and satisfaction had a negative statistically significant correlation ($r = -.41; p < .001$), as did burnout and satisfaction ($r = -.57; p < .001$). STS and age had a weak negative correlation ($r = -.18; p = .02$). The correlation between STS and years of experience was inverse but not significant. There was a significant difference in STS scores for individuals with childhood experiences of trauma and individuals who did not experience childhood trauma ($t = -6.96; p <. 000$). Individuals with a childhood trauma experience had a mean of 42.0 with a standard deviation of 13.0 in comparison with a 29.8 mean with a standard deviation 10.2 for individuals who did not. STS and burnout had a strong positive correlation ($r = .76; p < .001$) with 58 percent of shared variance. There were no relationships between STS and gender, education, or current job position.

The three measures were recoded into two categories of STS and burnout risk and satisfaction potential. Secondary traumatic stress and burnout were recoded into low risk and high risk. Satisfaction was recoded into low and high potential for satisfaction. Sixty-one participants were in the low-STS category. Fifty-four of them (88.5%) were also low burnout, and seven (11.5%) were high burnout. In contrast, 118 were at high risk for STS. Fifty-two participants (44.1%) were at low risk for burnout, and sixty-six (55.9%) were at high risk for burnout. Cross-tabulation and chi-square analysis were conducted between STS risk categories and burnout risk categories. A statistically significant association was found between the two vari-ables ($X^2 = 32.91; p = .001$). Overall, as STS increases in risk, burnout also increases in risk.

A statistically significant association was also found between STS and potential for compassion satisfaction ($X^2 = 7.45; p = .006$). Low satisfaction was associated with high STS for sixty child welfare workers (76.9%). High satisfaction was related to high STS for eighty-five (57.4%) participants and low STS risk for forty-three (42.6%) participants. There was a similar pattern in the distribution of State 3 and State 4 chi-square frequencies across the cells in that low satisfaction was more strongly associated with high STS. There was also a similar distribution for individuals with high satisfaction and low and high STS.

An item analysis was conducted to identify the ways in which participants were experiencing STS. Participants responded either no (never and rarely) or yes (a few times, somewhat often, often, and very often). A majority of respondents (76.4%) had experienced trauma firsthand as adults, and 128 (71.7%) had felt trapped by their work as child welfare practitioners, while 111 (62.8%) had flashbacks of clients, and 107 (60%) had been in danger when working with clients. One hundred four (59%) had difficulty falling or staying asleep, 100 (56.8%) reported avoiding certain thoughts or feelings that reminded them of a frightening experience, and 102 (57%) experienced intrusive thoughts of times spent with difficult clients. A similar number (56.9%) had a sense of hopelessness associated with working with clients, and 101 (56%) were preoccupied with more than one client. Ninety-six (53.6%) had had firsthand experience with traumatic events in their childhood. A little more than half of participants (52.3%) avoided certain activities or situations because they reminded them of a frightening experience, and ninety-one (52.1%) reported feeling estranged from others. Eighty-eight participants (50%) reported startling easily.

Participants were satisfied with the education they received. As in the prior group, several did not turn the evaluation form over to fill out the evaluation questions. Of the participants who completed the evaluation questions, 143 (91.6%) responded that the content of the workshop was relevant to their work, and 153 (97.5%) found the trainers to be knowledgeable. The majority (96.8%) felt encouraged to participate, and 142 (90.5%) responded that the presentation was interesting and held their attention. Many of the participants (84.7%) felt that the information would help them improve their self-care practices, and 140 (89.1%) believed the information would help them to manage STS. Most of the participants (86.5%) indicated that they would use the information in their work, and 122 (86%) reported that the handouts would be good future reference for them. The majority (94.2%) agreed that they had increased their knowledge of STS, and 138 (88.5%) thought that attending the workshop was a good investment of their time. One hundred forty-two (91%) indicated they would recommend the workshop to their colleagues.

State 4 Summary
This state was experiencing some tension due to the heavy demands of a court order. There was some concern that this might contribute to a lowered response rate, but that did not happen. There was a wide range of ages in this group. Several individuals chose not to report on their ages; one individual wrote for age: "Old and tired." The majority of the sample was made up of direct-service social workers and supervisors, individuals with the most client contact. Several individuals chose not

to share their position. There were few BSWs or MSWs in this group, and several individuals did not indicate their educational background. There were many individuals who were new to the work; 50 percent had less than three-and-a-half years on the job, and the remainder had four to twenty-seven years of experience, representing a fairly experienced group. As in most child welfare state agencies, the majority of child welfare workers were female. Several of the respondents chose not to report their gender. There seemed to be some reticence among participants to share their information regardless of the reassurances that only the researcher and research assistant would have access to it.

The reliability coefficients indicated that the three dimensions of the scale had good internal consistency. As in the previous findings, these workers were more affected by STS and less affected by burnout. As STS increased, satisfaction with work decreased. However, satisfaction with work was more affected by burnout with 33 percent shared variance. Younger workers were more affected by STS than older workers. While there was an inverse correlation between STS and years of experience, it was not significant. There was a strong correlation between STS and burnout. As STS increased, so did burnout, but this occurred for less than two-thirds of the sample.

The majority of the sample was in the extremely low-risk category for burnout. Interestingly, none of the participants was in the extremely high-risk category for burnout. The majority of workers scored high on compassion satisfaction. There was a strong association between STS and burnout. As STS increased among participants, burnout also increased. At the same time, the increase in burnout was only observed among a few individuals. Similarly, as STS increased, satisfaction with work decreased, but the relationship was stronger between burnout and compassion satisfaction. As in the prior analyses, workers were being affected by STS in certain ways, as shown in the item analysis. This group was similar in its symptoms of STS with the exception of having flashbacks connected to clients and experiencing intrusive thoughts of difficult times with especially difficult clients. They also reported startling easily, which only one other group reported. As were other groups, this group was satisfied with the training and thought it was a good investment of their time and that they would recommend it to their colleagues.

State 5

This state is located in the Midwest. The workshop was offered to several regions within the sate. The workshop had thirty-three participants. Twenty-seven participants elected to volunteer to fill out the Compassion Fatigue Self-Test. The short version was used. This version had six response options to the STS and burnout scales: never, rarely, a few times, somewhat often, and very often. The training proceeded as it had in the other states: participants were asked to fill out the instruments if they chose to do so or to read the items and reflect on them.

The mean age of the participants was 41.5 with a standard deviation of 9.7. The youngest participant was twenty-six and the oldest fifty-six. Two individuals chose not to report their age. Fifteen participants (55.6%) listed their current job functions as social worker, eight (29.6%) as social worker (advanced), and one (3.7%) as area social work supervisor; three (11.1%) listed their position as "other." The majority of these individuals provided direct services to clients. Twenty-two (8.15%) had non–social work bachelor's degrees, and three (11.1 %) had BSWs. One individual (3.7%) had a non–social work master's degree, and another individual (3.7%) responded "other" for education. The mean number of years working in child welfare was 5.1 with a standard deviation of 3.9. The range of years in child welfare was one to eighteen. More than half of the sample had four to eighteen years in the work. The majority of participants (80.8%) were female. One individual did not share his or her gender.

Scores on the STS scale scores ranged from 16 to 90. The mean was 44.2 with a standard deviation of 19.3. Approximately half of the sample had scores from 43 to 80. The burnout scale scores ranged from 20 to 70. The mean score was 40.2 with a standard deviation of 13.6. Skewness and kurtosis were divided by their standard errors to test for normalcy. Both of the variables had relatively normal distributions. Reliability analysis produced an alpha coefficient of .93 for the STS scale and .89 for burnout, indicating good internal consistency among items. The only significant correlation was between STS and burnout ($r = .81; p < .000$), producing 66 percent of shared variance. Years of experience and age of the worker were not significant, although there was an inverse relationship between age and STS. This is consistent with the other states, where younger workers were more affected by STS than older workers. Ten individuals (37%) had not experienced childhood trauma, and seventeen (63%) participants had. Participants who had were more affected by STS than those who had no childhood trauma ($t = 2.09; p = .05$), with a mean difference of 15.1. The small sample limits further comparisons of these factors.

Secondary traumatic stress and burnout were recoded into two risk categories, low and high risk. Nine participants (75.5%) were in the low-STS category. All of them were also in the low-burnout category. Eighteen participants were in the high-STS category. Fifteen of these individuals (83.3%) were in the high-burnout category. Fisher's Exact Test resulted in a p of .001, which was statistically significant. As in the other states' analyses, there were individuals with STS who were not affected by burnout, and as STS increased, so did burnout.

As in the other states, an item analysis was conducted to determine in what ways participants were affected by STS. Participants responded no (never and rarely) or yes (a few times, somewhat often, often, and very often). Twenty-four participants (88.9%) reported having firsthand experiences of trauma as adults. Twenty-two (81.4%) felt trapped in their child welfare work. Twenty participants (74%) avoided certain activities and situations because they brought up memories of a frightening experience. A majority of participants (70.3%) reported being in danger while working with clients. Many participants (66.6%) responded that they felt estranged from others and were preoccupied with more than one client. Seventeen respondents (62.9%) had thought about using violence against a perpetrator, had experienced firsthand trauma in childhood, and had experienced a sense of hopelessness working with some clients. Sixteen participants (59.2%) expressed the need to work through a traumatic experience. Many individuals (55.5%) reported having outbursts of anger or irritability with little provocation and being startled easily. Fourteen of the participants (51.8%) reported that they had lost sleep over clients' trauma and had been frightened of what a client had done.

Participant satisfaction with the workshop was not assessed. A snowstorm turned into a blizzard, resulting in an early end to the workshop.

State 5 Summary

This was a mature group of child welfare workers, two-thirds of whom had extensive experience in child welfare. The majority of participants were direct-service workers and had non–social work degrees. As in the other groups, the majority were female.

The reliability coefficients affirmed that the STS scale and burnout scale had good internal consistency. As in the other samples, there was a strong statistically significant correlation between STS and burnout. There was also a statically significant difference in STS between those who experienced childhood trauma and those who did not. Individuals who experienced childhood trauma had higher STS scores compared to individuals who did not. This finding is consistent with other studies' findings. As in the other groups, the majority of the participants were at low risk for burnout. In contrast, over half of the sample was at high risk for STS. There was a strong inverse association between the risk categories. The item analysis produced a pattern of effects of STS similar to the other groups. This was the only group to report thinking about committing a violent act against a perpetrator of child abuse and having been frightened of what a client said or did to them.

While this group was similar to the other groups, it was small and has limitations. It could be that these individuals were most affected by the work at the time and that this attracted them to the workshop. While their data are consistent with the other groups', regardless of size, this limitation limits generalization and should be considered.

WHAT 666 CHILD WELFARE WORKERS IN FIVE STATES ARE SAYING

The Compassion Fatigue Scale and Compassion Satisfaction and Fatigue Scale had good internal consistency confirmed by the strong alpha coefficients. The Skewness and kurtosis analysis supported the variables' having a relatively normal distribution in each state, regardless of sample size.

The 666 child welfare professionals in this study tell us that they are being affected by STS but are not as strongly affected by burnout. This can be seen in table 4. These findings are also supported by the strong correlations between STS and burnout. Further examination of STS and burnout risk categories in cross-tabulation demonstrated statistical significance in four states. The majority of participants in all states were in low-burnout risk categories, with one exception, State

2, where there was a group in the extremely high risk category. In all states, as STS increased, burnout increased. This suggests that STS is experienced before burnout. In some ways, this is a logical relationship. As hypothesized in the first chapter, it takes time to develop burnout. A worker does not get burned out during the first few days, weeks, or months on the job. Burnout is associated with organizational work stress and low personal rewards and takes time, in some cases years, to develop.

In contrast, a worker can be traumatized by particularly difficult cases in the first few weeks or months of child welfare work. STS can happen suddenly or develop over time, leading the worker to think he or she is burned out when this may not be. The nature of this work is such that workers can experience STS from overseeing the removal of children from a home where the floor is filthy with excrement; windows are broken; there is little furniture; and the children are dirty, malnourished, and clinging to their depressed mother, who quietly cries, saying she can't live without her babies. It can happen when a worker investigates the case of a baby who is dying in the hospital due to extreme malnourishment and the worker, after the third visit to the baby, starts crying and is told she is not maintaining professional objectivity. Workers can experience STS from listening to teenagers in foster care talk about the abuse they have experienced. They can experience STS as cases pile up and child and adolescent traumas accumulate. Once workers differentiate STS from burnout, they often remark that they knew something was wrong; they didn't think they were burned out, but they didn't have a name for what they were experiencing.

In two states, the Compassion Satisfaction and Fatigue scales were used for data collection. In the first state, STS and satisfaction had a modest negative statistically significant correlation; that result was the same in the second state, but the relationship was stronger. There was a similar finding of burnout and satisfaction, and it was stronger in both states than the relationship between STS and satisfaction. To some degree this finding is logical in that both satisfaction and burnout are more related to the organizational culture and work environment, while STS is more related to the worker's relationship with traumatized clients. It does raise the issue of what happens to the quality of the relationships with clients if STS is affecting the worker and compassion satisfaction is declining.

STS was analyzed in relation to personal characteristics. In State 2, there were significant associations with workers' personal characteristics. Younger and less experienced workers had negative correlations with STS. This was also true in State 4. States 1 and 5 had negative correlations between age and STS, but they were not significant. Years of experience also had a negative, but not significant, correlation in State 1 and State 3. These results are consistent with the findings of other studies that younger, less experienced practitioners are more affected by trauma work than are older, more experienced workers. In State 2, females had higher mean scores on STS than did males. Individuals with bachelor's degrees in social work scored higher on STS than did individuals with other degrees. This may be attributed to the ways in which social work education teaches students the importance of the use of empathy in relationships with clients. It could also be that empathy is one of the factors that attract students to social work, and the combination of having empathy and using it with traumatized clients makes the social worker more vulnerable to STS. In State 2, social workers had higher STS scores than did supervisors. This may reflect the fact that social workers have more direct contact with traumatized clients. States 1, 3, 4, and 5 all showed significant relationships between individuals who had experienced childhood trauma and individuals who had not. Those with childhood trauma had higher STS scores. This finding is also consistent with other studies and suggests that childhood trauma may promote vulnerability to STS.

An item analysis, shown in table 5, was conducted to determine if there are similarities in the ways in which child welfare workers experience STS. Under the diagnostic criteria for STS disorder as proposed by Figley (1995), workers are affected in all three areas. Workers reexperience traumatic events through recollection of experiences and feelings of distress in reaction to reminders of the events. They use avoidance and numbing when aroused by reminders. In all states, workers forced themselves to avoid certain thoughts and feelings reminding them of a frightening experience. In three states, workers avoided certain activities or situations because they brought up memories of frightening experiences. In four states, child welfare workers felt estranged from others; other people simply do not understand the work they do. And workers experienced persistent arousal. In four states, workers had difficulty falling and staying asleep; the fifth state was close to the 50 percent criterion at 48.1 percent. Workers in three states experienced outbursts of anger or irritability with little provocation. In four states, they reported startling easily. Child welfare workers also reported having firsthand experience of traumatic events in childhood and in adulthood. In all states, participants reported feeling trapped in child welfare work, had been in danger while working with clients, and had a sense of hopelessness associated working with clients, which is a hallmark feature of STS.

The evaluations of the STS workshop were consistently positive. Child welfare workers responded that this information was much needed and relevant to child welfare work. Participants consistently commented that learning the difference between STS and burnout was most useful to them. Several also commented that finding out that their feelings and responses to the work are normal was most important. Another frequent response was that learning that their colleagues felt the same way they did was most helpful. Many participants commented that the interaction in the groups and learning ways to cope and use social support were most helpful.

In conclusion, these results are consistent with the few studies of child welfare work and STS. The 666 child welfare workers we studied are being affected by STS, and many have ten of the seventeen symptoms of STS. These findings show that the impact of STS is greater than burnout and appears to precede burnout. Further research is needed in this area. Given the consistency in the results, the next step in this research project will be to use statistical modeling to deepen our understanding of the relationships among STS, burnout, and the other variables.

Table 4. Comparisons of States on Characteristics, STS, Burnout, and Compassion Satisfaction

	State 1 ($N = 24$)	State 2 ($N = 356$)	State 3 ($N = 80$)	State 4 ($N = 179$)	State 5 ($N = 27$)
Age	$X = 43.5$ SD = 8.3	$X = 37.5$ SD = 10.2	$X = 41.9$ SD = 8.0	$X = 36.8$ SD = 9.7	$X = 41.5$ SD = 9.7
Years of Experience	$X = 9.9$ SD = 6.1	$X = 8.6$ SD = 7.9	$X = 13.3$ SD = 8.4	$X = 6.0$ SD = 7.3	$X = 5.1$ SD = 3.9
Position					
Caseworker	10 (41.7%)	270 (77.2%)	41 (52.6%)	136 (79.0%)	23 (85.2%)
Supervisor	5 (20.8%)	54 (15.4%)	25 (32.0%)	23 (13.4%)	1 (3.7%)
Other	9 (37.5%)	26 (7.4%)	12 (15.4%)	13 (7.6%)	3 (11.1%)
STS Scores	$X = 43.8$ SD = 10.8	$X = 43.4$ SD = 11.5	$X = 33.3$ SD = 11.1	$X = 36.5$ SD = 13.3	$X = 44.2$ SD = 19.3
Burnout Scores	$X = 40.4$ SD = 9.7	$X = 38.7$ SD = 11.2	$X = 32.5$ SD = 9.1	$X = 34.7$ SD = 12.1	$X = 40.2$ SD = 13.6
Compassion Satisfaction Scores	N/A	N/A	$X = 90.2$ SD = 13.2	$X = 82.6$ SD = 16.0	Not Used

Table 5. Comparisons of States on Compassion Satisfaction Potential and STS and Burnout Risk Categories

	State 1 ($N = 24$)	State 2 ($N = 356$)	State 3 ($N = 80$)	State 4 ($N = 179$)	State 5 ($N = 27$)
STS Risk					
Extremely low	0	4 (1.1%)	22 (27.5%)	43 (24.0%)	7 (25.9%)
Low	2 (8.3%)	7 (7.6%)	11 (13.8%)	18 (10.1%)	2 (7.4%)
Moderate	4 (16.7%)	134 (37.6%)	14 (17.5%)	30 (16.8%)	2 (7.4%)
High	4 (17.7%)	0	10 (12.5%)	28 (16.6%)	2 (7.4%)
Extremely high	15 (58.3%)	191 (53.7%)	23 (28.8%)	60 (33.5%)	14 (51.9%)
Burnout Risk					
Extremely low	9 (34.6%)	174 (48.9%)	57 (71.3%)	106 (59.2%)	12 (44.4%)
Moderate	12 (46.2%)	128 (36.0%)	18 (22.5%)	54 (30.2%)	9 (33.3%)
High	3 (11.5%)	26 (7.3%)	5 (6.5%)	19 (10.6%)	6 (22.2%)
Extremely high	0	28 (7.9%)	0	0	0
Compassion Satisfaction Potential					
Low	N/A	N/A	3 (3.8%)	26 (15.5%)	N/A
Modest	N/A	N/A	13 (16.3%)	52 (29.1%)	N/A
Good	N/A	N/A	49 (61.3%)	78 (43.6%)	N/A
High	N/A	N/A	13 (16.3%)	23 (12.8%)	N/A
Extremely high	N/A	N/A	2 (2.5%)	0	N/A

Table 6. Effects of STS on Child Welfare Practitioners by State*

Compassion Fatigue Items	S1	S2	S3	S4	S5
1. Avoid thoughts and feelings	•	•	•	•	•
2. Avoid activities or situations			•	•	•
3. Have gaps in memory					
4. Feel estranged from others	•		•	•	•
5. Have difficulty falling or staying asleep	•	•	•	•	
6. Have outbursts of anger or irritability	•		•		•
7. Startle easily	•	•		•	•
8. Have thought about violence against perpetrator					•
9. Have flashbacks connected to my clients				•	
10. Experienced traumatic events in adult life	•	•	•	•	•
11. Experienced traumatic events in childhood	•		•	•	•
12. Need to work through a trauma	•	•			•
13. Am frightened of things a client said or did					•
14. Have troubling dreams related to client					
15. Have intrusive thoughts of difficult client sessions	•			•	
16. Sudden involuntary memory of event					
17. Am preoccupied with more than one client	•	•		•	•
18. Have lost sleep over client's trauma					•
19. Am infected by client's traumatic stress			•		
20. Am less concerned about clients' well-being					
21. Feel trapped in my work as a CW practitioner	•	•	•	•	•
22. Feel hopelessness associated working with clients	•	•	•	•	•
23. Have been in danger working with my clients	•	•	•	•	•

* In order to be included, each item had to be chosen by at least 50 percent of participants.

Appendix B

Syllabus of Primary and Secondary Traumatic Stress in Social Work: Practice, Supervision, and Organizations

I. COURSE DESCRIPTION AND GENERAL PURPOSE

This course will provide students an opportunity to explore a topic of special interest in social work practice. The course addresses primary and secondary traumatic stress. Students and instructors engage in a process of problem definition and specification, critical reading of pertinent theory and research, and an exploration of specialized social work responses and practices related to primary and secondary traumatic stress.

II. OBJECTIVES: UPON COMPLETION OF THE COURSE, THE STUDENT WILL BE ABLE TO

1. Describe the history of the study of trauma and the evolution of the study of posttraumatic stress disorder (PTSD), primary traumatic stress (PTS), and secondary traumatic stress (STS)

2. Demonstrate competent knowledge of STS by mastering the appropriate literature with a focus on theory

3. Examine empirical research on STS in social workers and other helping professionals

4. Identify appropriate prevention and intervention strategies for social workers

5. Describe selected professional and personal approaches to STS that are currently in practice

6. Describe what is known about how diversity factors are related to STS

7. Identify and understand the roles and functions of supervision and administration in assessing and managing STS in the agency, including policy and legal implications

8. Describe the research needed to improve social work clinical practice and supervision and organizational management in relation to STS

9. Relate this content to the education of social workers and their preparation for practice

III. MAJOR AREAS OF CONTENT

1. Historical background of the study of traumatic stress, PTS, PTSD, and STS
2. Theoretical explanations of direct and indirect traumatic stress
3. Empirical studies of the effects of STS on social workers and clients
4. Impact of STS on social work practice and client relationships
5. Prevention and intervention of STS in social work practice and organizations through education, supervision, coping skills, and institutional social support
6. STS as occupational hazard: policy and legal implications

IV. STS COURSE READING MATERIALS

Primary and Required Texts

Figley, C. R. (Ed.). (1995). *Compassion fatigue: Coping with secondary traumatic stress disorder in those who treat the traumatized.* New York: Brunner/Mazel.

Pryce, Josephine, Shackelford, Kimberly K., & Pryce, David H. (2007). *Secondary traumatic stress and the child welfare professional.* Chicago: Lyceum Books.

Web Sites

Figley, C. R., & Stamm, B. H. (1996). Psychometric review of the Compassion Fatigue Self-Test. In B. H. Stamm (Ed.), *Measurement of stress, trauma, and adaptation.* Lutherville, MD: Sidran Press. Available from http://www.isu.edu/~bhstamm/pdf/

Stamm, B. H. (1997–2005). *Rural care: Crossroads of culture, healthcare, traumatic stress, and technology.* Retrieved from http://www.isu.edu/irh~bhstamm

All additional readings will be on reserve in the library.

V. COURSE OVERVIEW

This course will explore the phenomenon of traumatic stress as a topic of increasing importance in social work practice. Self-care issues that are of longstanding interest to social work practitioners are usually studied from the perspective of burnout and organizational stress. Burnout has its origins in organizational demands, limited resources, and unsupportive environments. In contrast, STS is derived from the social worker–client relationship. Through empathic engagement, the social worker absorbs the client's emotional distress, particularly emotions related to traumatic stress and events. STS affects social service organizations, administrators, social workers, social work supervisors, and clients. If STS is unattended, it may compromise professional competence and create distress in interpersonal relationships. The knowledge derived from this course will allow social workers to prevent and intervene in STS in themselves, colleagues, clients, and organizations. It will also contribute to competent supervision of social workers, especially those working in trauma and crisis environments. A variety of instructional techniques (lecture, videotapes, films, active and collaborative learning exercises, along with other activities) will be used to achieve the course objectives. Case scenarios will be presented for students to analyze and apply the content of the course to traumatic events. These exercises involve group work.

Throughout this course, we will be learning about and discussing traumatic experiences. If at any time the topic becomes distressing to you, please take appropriate action to protect yourself. This may include leaving the room for a period of time. You may want to reflect on your distress and consider discussing it with a counselor in the student health center.

VI. EXPECTATIONS AND EVALUATION

A	90–100
B	80–89
C	70–79
D	60–69
F	0–59

Fifty percent of your grade will be based on an application paper. The other 50 percent is based on an oral presentation. Instructions for both are at the end of this syllabus. There is no final examination. Papers should follow APA style unless otherwise indicated by the instructor. Please do not hesitate to ask if you have questions about the writing requirements.

VII. COURSE OUTLINE AND CALENDAR (SUBJECT TO CHANGE AS NEEDED)

Week 1

Introduction to class, syllabus review, and course assignments
Shared and individual traumatic experience
History of the study of trauma
Direct and indirect trauma and types of trauma
History of posttraumatic stress disorder (PTSD)
Definition of PTSD, clinical symptoms
Treatment of PTSD
Film: *Combat and Hospital Trauma.* Walter Reed Medical Service (5 min.)
Film: *The Doctor Is In: Post-traumatic Disorder* (28 min.)
Reading assignment: Figley, chapter 1
Pearlman, L. A. (1998). Trauma and the self: A theoretical and clinical perspective. *Journal of Emotional Abuse, 1*(1), 7–25

Week 2

Film: *The General's Daughter* (116 min.)
Discussion of a primary trauma and consequences in main characters. We will analyze what features of PTSD are present.

Week 3

Secondary traumatic stress
Identification of the phenomenon
Theory of vicarious traumatization and compassion fatigue
Conceptual confusion in definitions and terms
Differentiation of STS from burnout
Key terminology: PTSD and STS
Barriers to interventions and support
Video: *When Helping Hurts: Sustaining Trauma Workers* (40 min.)
Reading assignment: Figley, chapters 2, 6, 7

Week 4

Recovering from trauma: Clinician's roles and responsibilities and healing activities
Reactions to trauma: Normal responses to abnormal events
Human-induced versus nature-induced traumatic stress
Crisis intervention and debriefing
Psychoeducational interventions
Clinician trauma history
Ethical issues and professional boundaries
Film: *Recovering from Traumatic Events: The Healing Process* (50 min.)
Case application: Analysis of clinician's roles and responsibilities through case scenarios
Reading assignment: McCann, I. L., & Pearlman, L. A. (1990). The disruption of psychological needs and related cognitive schemas. In *Psychological trauma and the adult survivor: Theory, therapy, and transformation* (pp. 57–82). New York: Brunner/Mazel.
McCann, I. L., & Pearlman, L. A. (1990). Vicarious traumatization: A framework for understanding the psychological effects of working with victims. *Journal of Traumatic Stress, 3*(1), 131–149.
McCann, L., & Pearlman, L. A. (1993). Vicarious traumatization: The emotional costs of working with survivors. *Treating Abuse Today, 3*(5), 28–31.

Week 5

Film: *Hotel Rwanda*
Discussion of primary and secondary trauma in characters. We will analyze what features of PTSD and STS are present.

Week 6

Traumatic impact and disruption of psychological needs
Changes in cognitive schemata
Assessment of disrupted psychological needs and cognitive schemata
Assessment of ego resources and self-capacities
Assessment measures
Film: *Vicarious Traumatization: The Cost of Empathy* (46 min.)
Turn in paper abstract, outline, and proposed reference list for instructor review and comment
Case application: Assessment of primary and secondary trauma in a case scenario
Reading assignment: Figley, chapter 8

Week 7

STS and clinical issues
Factors influencing STS
Transference and countertransference
Impact of personal trauma history
Film: *When Helping Hurts: Sustaining Trauma Workers* (50 min.)
Case scenario and analysis
Reading assignment: Figley, chapter 4
Calhoun, L. G., & Tedeschi, R. G. (1999). Helping clients toward philosophical and spiritual growth. *Facilitating posttraumatic growth: A clinician's guide* (pp. 104–124). Mahwah, NJ: Lawrence Erlbaum.
Pearlman, L. A., & Mac Ian, P. S. (1993). Vicarious traumatization among trauma therapists: Empirical findings on self-care. *Traumatic Stress Points: News for the International Society for Traumatic Stress Studies, 7*(3), 5.
Pearlman, L. A., & Mac Ian, P. S. (1995). Vicarious traumatization: An empirical study of the effects of trauma work on trauma therapists. *Professional Psychology: Research and Practice, 26*(6), 558–565.
Chrestman, K. R. (1995). Secondary exposure to trauma and self reported distress among therapists. In B. H. Stamm (Ed.), *Secondary traumatic stress: Self-care issues for clinicians, researchers, and educators* (pp. 29–48). Lutherville, MD: Sidran Press.
Empirical measures: Mac Ian, P. S., & Pearlman, L. A. (1992). Development and use of the TSI Life Event Questionnaire. *Treating Abuse Today: The International News Journal of Abuse, Survivorship, and Therapy, 2*(1), 9–11.
TSI Belief Scale (Revision L): An 80-item Likert-scale measure of disrupted cognitive schemas
TSI Life Event Questionnaire (Revision 1): 204-item inventory of traumatic life events
TSI Life Event Questionnaire, short form (Revision 2): 18-item inventory of traumatic life events
Compassion Fatigue Self-Test for Psychotherapists

Week 8

Empirical evidence of STS in various helping professionals
The psychobiology of trauma: Questions and issues
Presentation of child welfare STS studies and item analysis
Film: Overcoming the Tyranny of the Past: The Psychobiology of Violence and Recovery (67 min.)
Reading assignment: Figley, chapter 9
Catherall, D. R. (1995). Coping with secondary traumatic stress: The importance of the therapist's professional peer group; In B. H. Stamm (Ed.), *Secondary traumatic stress: Self-care issues for clinicians, researchers, and educators* (pp. 80–94). Lutherville, MD: Sidran Press.
Mitchell, J. T., & Everly, G. S. (1996). Critical incident stress debriefing from start to finish. *Critical incident stress debriefing—CISD: An operations manual for the prevention of traumatic stress among emergency service and disaster workers* (Rev. 2nd ed., pp. 77–119). Ellicott City, MD: Chevron Publishing Corporation.
Pearlman, L. A. (1995). Self care for trauma therapists: Ameliorating vicarious traumatization. In B. H. Stamm (Ed.), *Secondary traumatic stress: Self-care issues for clinicians, researchers, and educators* (pp. 51–64). Lutherville, MD: Sidran Press.

Week 9

STS prevention and intervention
Education and ongoing training
Individual coping, social support, supervision
Critical incident stress debriefing
Individual and group counseling
Film: Vicarious Traumatization II: Transforming the Pain (40 min.)
Reading assignment: Figley, chapters 10 and 11
Munroe, J. F. (1995). Ethical issues associated with secondary trauma in therapists. In B. H. Stamm (Ed.), *Secondary traumatic stress: Self-care issues for clinicians, researchers, and educators* (pp. 211–229). Lutherville, MD: Sidran Press.
Shulman, L. (1993). Helping staff cope with trauma. *Interactional supervision* (pp. 258–283). Washington, DC: NASW Press.

Week 10

STS and social work agencies and institutions and responsibility for STS
Supervision as a factor in promotion of well-being
STS and ethical issues
Exercises in ethics: CODE TRAIN training module
Reading assignment: Munroe, J. F. (1999). Ethical issues associated with secondary trauma in therapists. In B. H. Stamm (Ed.), *Secondary traumatic stress:*

Self-care issues for clinicians, researchers, and educators (pp. 211–229). Lutherville, MD: Sidran Press.

Bloom, S. L. (1999). The germ theory of trauma: The impossibility of ethical neutrality. In B. H. Stamm (Ed.), *Secondary traumatic stress: Self-care issues for clinicians, researchers, and educators* (pp. 257–276). Lutherville, MD: Sidran Press.

Week 11

STS as an occupational hazard and occupational stress strain in social work
Legal issues and employers' responsibility for mental health policies
The importance of social work advocacy for interventions for STS

Week 12

What do we need to know?
Future research needs areas for discovery
Review of organization of presentations

Weeks 13–15

Presentations and papers due

ASSIGNMENTS

Paper

You will choose a topic of interest to you on which to write your paper. You may choose a personal traumatic experience or one to which you were a witness. You may develop a fictional traumatic situation or use a film or book that involves a traumatic situation as the topic for your paper. Find sources to expand your knowledge of your topic. Please include empirical literature in your review. You will apply the content of the course, where appropriate, to your paper. Your paper should cover the following course content: PTSD, STS, constructivist self-development theory, cognitive schemata, psychological needs, changes in cognitive schemata, ego resources and self-capacities, social support, coping, supervision, and organizational interventions. Write an outline of your paper and include your references. Turn your outline in and be prepared to discuss your paper with your professor before you complete it and turn it in.

You will receive your outline with comments from your professor, after which you should begin writing your paper. If you have any questions, please ask them. You may share drafts with peers or the professor for review and suggestions. In your paper, you should reflect on how writing the paper affected you.

Oral Presentation

You will provide a handout to your peers and professor. The information you provide will explain the topic and any visual or graphic material you will be presenting. You may have guests who have some familiarity with your topic and are willing to participate in your presentation. For example, in one presentation, the student's topic was traumatic stress and tornadoes. The student invited two members from a community that had been devastated by an F5-class tornado to share their experience and recovery with the class. You may use any resources you desire for your presentation. If you need any assistance with equipment, please discuss with your professor the day before your presentation. Presentations will be fifteen to twenty minutes in length.

Appendix C

Glossary

Burnout "A syndrome of emotional exhaustion, depersonalization, and reduced personal accomplishment that can occur among individuals who do 'people-work' of some kind. It is a response to the chronic emotional strain of dealing extensively with other human beings, particularly when they are troubled or having problems" (Maslach, 2003, p. 2); "A state of physical, emotional, and mental exhaustion caused by long term involvement in emotionally demanding situations" (Pines & Aronson, 1988, p. 9)

Compassion fatigue Another term for secondary traumatic stress disorder (Figley, 2002, p. 3)

Countertransference "A set of conscious or unconscious emotional reactions to a client experienced by the social worker or other professional, usually in a clinical setting. According to psychodynamic theory, these feelings originate in the professional's own developmental conflicts and are projected onto the client" (Barker, 2003, p. 100); the process of seeing oneself in the client, of overidentifying with the client, or of meeting one's own needs through the client (Corey, 1986)

Posttraumatic stress disorder (PTSD) "A delayed psychological reaction to experiencing an event that is outside the range of usual human experience" (Barker, 2003, p. 333); "Symptoms following exposure to an extreme traumatic stressor involving direct personal experience of an event that involves actual or threatened death or serious injury, or other threat to one's physical integrity; or witnessing an event that involves death, injury, or a threat to the physical integrity of another person; or learning about unexpected or violent death, serious harm, or threat of death or injury experienced by a family member or other close associate" (American Psychiatric Association, 2000, p. 463)

Secondary trauma "Also known as 'vicarious trauma' the sense of trauma that comes often to those who are close to the victim of trauma, such as a family member, helping professional, or bystander near the trauma site" (Barker, 2003, p. 385)

Secondary traumatic stress (STS) "The natural consequent behaviors and emotions resulting from knowing about a traumatizing event experienced by a significant other—the stress resulting from helping or wanting to help a traumatized or suffering person" (Figley, 1995, p. 7)

Secondary traumatic stress disorder (STSD) According to Charles Figley, the cluster of symptoms that characterize posttraumatic stress disorder, as delineated in the *DSM-IV*, when the symptoms afflict a person who has experienced trauma indirectly by knowing about a traumatic event experienced by a significant other, or by wanting to help a traumatized person; also known as compassion fatigue (Figley, 1995, 2002)

Social work The applied science of helping people achieve an effective level of psychosocial functioning and effecting social change to enhance the well-being of all people; according to the National Association of Social Workers, "the professional activity of helping individuals, groups, or communities enhance or restore their capacity for social functioning and creating societal conditions favorable to this goal" (Barker, 2003, p. 408)

Social work education "The formal training and subsequent experience that prepares social workers for their professional roles. The formal training takes place primarily in accredited colleges and universities at the *baccalaureate social work* (bachelor's degree in social work) level and in accredited professional schools of social work in *MSW, DSW,* PhD, and other *doctoral programs.*" (Barker, 2003, pp. 408–409)

Trauma "An injury to the body or *psyche* by some type of shock, violence, or unanticipated situation" (Barker, 2003 p. 441)

Trauma workers Persons such as mental health professionals, lawyers, victims' advocates, caseworkers, judges, physicians, and applied researchers, who work directly with or have direct exposure to trauma victims (Dutton & Rubinstein, 1995, p. 83)

Vicarious traumatization "A transformation in the therapist's (or other trauma worker's) inner experience resulting from empathetic engagement with clients' trauma material" (Pearlman & Saakvitne, 1995, p. 151)

References

Alabama, State of, Department of Labor. (2005). Workers' compensation information [Poster], Montgomery, AL: Labor Law Poster Service.

American Psychiatric Association. (1980). *Diagnostic and statistical manual of mental disorders* (3rd ed.). Washington, DC: Author.

American Psychiatric Association. (2000). *Diagnostic and statistical manual of mental disorders* (4th ed. text revision). Arlington, VA: Author.

American Public Human Services Association. (2005). Report from the 2004 child welfare workforce survey. Washington, DC: Author.

Anderson, D. G. (2000). Coping strategies and burnout among veteran child protection workers. *Child Abuse & Neglect, 24*(6), 839–849.

Archibald, H. C., Long, D. M., Miller, C., & Tudenham, R. D. (1962). Gross stress reaction in combat: A 15-year follow-up. *American Journal of Psychiatry, 119,* 317–322.

Archibald, H. C., & Tuddenham, R. D. (1965). Persistent stress reactions after combat. *Archives of General Psychiatry, 12,* 475–481.

Bandura, A. (1997). Self-efficacy: The exercise of control. New York: W. H. Freeman.

Baranowsky, A. B. (2002). The silencing response in clinical practice: On the road to dialogue. In C. R. Figley (Ed.), *Treating compassion fatigue* (pp. 155–170). New York: Brunner-Routledge.

Bargal, D. (2000). The manager as leader. In R. J. Patti (Ed.), *The handbook of social welfare management* (pp. 303–319). Thousand Oaks, CA: Sage.

Barker, R. L. (2003). *The social work dictionary.* Washington, DC: NASW Press.

Beaver, A. A. (1999). Client violence against professional social workers: Frequency, worker characteristics, and impact on worker job satisfaction, burnout, and health. Doctoral dissertation, University of Arkansas, 1999). *Dissertation Abstracts International, 60*(06), 2227. (UMI No. 9932738)

Bell, H., Kulkarni, S., & Dalton, L. (2003). Organization prevention of vicarious trauma. *Families in Society: The Journal of Contemporary Human Services, 84*(4), 463–470.

Bennis, W. (1982). The artform of leadership. *Training and Development Journal, 36*(4), 44–46.

Bernotavicz, F. (1997). Retention of child welfare caseworkers: A report. Retrieved August 30, 2004, from http://muskie.usm.maine.edu/helpkids/pubstext/retention.html

Bernstein, D., & Fink, L. (1998). *Childhood Trauma Questionnaire: A retrospective self-report: Manual.* Orlando, FL: Psychological Corporation, Harcourt Brace.

Bhana, A., & Haffejee, N. (1996). Relation among measures of burnout, job satisfaction, and role dynamics for a sample of South African child-care workers. *Psychological Reports, 79,* 431–434.

Black, P. N., Jeffreys, D., & Hartley, E. K. (1993). Personal history of psychosocial trauma in the early life of social work and business students. *Journal of Social Work Education, 29*(2), 171–181.

Bloom, B. S. (1956). *Taxonomy of educational objectives.* New York: Longman.

Blumenthal, J. A., Babyak, M. A., Moore, K. A., Craighead, W. E., Herman, S., Khatri, P., et al.

(1999). Effects of exercise training in older patients with major depression. *Archives of Internal Medicine, 159,* 2349–2356.

Bride, B. E. (2004). The impact of providing psychosocial services to traumatized populations. *Stress, Trauma, and Crisis, 7,* 29–46.

Bride, B. E. (in press). Prevalence of secondary traumatic stress among social workers. *Social Work.*

Bride, B. E., Jones, J. L., & MacMaster, S. A. (in press). Correlates of secondary traumatic stress in child protective services workers. *Journal of Evidence-Based Social Work Practice.*

Bride, B. E., Robinson, M. M., Yegidis, B., & Figley, C. R. (2004). Development and validation of the secondary traumatic stress scale. *Research on Social Work Practice, 14*(1), 27–35.

Brown, S. P., & Leigh, T. W. (1996). A new look at psychological climate and its relationship to job involvement, effort, and performance. *Journal of Applied Psychology, 81*(4), 358–368.

Butler, D. (2002). *Employer liability for workplace trauma.* Hants, UK: Ashgate.

Butler, S. D. (1935). *War is a racket.* Los Angeles: Feral House.

Calhoun, L. G., & Tedeschi, R. G. (1999). *Facilitating posttraumatic growth: A clinician's guide.* Mahwah, NJ: Lawrence Erlbaum.

Catherall, D. R. (1995). Preventing institutional secondary traumatic stress disorder. In C. R. Figley (Ed.), *Compassion fatigue* (232–249). Bristol, PA: Brunner/Mazel.

Child Welfare League of America, Alliance for Children and Families, American Public Human Services Association. (2001, May). The child welfare workforce challenge: Results from a preliminary study. Paper presented at the Finding Better Ways Conference, Dallas, TX.

Chrestman, K. R. (1995). Secondary exposure to trauma and self-reported distress among therapists. In B. H. Stamm (Ed.), *Secondary traumatic stress: Self-care issues for clinicians, researchers, and educators* (pp. 29–36). Lutherville, MD: Sidran.

Cohen, S. (2002). Psychosocial stress, social networks, and susceptibility to infection. In H. G. Koenig & H. J. Cohen (Eds.), *The link between religion and health: Psychoneuroimmunology and the faith factor* (pp. 101–123). Oxford: Oxford University Press.

Collins-Camargo, C. (2002). *Southern Regional Quality Improvement Center for Child Protection review of literature associated with social work supervision.* Lexington: University of Kentucky, School of Social Work, Training Resource Center.

Comstock, A., & McDaniel, N. (2004). The casework process. *Helping in Child Protective Services: A Competency-Based Casework Handbook* (pp. 49–75). New York: Oxford University Press.

Corey, G. F. (1986). *Theory and practice of counseling psychotherapy.* Monterey, CA: Brooks/Cole.

Courtney, M. E., Needell, B., & Wulczyn, F. (2004). Unintended consequences of the push for accountability: The case of national child welfare performance standards. *Children and Youth Services Review, 26*(12), 1141–1154.

Craft, L. L. (2005). Exercise and clinical depression: Examining two psychological mechanisms. *Psychology of Sport & Exercise, 6*(2), 151–172.

Crosson-Tower, C. (2004). *Exploring child welfare: A practice perspective.* Boston: Pearson.

Cunningham, M. (2003). Impact of trauma work on social work clinicians: Empirical findings. *Social Work, 48*(4), 451–459.

Cunningham, M. (2004). Teaching social workers about trauma: Reducing the risks of vicarious traumatization in the classroom. *Journal of Social Work Education, 40*(2), 305–317.

Curl, A. (1998). *A quantitative report of child protective service worker characteristics and physical safety responses.* Unpublished manuscript, University of Alabama, Tuscaloosa.

Daley, M. R. (1979). Burnout: Smoldering problem in protective services. *Social Work, 24,* 375–379.

Dane, B. (2000). Child welfare workers: An innovative approach for interacting with secondary trauma. *Journal of Social Work Education, 36,* 27–38.

Danieli, Y. (1984). Psychotherapists' participation in the conspiracy of silence about the Holocaust. *Psychoanalytic Psychology, 1,* 23–42.

Denison, D. R. (1996). What is the difference between organizational culture and organizational climate? A native's point of view on a decade of paradigm wars. *Academy of Management Review, 21,* 619–654.

Desphandé, R., & Webster, F., Jr. (1989). Organizational culture and marketing: Defining the research agenda. *Journal of Marketing, 53,* 3–15.

Dickinson, N. S., & Perry, R. E. (2002). Factors influencing the retention of specially educated public child welfare workers. *Journal of Health & Social Policy, 15*(3/4), 89–103.

Dienstbier, R. A. (1989). Arousal and psychological toughness: Implications for mental and physical health. *Psychological Review, 96*(1), 84–100.

Dilworth, D. C. (1991a, January). Psychologists seek ways to reduce workplace stress. *TRIAL,* 14–15.

Dilworth, D. C. (1991b, February). Stress problems increase as workplace changes. *TRIAL,* 11–12.

Donovan, D. (1991). Traumatology: A field whose time has come. *Journal of Traumatic Stress, 4,* 433–436.

Drake, B., and Yadama, G. N. (1996). A structural equation model of burnout and job exit among child protective service workers. *Social Work Research, 20,* 179–187.

Dutton, M. A., & Rubinstein, F. L. (1995). Working with people with PTSD: Research implications. In C. R. Figley (Ed.), *Compassion fatigue: Coping with secondary traumatic stress disorder in those who treat the traumatized* (pp. 82–100). New York: Brunner-Routledge.

Dyregrov, A. (1989). Caring for helpers in disaster situations: Psychological debriefing. *Disaster Management, 2*(1), 25–30.

Dyregrov, A. (1997). The process in psychological debriefings. *Journal of Traumatic Stress, 10*(4), 589–605.

Einarsen, S. (1999). The nature and causes of bullying at work. *International Journal of Manpower, 20*(1/2), 16–27.

Ellett, A. J. (2001, March). Self-efficacy beliefs and employee retention in child welfare: A multistate study. Paper presented at the Council on Social Work Education Annual Program Meeting, Dallas, TX.

Ellett, A. J. (2005). Linking self-efficacy beliefs to employee retention in child welfare: Implications for supervision, theory, and research. Submitted for publication in *Journal of Evidenced Based Social Work.*

Ellett, A. J., & Leighninger, L. (1998, March). De-professionalization in child welfare: Historical analysis and implications for social work education. Paper presented at Council on Social Work Education Annual Program Meeting, Orlando, FL.

Ellett, A. J., & Millar, K. I. (2001, March). Organizational culture and intent to remain employed in child welfare: A two-state study. Paper presented at Council on Social Work Education Annual Program Meeting, Dallas, TX.

Ellett, A. J., & Millar, K. I. (2005). Professional organizational culture and retention in child welfare: Implications for continuing education for supervision and professional development. Unpublished manuscript.

Fairfax County Fire and Rescue Department v. Mottram, 263 Va. 365, 559 S.E. 2d 698, 113 A.L.R. 5th 665 (2002).

Farkas, G. M. (1989). The impact of federal rehabilitation laws on the expanding role of employee assistance programs in business and industry. *American Psychologist, 44*(12), 1482–1490.

Felton, J. S. (1998). Burnout as a clinical entity: Its importance in health care workers. *Occupational Medicine, 48,* 237–250.

Figley, C. R. (1989). *Helping traumatized families.* San Francisco: Jossey-Bass.

Figley, C. R. (Ed.). (1995). *Compassion fatigue: Coping with secondary traumatic stress disorder in those who treat the traumatized.* New York: Brunner/Mazel.

Figley, C. R. (Ed.). (2002). *Treating compassion fatigue.* New York: Brunner-Routledge.

Figley, C. R., & Stamm, B. H. (1996). Psychometric review of the Compassion Fatigue Self-Test. In B. H. Stamm (Ed.), *Measurement of stress, trauma, and adaptation.* Lutherville, MD: Sidran Press. Available from http://www.isu.edu/~bhstamm/pdf/

Flannery, R. B. (1990). Social support and psychological trauma: A methodological review. *Journal of Traumatic Stress, 3*(4), 593–611.

Follette, V. M., Polusny, M. M., & Milbeck, K. (1994). Mental health and law enforcement professionals: Trauma history, psychological symptoms, and impact of providing services to child sexual abuse survivors. *Professional Psychology: Research and Practice, 25,* 275–282.

Fournier, R. R. (2002). A trauma education workshop on posttraumatic stress. *Health & Social Work, 27*(2), 113–125.

Frank, H., & Paris, J. (1987). Psychological factors in the choice of psychiatry as a career. *Canadian Journal of Psychiatry, 32*(March), 118–122.

Frayne, S. M., Seaver, M. R., Loveland, S., Christiansen, C. L., Spiro, A., Parker, V. A., et al. (2004). Burden of medical illness in women with depression and posttraumatic stress disorder. *Archives of Internal Medicine, 164,* 1306–1312.

Freudenberger, H. J. (1974). Staff burnout. *Journal of Social Issues, 30*(1), 159–165.

Friedman, M. J. (2001). *Post-traumatic stress disorder: The latest assessment and treatment strategies.* Kansas City, MO: Compact Clinicals.

Friedman, M. J., & Schnurr, P. P. (1995). The relationship between trauma, post-traumatic stress disorder, and physical health. In M. Friedman, D. Charney, & A. Deutch (Eds.), *Neurobiological and clinical consequences of stress: From normal adaptation to PTSD* (pp. 518–524). Philadelphia: Lippincott-Raven.

Fromm, S. (2001). Total estimated cost of child abuse and neglect in the United States: Statistical evidence. Prevent Child Abuse America. Retrieved on March 17, 2005, from www.preventchildabuse.org/learn_more/research_docs/cost_analysis

Fryer, G. E., Jr., Miyoshi, T. J., & Thomas, P. J. (1989). The relationship of child protection worker attitudes to attrition from the field. *Child Abuse & Neglect, 13,* 345–350.

Gabbard, G., & Pope, K. S. (1989). Sexual intimacies after termination: Clinical, ethical, and legal aspects. In G. Gabbard (Ed.), *Sexual exploitation in professional relationships* (pp. 115–127). Washington, DC: American Psychiatric Press.

Gelman, J. L. (1989). Stress in the workplace: The availability of workers' comp benefits. Retrieved June 20, 2005, from www.gelmans.com/Articles/Stress89.htm

General Accounting Office. (2003, March). *HHS could play a greater role in helping child welfare agencies recruit and retain staff.* GAO-03-357.

Gibelman, M., & Schervish, P. H. (1997). *Who we are.* Washington, DC: NASW Press.

Glisson, C. (2000). Organizational climate and culture. In R. J. Patti (Ed.), *The handbook of social welfare management* (pp. 195–218). Thousand Oaks, CA: Sage.

Glisson, C., & Hemmelgarn, A. (1998). The effects of organizational climate and interorganizational coordination on the quality and outcomes of children's service systems. *Child Abuse & Neglect, 22*(5), 401–421.

Gold, N. (1998). Using participatory research to help promote the physical and mental health of female social workers in child welfare. *Child Welfare, 77*(6), 701–724.

Graef, M. I., & Hill, E. L. (2000). Costing child protective services staff turnover. *Child Welfare, 79*(5), 517–534.

Harkness, D., & Poertner, J. (1989). Research and social work supervision: A conceptual review. *Social Work, 34*(2), 115–119.

Harmon, M. B. (2002). Antarctic quest. *Biography, 6*(4), 80–84.

Harrison, S. G. (1995). Exploration of factors related to intent to leave among child welfare caseworkers. Doctoral dissertation, Ohio State University, 1995.

Harrison, W. D. (1980). Role strain and burnout in child-protective service workers. *Social Service Review, 54,* 31–44.

Harrison, W. D. (1983). A social competence model of burnout. In B. A. Farber (Ed.), *Stress and burnout in the human service professions* (pp. 29–39). New York: Pergamon.

Herman, J. L. (1992). *Trauma and recovery.* New York: Basic Books.

Hewitt, A. S., LaLiberte, T. L., Kougl-Lindstron, J., & Larson, S. A. (2005). Fostering commitment and skill through mentoring programs. In S. A. Larson & A. S. Hewitt (Eds.), *Staff recruitment retention and training strategies for community human services organizations* (pp. 177–191). Baltimore: Paul H. Brookes.

Hewitt, A. S., Larson, S. A., O'Nell, S. N., & Sauer, J. (2005). Orientation, socialization, networking, and professionalization. In S. A. Larson & A. S. Hewitt (Eds.), *Staff recruitment retention and training strategies for community human services organizations* (pp. 105–122). Baltimore: Paul H. Brookes.

Himle, D. P., Jayaratne, S., & Thyness, P. (1991). Social support and social worker burnout. *Social Work Research and Abstracts, 27*(1), 22–27.

Hodge, D. R. (2004). Who are we, where do we come from, and some of our perceptions: Comparison of social workers and the general population. *Social Work, 49*(2), 261–269.

Horwitz, M. (1998). Social worker trauma: Building resilience in child protection social workers. *Smith College Studies in Social Work, 68*(3), 363–377.

Howe, P., & McDonald, C. (2001). Traumatic stress, turnover and peer support in child welfare. Presented at the 2001 Finding Better Ways Conference, *Child Welfare League of America.* Retrieved from www. cwla.org/programs/trieschman/2001fbwPhilHowe.htm

Janoff-Bulman, R. (1989). Assumptive worlds and the stress of traumatic events: Applications of the schema construct. *Social Cognition, 7*(2), 113–136.

Jaskyte, K. (1999). Socialization of newly hired social workers into human service organizations. Unpublished paper, University of Alabama, Tuscaloosa.

Jayaratne, S., & Chess, W. A. (1984). Job satisfaction, burnout, and turnover: A national study. *Social Work,* 448–453.

Jones, L. (2002). A follow-up study of a Title IV-E program's graduates' retention rates in a public child welfare agency. *Journal of Health & Social Policy, 15*(3/4), 39–51.

Kadushin, A. (1980). *Child welfare services.* New York: Columbia University Press.

Kadushin, A. (1985). *Supervision in social work* (2nd ed.). New York: Columbia University Press.

Kools, S. M. (1997). Adolescent identity development in foster care. *Family Relations, 46*(3), 263–272.

Kouzes, J. M., & Posner, B. Z. (2002). *The leadership challenge* (3rd ed.). San Francisco: Jossey-Bass.

Krucoff, C., & Krucoff, M. (2000). Peak performance. *American Fitness, 19,* 32–36.

Landsman, M. J. (2001). Commitment in public child welfare. *Social Services Review, 75*(3), 386–419.

Larson, L. K., & Larson, A. (2000). *Workers' compensation law: Cases, materials, and text.* New York: Matthew Bender.

Lee, S. D. (1979). Staying alive in child protective services: Survival skills for worker and supervisor. Part II. *Arete, 5,* 243–253.

Lee, S. S., & Waters, C. (2003). Impact of stressful life experiences and of spiritual well-being on trauma symptoms. *Journal of Prevention & Intervention in the Community, 26*(1), 39–47.

Lerner, M. J. (1980). *The belief in a just world.* New York: Plenum Press.

Levine, E. S., & Sallee, A. L. (1999). *Child welfare: Clinical theory and practice.* Dubuque, IA: Eddie Bowers.

Lewis, G. W. (1994). *Critical incident stress and trauma in the workplace: Recognition, response, recovery.* Levittown, PA: Accelerated Development.

Lindahl, M. W. (2004). A new development in PTSD and the law: The case of *Fairfax County v. Mottram. Journal of Traumatic Stress, 17*(6), 543–546.

Littner, N. (1957). *The strains and stresses on the child welfare worker.* New York: Child Welfare League of America.

Lyon, E. (1993). Hospital staff reactions to accounts by survivors of childhood abuse. *American Journal of Orthopsychiatry, 63,* 410–416.

Maidment, J. (2003). Problems experienced by students on field placement: Using research findings to inform curriculum design and content. *Australian Social Work, 56*(1), 50–60.

Marsh, S. R. (1988). Antecedents to choice of a helping career: Social work vs. business majors. *Smith College Studies in Social Work, 58*(2), 85–100.

Martin, J. (2005, February 17). Father slain after machete attack on social worker. *Seattle Times.* Retrieved February 24, 2005, from http://seattletimes.nwsource.com

Maslach, C., & Jackson, S. E. (1981). The measurement of the experienced burnout. *Journal of Occupational Behavior, 2*(2), 99–113.

Maslach, C. (1982). *Burnout: The cost of caring.* Englewood Cliffs, NJ: Prentice-Hall.

Maslach, C. (2003). *Burnout: The cost of caring.* Cambridge, MA: Malor Books.

Matthiesen, S. B., & Einarsen, S. (2004). Psychiatric distress and symptoms of PTSD among victims of bullying at work. *British Journal of Guidance & Counseling, 32*(3), 335–356.

McCammon, S. L. (1999). Painful pedagogy: Teaching about trauma in academic and training settings. In B. H. Stamm (Ed.), *Secondary traumatic stress: Self-care issues for clinicians, researchers, and educators* (pp. 105–120). Lutherville, MD: Sidran.

McCann, I. L., & Pearlman, L. A. (1990). *Psychological trauma and the adult survivor: Theory, therapy, and transformation.* New York: Brunner/Mazel.

McCann, I. L., Sakheim, D. K., & Abrahamson, D. J. (1998). Trauma and victimization: A model of psychological adaptation. *The Counseling Psychologist, 16*(4), 531–594.

McDaniel, N., & Lescher, C. L. (2004). The history of child protective services. In C. R. Brittain & D. E. Hunt (Eds.), *Helping in child protective services: A competency-based casework handbook* (pp. 31–47). New York: Oxford University Press.

McElroy, J. C. (2001). Managing workplace commitment by putting people first. *Human Resource Management Review, 11,* 327–335.

McFarlane, A. C., & Van der Kolk, B. A. (1996). Trauma and its challenge to society. In B. A. van der Kolk, A. C. McFarlane, & L. Weisaeth (Eds.), *Traumatic stress: The effects of overwhelming experience on mind, body, and society* (pp. 24–46). New York: Guilford Press.

McMillen, J. C. (1999). Better for it: How people benefit from adversity. *Social Work, 44*(5), 455–468.

Meyers, T. W. (1996). *The relationship between family of origin functioning, trauma history, exposure to children's traumata, and secondary traumatic stress symptoms in child protective service workers.* Unpublished doctoral dissertation, Florida State University, Tallahassee.

Meyers, T. W., & Cornille, T. A. (2002). The trauma of working with traumatized children. In C. R. Figley (Ed.), *Treating compassion fatigue* (pp. 39–56). New York: Brunner-Routledge.

Millar, J. D. (1990). Mental health and the workplace: An interchangeable partnership. *American Psychologist, 45*(10), 1165–1166.

Miller, P. M., Gorski, P. A., Borchers, D. A., Jenista, J. A., Johnson, C. D., Kaufman, N. D., et al. (2000). Developmental issues for young children in foster care. *Pediatrics, 106*(5), 1145–1152.

Minnesota. (2004a). *Employee assistance program (EAP)*. Retrieved May 16, 2005, from http://www.doer.state.mn.us/eap/eap.htm

Minnesota. (2004b). *Supervisor's guide to EAP referrals*. Retrieved May 16, 2005, from http://www.doer.state.mn.us/eap/refrl-gd.htm

Mitchell, J. T., & Everly, G. S. (1996). *Critical incident stress debriefing—CISD: An operations manual for the prevention of traumatic stress among emergency service and disaster workers* (Rev. 2nd ed.). Ellicott City, MD: Chevron Publishing Corporation.

Moran, C. C. (2002). Humor as a moderator of compassion fatigue. In C. R. Figley (Ed.), *Treating compassion fatigue* (pp. 139–154). New York: Brunner-Routledge.

Morrison, T. (1990). The emotional effects of child protection work on the worker. *Practice, 4,* 253–271.

Morrissette, P. J. (2004). *The pain of helping.* New York: Brunner-Routledge.

Munson, C. E. (1993). *Clinical social work supervision.* New York: Haworth Press.

Myung-Yong, U., & Harrison, D. F. (1998). Role stressors, burnout, mediators, and job satisfaction: A stress-strain-outcome model and an empirical test. *Social Work Research, 22,* 100–116.

National Association of Social Workers. (1996). *Code of ethics.* Washington, DC: NASW Press.

Nelson-Gardell, D., & Harris, D. (2003). Childhood abuse history, secondary traumatic stress, and child welfare workers. *Child Welfare, 82*(1), 5–26.

Nissly, J. A., Mor Barak, M. E., & Levin, A. (2005). Stress, social support, and workers' intentions to leave their jobs in public child welfare. *Administration in Social Work, 29*(1), 79–101.

O'Brien, J. (n.d.). Post-traumatic stress disorder in the workers' compensation setting. Retrieved June 20, 2005, from www.beachnet.com/~jobrien/Ptsd.htm

Osborne, D., & Gaebler, T. A. (1992). *Reinventing government.* Reading, MA: Addison-Wesley.

Paton, D. & Smith, L. (1996). Psychological trauma in critical occupations: Methodological and assessment strategies. In D. Paton & J. Violante (Eds.), *Traumatic stress in critical occupations: Recognition, consequences, and treatment* (pp. 15–57). Springfield, IL: Charles C. Thomas.

Patti, R. (1987). Managing for effectiveness in social welfare agencies: Toward a performance model. *Administration in Social Work, 11*(3/4), 7–21.

Payne, R. L., & Jones, J. G. (1987). Measurement and methodological issues in social support. In S. V. Kasl & C. L. Cooper (Eds.), *Stress and health: Issues in research methodology* (pp. 167–205). New York: John Wiley & Sons.

Pear, R. (2004, April 26). U.S. finds fault in all 50 states' child welfare programs. *New York Times.* Retrieved January 7, 2005, from http://www.nytimes.com/2004/04/26/politics/26CHIL.html

Pearlman, L. A., & Mac Ian, P. S. (1995). Vicarious traumatization: An empirical study of the effects of trauma work on trauma therapists. *Professional Practitioner: Research and Practice, 26*(6), 558–565.

Pearlman, L. A., & Saakvitne, K. W. (1995). *Trauma and the therapist: Countertransference and vicarious traumatization in psychotherapy with incest survivors.* New York: W. W. Norton.

Pecora, P. J., Kessler, J. W., O'Brien, K., Downs, C., English, D., White, J., et al. (2005). *Improving family foster care: Findings from the northwest foster care alumni study.* Casey Family Programs, Seattle.

Peirce, J. M., Newton, T. L., Buckley, T. C., & Keane, T. M. (2002). Gender and the psychophysiology of PTSD. In R. Kimerling, P. Ouimette, & J. Wolf (Eds.), *Gender and PTSD* (pp. 177–204). New York: Guilford Press.

Peters, J. K. (2001). *Representing children in child protective proceedings: Ethical and practical dimensions* (2nd ed.). Charlottesville, VA: Lexis Law Publications.

Peterson, M. (1992). At personal risk: Boundary violations in professional-client relationships. New York: Norton.

Pines, A., & Aronson, E. (1988). *Career burnout: Causes and cures.* New York: Free Press.

Pitman, R. K., Sparr, L. F., Saunders, L. S., & McFarlane, A. C. (1996). Legal issues in posttraumatic stress disorder. In B. A. van der Kolk, A. C. McFarlane, & L. W. Weisaeth (Eds.), *Traumatic stress: The effects of overwhelming experience on mind, body, and society* (pp. 378–397). New York: Guilford Press.

Poulin, J., & Walter, C. (1993). Social worker burnout: A longitudinal study. *Social Work Research & Abstracts, 29*(4), 5–18.

Pryce, D., & Knox, J. (1999, March). *Secondary traumatic stress and social work: The need for prevention education.* Paper presented at the 45th Annual Program Meeting of the Council on Social Work Education, San Francisco.

Pryce, J. G., & Pryce, D. H. (2000). Healing psychological wounds of war veterans: Vet centers and the social contract. *Tulane Studies in Social Welfare, 21–22*, 267–283.

Reagh, R. (1994). Public child welfare professional: Those who stay. *Journal of Sociology and Social Welfare, 21*(3), 69–78.

Reamer, F. G. (1989). Liability issues in social work supervision. *Social Work, 34*(5), 445–449.

Regehr, C., Chau, S., Leslie, B., & Howe, P. (2002). Inquiries into deaths of children in care: The impact on child welfare workers and their organization. *Children and Youth Services Review, 24*(11), 641–658.

Robbins, S. (2002). The rush to counsel: Lessons of caution in the aftermath of disaster. *Families in Society, 83*, 113–116.

Rogers, D. F. (2002). *Pastoral care for post-traumatic stress disorder: Healing the shattered soul.* New York: Haworth Pastoral Press.

Rompf, E. L., & Royse, D. (1994). Choices of social work as a career: Possible influences. *Journal of Social Work Education 30*(2), 163–172.

Rousseau, D. M. (1990). Assessing organization culture: The case for multiple methods. In B. Schneider (Ed.), *Organizational climate and culture* (pp. 153–192). San Francisco: Jossey-Bass.

Rubenstein, H., & Bloch, M. H. (1982). *Things that matter: Influences on helping relationships.* New York: Macmillan.

Rudolph, J. M., & Stamm, B. H. (1999). Maximizing human capital: Moderating secondary traumatic stress through administrative and policy action. In B. H. Stamm (Ed.), *Secondary traumatic stress: Self-care issues for clinicians, researchers, and educators* (pp. 277–292). Lutherville, MD: Sidran.

Russel, M. (1987). *National study of public child welfare job requirements.* Portland: University of Southern Maine, National Child Welfare Resource Center for Management and Administration.

Russell, C. S., & Peterson, C. M. (1998). The management of personal and professional boundaries in marriage and family therapy training programs. *Contemporary Family Therapy, 20*(4), 457–470.

Russell, R., Gill, P., Coyne, A., & Woody, J. (1993). Dysfunction in the family of origin of MSW and other graduate students. *Journal of Social Work Education, 29*(1), 121–129.

Rycraft, J. (1994). The party isn't over: The agency role in the retention of public child welfare caseworkers. *Social Work, 39*(1), 75–81.

Saakvitne, K. W., & Pearlman, L. A. (1996). *Transforming the pain: A workbook on vicarious traumatization.* New York: W. W. Norton.

Samantrai, K. (1992). Factors in the decision to leave: Retaining social workers with MSWs in public child welfare. *Social Work, 37*(5), 454–459.

Scaer, R. C. (2001). *The body bears the burden: Trauma, dissociation, and disease.* New York: Haworth Medical Press.

Schein, E. (1985). *Organizational culture and leadership: A dynamic view.* San Francisco: Jossey-Bass.

Schein, E. (1992). *Organizational culture and leadership: A dynamic view* (2nd ed.). San Francisco: Jossey-Bass.

Schnurr, P. P. (1996). Trauma, PTSD, and physical health. *PTSD Research Quarterly, 7*(3), 1–6.

Schwartz, W. (1961). The social worker in the group. In B. Sanders (Ed.), *New perspectives on services to groups: Theory, organization, practice* (pp. 7–34). New York: National Association of Social Workers.

Schwartz, W. (1976). Between client and system: The mediating function. In R. W. Roberts & H. Northern (Eds.), *Theories of social work with groups* (pp. 171–197). New York: Columbia University Press.

Scott, W. J. (1993). *The politics of readjustment: Vietnam veterans since the war.* New York: Walter de Gruyter.

Seretean, T. (Producer/Director). (2000). *Big mama* [Motion picture]. United States: California Newsreel.

Shackelford, K. (2006). *Preparation of undergraduate social work students to cope with the effects of indirect trauma.* Unpublished doctoral dissertation, University of Mississippi, Oxford.

Shinn, M., Rosario, M., Morch, H., & Chestnut, D. E. (1984). Coping with job stress and burnout in the human services. *Journal of Personality and Social Psychology, 46*, 864–876.

Shulman, L. (1993). *Interactional supervision.* Washington, DC: NASW Press.

Simon, C. (1997). Psychoeducation: A contemporary approach. In T. R. Watkins & J. W. Callicutt (Eds.), *Mental health policy and practice today* (pp. 129–145). Thousand Oaks, CA: Sage.

Simon, C. E., McNeil, J. S., Franklin, C., & Cooperman, A. (1991). The family and schizophrenia: Toward a psychoeducational approach. *Families in Society, 72*, 323–333.

Skovholt, T. M. (2001). *The resilient practitioner: Burnout prevention and self-care strategies for counselors, therapists, teachers, and health professionals.* Needham Heights, MA: Allyn & Bacon.

Skovholt, T. M., & Ronnestad, M. H. (1995). *The evolving professional self: Stages and themes in therapist and counselor development.* New York: John Wiley & Sons.

Smith, B. D. (2004). Job retention in child welfare: Effects of perceived organizational support, supervisor support, and intrinsic job value. *Children and Youth Services Review, 27*, 153–169.

Smith, M. (2000). Supervision of fear in social work: A re-evaluation of reassurance. *Journal of Social Work Practice, 14*(1), 17–26.

Soderfeldt, M., Soderfeldt, B., & Warg, L. (1995). Burnout in social work. *Social Work, 40*, 638–646.

Stamm, B. H. (Ed.). (1995). *Secondary traumatic stress: Self-care issues for clinicians, researchers, and educators.* Lutherville, MD: Sidran Press.

Stanley J., & Goddard, C. (2002). *In the firing line: Violence and power in child protection work.* New York: John Wiley & Sons.

Staten, N., & Yeager, S. (2003). Four workouts to improve your love life. *Prevention, 55,* 76–78.

Stress at work 1: Statutory and common duties of care. (1995, August). *Industrial relations law bulletin,* 2–10.

Struebing, L. (1996). GAO symposium uncovers eight principles for managing people. *Quality Progress, 29*(4), 21–23.

Summit, R. (1983). The child sexual abuse accommodation syndrome. *Child Abuse & Neglect, 7,* 177–193.

Tedeschi, R. G., & Calhoun, L. G. (1995). *Trauma and transformation: Growing in the aftermath of suffering.* Thousand Oaks, CA: Sage.

Tehrani, N. (2004). *Workplace trauma: Concepts, assessment, and interventions.* New York: Brunner-Routledge.

Tolin, D. F., & Foa, E. B. (2002). Gender and PTSD. In R. Kimerling, P. Ouimette, & J. Wolf (Eds.), *Gender and PTSD* (pp. 76–97). New York: Guilford Press.

U.S. Department of Health and Human Services, Administration for Children and Families, Children's Bureau. (2004). The AFCARS Report. Washington, DC. Retrieved on March 17, 2005, from www.acf.hhs.gov/programs/cb

U.S. Department of Veterans Affairs. (1994). *Annual report of the secretary of veteran affairs: Fiscal year 1993.* Washington, DC: Author.

Van der Kolk, B. A. (1984). *Post-traumatic stress disorder: Psychological and biological sequelae.* Washington, DC: American Psychiatric Press.

Van der Kolk, B. A. (1996). The body keeps the score: Approaches to the psychobiology of post-traumatic stress disorder. In B. A. van der Kolk, A. C. McFarland, & L. Weisaeth (Eds.), *Traumatic stress: The effects of overwhelming experience on mind, body, and society* (pp. 214–241). New York: Guilford Press.

Van der Kolk, B. A., Weisaeth, L., & Van der Hart, O. V. (1996). History of trauma in psychiatry. In B. A. van der Kolk, A. C. McFarlane, & L. Weisaeth (Eds.), *Traumatic stress: The effects of overwhelming experience on mind, body, and society* (pp. 47–74). New York: Guilford Press.

Vaux, A. (1988). *Social support: Theory, research, and intervention.* New York: Praeger

Wagner, A. W., Wolfe, J., Rotnitsky, A., Proctor, S. P., & Erickson, D. J. (2000). An investigation of the impact of posttraumatic stress disorder on physical health. *Journal of Traumatic Stress, 13*(1), 41–55.

Wanous, J. P. (1980). *Organizational entry: Recruitment, selection, and socialization of newcomers.* Reading, MA: Addison-Wesley.

Weisaeth, L. (2002). The European history of psychotraumatology. *Journal of Traumatic Stress, 15,* 443–452.

Workers' comp injury settlement. (2004). *The Concise Law Encyclopedia.* Retrieved June 20, 2005, from www.thelawencyclopedia.com/term/workers_comp_injury_settlement

Index

CPSIA information can be obtained
at www.ICGtesting.com
Printed in the USA
LVHW021137160721
692841LV00007B/58